"This book provides an excellent, engaging borderline personality disorder (BPD), and anyone wishing to learn more about the complexity of the disorder and its clinical manifestations. Daniel J. Fox skillfully distills a wealth of complex information and years of practice into an easy-to-read narrative. The manual offers an outstanding guide for fostering deeper understanding and supplementing clinical practice."

> —**Anka A. Vujanovic, PhD**, associate professor of psychology, and director of the Trauma and Stress Studies Center at the University of Houston

"Daniel J. Fox has created a tremendously valuable resource for those struggling with BPD symptoms, alone or along with co-occurring issues. This book serves as a great tool for helping individuals understand the issues they deal with on a daily basis, and also as a map that provides direction on how to get to a place of meaningful and fulfilling relationships, as well as greater peace and acceptance of oneself."

> —**Russ Wood, PhD**, founder and director of Clear Fork Psychology Services

"Knowledge is empowerment! Fox's book is exceptional in providing a road map to understanding the often-misunderstood journey of those with complex borderline personality disorder (CBPD). Fox provides tools to identify symptoms (surface structure), as well as core content that must be addressed to manage CBPD and live a meaningful life. This self-help resource is filled with lots of strategies and up-to-date research needed to achieve wellness."

—**Diane Stoebner-May, PhD**, training director at the
counseling center, and clinical assistant professor in the
department of psychology at Sam Houston State University

"In this highly accessible and clearly written book, Fox takes on one of the most complex manifestations of the mind—our personality function. Drawing on years of clinical experience with complex patients, he delivers an essential guide for those hoping to understand and manage their BPD and its overlap with other mental health problems."

—**Carla Sharp, PhD**, professor of clinical psychology at
the University of Houston; internationally known for her
work on the development, phenomenology, and treatment
of personality disorders

Complex Borderline Personality Disorder

HOW COEXISTING CONDITIONS

AFFECT YOUR BPD *and* HOW YOU CAN

GAIN EMOTIONAL BALANCE

DANIEL J. FOX, PhD

New Harbinger Publications, Inc.

Publisher's Note

This publication is designed to provide accurate and authoritative information in regard to the subject matter covered. It is sold with the understanding that the publisher is not engaged in rendering psychological, financial, legal, or other professional services. If expert assistance or counseling is needed, the services of a competent professional should be sought.

Distributed in Canada by Raincoast Books

NEW HARBINGER PUBLICATIONS is a
registered trademark of New Harbinger Publications, Inc.

New Harbinger Publications is an employee-owned company.

Cover design by Amy Shoup; Acquired by Elizabeth Hollis Hansen;
Edited by Gretel Hakanson

Library of Congress Cataloging-in-Publication Data

Names: Fox, Daniel J., Psychologist, author.
Title: Complex borderline personality disorder : how coexisting conditions affect your
    BPD and how you can gain emotional balance / Daniel J. Fox, PhD.
Description: Oakland, CA : New Harbinger Publications, [2022] | Includes bibliographi-
    cal references.
Identifiers: LCCN 2021031369 | ISBN 9781684038558 (trade paperback)
Subjects: LCSH: Borderline personality disorder. | Borderline personality
    disorder--Treatment.
Classification: LCC RC569.5.B67 F693 2022 | DDC 616.85/852--dc23
LC record available at https://lccn.loc.gov/2021031369

Printed in the United States of America

25   24   23

10   9   8   7   6   5   4   3

This book is dedicated to my three heartbeats:
my wife, Lydia, and my two children, Alexandra and Sebastian

Contents

Not Another Rabbit Hole

No one ever reads the introduction, but you should read this one.

This book is designed to bring you value and not to waste your time or send you down a useless rabbit hole of unnecessary information. This introduction is the meet-and-greet between you and how this book is constructed. Skipping this short section could cause confusion that leads to frustration that concludes with you putting down the book and missing out on a resource that could be a central part of building insight and knowledge, as well as the skills and abilities, to manage your BPD and co-occurring conditions.

How This Book Is Structured

This book is designed to provide foundational knowledge of BPD and what makes it a disorder. Chapter 1 includes an exercise to help you identify not only general personality symptoms and issues but also those related to your BPD so you gain valuable insight. Chapter 2 explores the difference between pure BPD and complex BPD (CBPD). You might be surprised by what you learn.

In chapters 3 through 12, we'll explore the various disorders that likely co-occur with BPD, which causes CBPD. These include bipolar disorder, depression, psychosis, attention deficit/hyperactivity disorder (ADHD), post-traumatic stress disorder (PTSD), and complex PTSD (C-PTSD). In these chapters, you'll first learn about the details and symptoms for each co-occurring condition. Then, you'll do activities to help you manage and control not only the BPD symptoms but the co-occurring conditions as well.

Chapter 13 pulls it all together and helps you identify the top ten symptoms related to your CBPD as it pertains to all the likely co-occurring disorders discussed in the book. This helps you direct your efforts at decreasing the most troublesome symptoms while increasing the probability of success and sense of empowerment going forward. It doesn't stop there; this chapter also gives you resources to help you avoid feeling overwhelmed by your symptoms and issues, ways to build clarity for success, methods for challenging negative self-value judgments, and a leg up to grow beyond your CBPD.

The final chapter helps you find a mental health professional who can accompany you on this journey by giving you questions to ask and tips on what to look for to get the help you need and find a good therapeutic fit. It also addresses common blockades to treatment that you can and need to address before working on CBPD symptoms and issues.

This book uses an approach that considers not only the underlying disorder, BPD, but the co-occurring conditions as well to address your unique symptoms, issues, expression, and experience that make up your CBPD. Your uniqueness is an asset, not a liability. Accessing that part of you through these pages will assist you in not only learning more about yourself but your world as well.

Consider This… In each chapter, there are "Consider This" exercises and activities to learn more about your CBPD symptoms and issues that will help you learn strategies to lessen their adverse impact. These are concrete and applicable skills and abilities you can use as you move away from the challenging symptoms and toward a life of self-determination on your terms, in an adaptive, healthy, and productive way.

Your CBPD Journal

You'll need a composition book or another notebook to serve as your CBPD journal. This will be where you enter all the information you learn about yourself, your symptoms and conditions, and your CBPD. You'll also have a place to put your responses and any insights you glean from the "Consider This" exercises and activities.

Your journal will quickly become a valuable resource as it will provide you a space to review all the information about yourself and your CBPD, as opposed to having to flip back and forth to find it here or there. You may want to find a journal that's decorated in a particular way or that has a certain cover or material that speaks to you. Make it unique, as it can become a very special tool as you go through this process of discovery and growth.

Suicidal Ideation or Intent*

Exploring CBPD symptoms and issues may lead to thoughts or plans of self-harm. If you or someone you know is thinking about harming themselves:

- Call the local authorities for help to intervene.

- Call the National Suicide Prevention Lifeline at 1-800-273-8255.

- Visit their website at http://www.suicidepreventionlifeline.org.

- Text the word "home" to 741741 (US and Canada only) to connect to a counselor or visit their website at http://www.crisistextline.org. If you're in the UK, text 85258, or in Ireland, text 50808.

- Reach out to the International Association for Suicide Prevention (IASP) at https://www.iasp.info/resources/Crisis_Centres.

It's important that you identify the people and resources you can reach out to if this should arise.

As you go through the book, you'll see certain symptoms followed by an asterisk (*) to remind you to return to this section to access self-harm or suicidal ideation or intent resources for help. Remember, you're using the knowledge in this book to push back on your CBPD and do your life differently. Though this isn't easy, it is a valuable endeavor, and everyone needs help sometimes to get through life-changing circumstances.

Consider This: Your First Journal Entry

On the first page of your journal, list two or three people you can call or contact via text if you're thinking about hurting yourself or ending your life. Add their numbers and email addresses after their names. If you can't think of anyone, write down the National Suicide Prevention Lifeline number and the crisis text number listed above in your journal and also add them to your phone.

As you go through this process, you're going to learn a lot about yourself and the people in your life. It's my sincere hope that you recognize your value, uniqueness, power, and ability to change the life you feel trapped in by the distortion created by your CBPD. You're more than your diagnosis, and this book is going to help you see that and grow beyond it.

Let's Do This

Every great endeavor starts with a first step. This introduction is that initial motion forward. You'll be surprised what you learn about yourself and the people and situations in your life. I admire those I've worked with and those who read my books who strive to overcome their symptoms and concerns to make their life better. This book embodies the belief and hope I have for those with CBPD. Know your efficacy, know your strength, and embrace your tenacity to do your life differently. As you go forward, do so remembering a statement I've found to be true over and over in my professional and personal life: *knowledge is empowerment.*

CHAPTER 1

What Is BPD and What Makes It a Disorder?

"Something inside me isn't working, and you're not seeing it."

—Pam, 28

Pam is a single woman who has been in and out of therapy since she was fifteen years old. Pam began therapy again after a fight with her boyfriend Marcus that resulted in a breakup. After this breakup, and all the breakups before, she feels desolate, hopeless, empty, unfulfilled, directionless, and unknown. In therapy, she describes herself as "unknown" because she doesn't know who she is without being in a relationship or close to someone. She'll often binge-eat and spend money recklessly to help herself feel better, but these behaviors are very short-lived, lasting maybe a day or two, and she feels helpless about feeling better about herself and managing her relationships.

She has no friends to turn to as Pam is often unreliable and argues with them over the smallest perceived offense. She's no longer talking to Cathy because she sent a text after the breakup, and it took Cathy four hours to respond. When Pam confronted Cathy, she told her that she was working and couldn't answer, which Pam didn't believe and accused her of ghosting her. Cathy eventually told Pam that she's a user and only reaches out to her friends when she's not dating someone and even then, only when she's in distress.

In therapy, Pam describes how she feels a constant inner rage boiling inside her that prevents her from concentrating and focusing and how the smallest stressor drives her to "turn into an inferno of hate." This has caused her to lose many jobs, friends, romantic partners, and contact with her family. Throughout therapy, her medications often changed and provided only limited relief. Pam often stated how she felt the same, that she hated feeling stuck, and that medication changes didn't matter and weren't working. Her therapist diagnosed her with major depressive disorder, generalized anxiety disorder, bipolar disorder, and an impulse-control disorder at various times. Pam was frustrated with the process and her therapist. She wanted answers and direction but was having trouble getting help to see and understand herself and her life. After two years, Pam left this therapist feeling hopeless, empty, and even more unknown.

Pam Is Misdiagnosed and Not Alone

As you read Pam's story, you may have said, "Yep, that's me." This is because it illustrates issues that people with borderline personality disorder (BPD) often face every day in many of their relationships and their quest for treatment. For example, you may recognize Pam's confusion and frustration not only with those around her but also with herself. The difficulty she has understanding her feelings, thoughts, and behaviors and how she relies on the reactions from others to define her mood and self-worth are very common in those with BPD. She's frustrated with her therapist and feels as if she's going nowhere, stuck in a rut.

All of Pam's diagnoses may sound like they fit, but they don't. There isn't enough evidence for her to qualify for any of those diagnoses. Regretfully, this occurs too often in the treatment of BPD. Bits and pieces of symptoms are projectiles in a wide and random pattern. This causes mental health providers to get overwhelmed, and their tendency is to reach out and grab at diagnostic straws to try to understand and help their clients. This sense of being overwhelmed is widespread, and these providers are doing their best to manage and treat a disorder that's a chameleon in many ways. BPD presents differently in different people and in varying degrees, and recognizing this makes it easy to see that *BPD isn't a simple disorder but a complex one.*

Pam's therapist is overwhelmed, looking for a disorder to account for all of these symptoms. In doing this, the therapist loses sight of the client, the symptoms, and what's causing the symptoms. You can't say that everything Pam is experiencing is her fault or choice, because it's not. It's what's underneath these symptoms and behaviors and how they drive the patterns that're continually disrupting Pam's life.

Helping you discover those patterns for yourself is the goal of this book. Understanding the complexity of BPD will lead to better diagnoses and treatments that're more impactful, take less time, and are more cost-effective.

Leaving her therapist isn't the end of Pam's story. She resumed therapy with another therapist, and they are looking not only at all the things Pam's doing, but also at the things that cause Pam to react in unhelpful ways. Pam's therapist noted that Pam has many of the symptoms seen in individuals with BPD, such as:

- unbalanced and intense interpersonal relationships (with her significant other and friends)

- an unstable self-image (she sees herself as unknown and uses relationships to define herself)

- feelings of emptiness (a hole inside her she can't seem to fill, and she feels empty when not in a relationship)

- a self-damaging impulsivity (spending and binge-eating)

- intense irritability and anger

- fluctuations in mood that cause severe consequences (loss of jobs, friends, and contact with her family due to outbursts and aggression)

Pam remained in treatment for two years with this therapist, focusing on her emptiness and feeling unknown, which drives her to instinctively see and react toward herself, others, and the world around her in erratic and dramatic ways. This therapist helped Pam learn about her symptoms and what drives her reactions. Her successful treatment required an understanding of the complexity of BPD to recognize that she can be in control of herself and that she doesn't need to relent to unhealthy and destructive impulses. At the conclusion of treatment, Pam was better able to manage her behaviors and responses to life stressors and circumstances by learning about herself, accurately understanding her condition, and learning new, helpful strategies.

The Complexity of Personality

Personality and its influence on behavior is a complicated part of human functioning, and people have been studying human personality continually for almost a century to try to understand it (Allport 1937). We each have a unique personality, and your personality isn't the same as those with whom you share DNA, a home, or even your life. Personality isn't set in stone and changes over time due to biology, experiences, losses, successes, and failures. Although diversity in personality is universal, there are similarities across people that help us understand and, to a certain degree, predict people's behavior using what are called *personality traits.*

Your personality is made up of a combination of these traits that form a pattern of thoughts, feelings, and behaviors that are stable across time and circumstances. These combinations create differences that vary in all of us, which adds to the complexity to not only understanding yourself but also to understanding others and your world.

Researchers have broken down personality traits into five factors. Each of these factors, like all traits, disorders, and conditions, exists on a spectrum that ranges from absent to extreme. To help you learn more about them, here are the descriptions so you can get a sense of whether you're high or low on each factor.

Openness to experience. If you were at the high end of this factor, you'd have an intense interest in art and adventure and be very imaginative and creative, intellectually curious, and willing to try new things. For example, you might try snowboarding, enjoy going to a new museum or restaurant just to check it out, and revel in traveling to unique and unusual places. If you're at the low end, you'd be a practical, concrete, and focused thinker who makes decisions based on evidence, data, and analysis. For example, you might look at reviews for a restaurant before you go, or you might analyze cost and benefit of each interaction, whether it's about a new romantic partner or buying a new vehicle.

Conscientiousness. If you were at the high end of this factor, you'd be very self-disciplined, achievement oriented, goal focused, and stubborn. For example, you might be organized in how you prepare and execute tasks and driven to follow through until completion. At the low end, you'd be highly spontaneous, flexible, and unreliable as well as inconsistent and disorganized regarding your tasks, schedule, and follow-through with others. You might often show up late, cancel appointments at the last minute, and lose things routinely.

Extraversion. If you were at the high end of this factor, you'd be highly enthusiastic about many different things, have multiple interests, and be talkative and assertive. Your energy level would increase or decrease based upon the number of people around you, and you'd take action when presented with a problem or solution. You'd probably like being around others, doing things, socializing, getting to know many people, and working to resolve problems. At the low end, you'd likely be reluctant to socially engage, tend to be quiet and restrained, and need less social stimulation. You might feel "fine" being by yourself, not like drawing attention to yourself, and be quiet around those you don't know well.

Agreeableness. If you were high on this trait, you'd tend to get along with others and be considerate, generous, trusting, optimistic, helpful, and willing to compromise. You'd perhaps be a solution-focused person who wants others to feel included, and you'd believe in the goodness of those around you. At the low end, you'd tend to place self-interest above others and be skeptical, unfriendly, and suspicious of others while being unconcerned about how others feel or what they think. You'd be less likely to "put yourself out" or to be inconvenienced for others. You might tend to believe others only do things for the good of themselves, care little for those in your life, and feel highly annoyed or outright refuse to be inconvenienced to help another person.

Neuroticism. If you're at the high end of this factor, you'd tend to experience a preponderance of anxiety, depression, and anger as well as other negative emotions and have difficulty managing your emotional reactions to external and internal stimuli. You'd also have a low stress tolerance, be likely to interpret benign situations as threatening and harmful, and be pessimistic and likely to brood, hold grudges, and be "grumpy." For example, you'd see the world as a negative, stress-inducing, discordant mixture of experiences and let-downs, and that outlook would be exacerbated by a hopeless attitude that it'll never change. At the low end, you'd be less likely to get highly irritated with others over minor slights, less emotionally reactive, and likely to be calm, relaxed, and positive about yourself and others and the situations you're in. For example, you might feel that the world is a place to grow and build a life for yourself that's satisfying, and you'd have a strong sense of inner peace, an objective outlook, and a high tolerance for stressful situations and adverse comments.

These five factors are often used to understand individual differences in human functioning, and they provide a valuable basis for understanding not only "unimpaired" personality functioning but disordered personality as well (Costa and Widiger 1994). Learning more about your five factors and where you fall along the spectrum for each can provide great insight into not only how you see yourself but how you see others and your world as well.

Consider This: Your Five Factors

Let's get a sense of where you fall along the five factors. On a new page in your journal, write "My Five Factors" at the top and list each of the five factors down the left side of the page, leaving four spaces for your response ratings between each. Below each factor, write the numbers 1 to 4, so you can note your rating of how much each of these characteristics is or isn't like you using the scale below.

1 = Not at All Like Me, 2 = A Little Like Me, 3 = Neutral/Undecided, 4 = Somewhat Like Me, 5 = A Lot Like Me

Openness to Experience

1. I come up with original ideas.

2. I'm curious about many different things.

3. I'm a deep thinker.

4. I have an active imagination.

Conscientiousness

1. I'm very thorough with tasks and assignments.

2. I'm meticulous, attentive, and careful.

3. I'm reliable.

4. I'm perseverant.

Extraversion

1. I like to talk to other people.

2. I'm outgoing.

3. I have a lot of energy.

4. I'm assertive.

Agreeableness

1. I get satisfaction from helping others.

2. I'm forgiving and don't hold grudges.

3. I'm kind to most people.

4. I'm cooperative with others.

Neuroticism

1. I often feel sad, angry, and anxious.

2. I'm easily overwhelmed by stress.

3. I get upset easily.

4. I worry a lot about many different things.

Now that you've gotten your ratings, add up your responses for each of the five factors. The lowest score you can get for a factor is 4, whereas the highest score is 20. Like all traits and disorders, these factors are on a spectrum, so you may find that you scored an 8 on openness to experience, but a 16 on neuroticism. This means that your tendency to have and be reactive to negative emotions is higher than your tendency to have an active imagination and try new things.

This isn't an assessment to diagnose your personality, but an exercise to help you build insight into where you may fall on each of these factors. This information is useful for providing a foundation of personality traits. This can help you focus on areas you want to improve, such as being more trusting and cooperative if you feel you're often pessimistic and angry.

Based on your results, you may be wondering how to improve, lessen, or balance your personality factor results. This book is going to help you do that as you move forward exploring topics and working through the included activities and exercises.

Now that you've gotten a sense of your five factors and the complexity of personality, let's take a look at disordered personality. Before we dive into BPD and its complexity, knowing the mental health perspective of personality disorders will provide you with insight as to how your mental health or other providers are likely to see your functioning, perceptions, and actions and reactions.

Is Your Personality Disordered?

As if personality weren't complex enough, the traits that make up your personality aren't the only determinants of a disordered or nondisordered personality. Nondisordered personality is *the ability to adjust your thoughts and behavior based upon the environment that you're in.* That definition is the true basis for the identification of disordered or nondisordered personality. This is because your behavior across situations and environments gives important information about you and how you function. How flexible you are in situations is an important part of adaptive and healthy functioning, which you'll revisit throughout this book, and it's central to your understanding of and distinguishing between disordered personality and nondisordered personality.

Personality disorders are best defined as *the inability to adjust your thoughts and behaviors based upon the environment you're in.* This definition encompasses the central features of the "five-factor model of personality" (which were described above) as well as the characteristics of nondisordered and disordered personalities. To determine whether a personality trait or a disorder is present, mental health and other treatment providers may ask you:

- Do you use adaptive or maladaptive (destructive) interpersonal strategies to manage situations?

- To what degree do you consider the costs and benefits of situations?

- What memories and emotions are activated from your various experiences?

- How intensely does the activation drive you to respond?

- How inflexible and maladaptive is your perception of your environment and yourself?

- What adaptive and maladaptive strategies are used when you're relating to and thinking about yourself and others?

- To what degree do your maladaptive thoughts and behaviors cause functional impairment or subjective distress?

Let's put this knowledge to practical use with an example. Imagine talking to your boss during a performance review the same way you talk to your children when they tell you about their grades in school. You may speak in a tone of annoyance if the grades are bad or in an excited and childlike tone if the grades are good, but either of these would likely cause conflict between you and your boss and could even put your job at risk. Those with disordered personality don't recognize the way they're speaking—to their boss or their children—so they engage in the same manner of speaking with everyone they know, even though they may have lost jobs because of it.

Now that you have an understanding of nondisordered and disordered personalities, let's take a look at how they're classified and understood by the medical and mental health community. Through decades of research and clinical experience, the field of psychology and psychiatry has attempted to lessen the confusion related to personality disorders. In doing so, the field has identified ten personality disorders in the "Diagnostic Criteria and Codes" section of the *Diagnostic and Statistical Manual,* now in its fifth edition (APA 2013).

These identified personality disorders are broken down into three groupings, or clusters, of personality disorders, labeled A, B, and C.

- Cluster A is composed of paranoid, schizoid, and schizotypal personality disorders. Individuals within this cluster tend to exhibit odd or eccentric behaviors and thoughts.

- Cluster B includes histrionic (exaggerated displays of emotions and excessive attention seeking), narcissistic, antisocial, and *borderline personality disorders.* Individuals who fall into this category tend to have and exhibit erratic and dramatic behavior and thoughts.

• Cluster C is made up of avoidant, dependent, and obsessive-compulsive personality disorders. Anxious and fearful thoughts and behaviors are often experienced and observed in individuals classified in this cluster.

The most common, most complex, most studied, and certainly one of the most challenging of all the personality disorders is BPD (Gunderson and Berkowitz 2011). Let's explore why this is, embrace it to understand it, and then dismantle it to make it simpler by going through this book and learning and using the included activities and exercises.

Why Your BPD Is So Confusing

BPD is confusing to many mental health and medical providers, but it's probably substantially more so for you, as someone living with the disorder, and for the people who know and interact with you on a regular basis. This confusion comes from the overlap and similarities in symptoms associated with BPD. For example, criteria for BPD include intense and erratic interpersonal relationships characterized by alternating between seeing others as either heroes or zeros. But this has many similarities with those in a manic, hypomanic, or depressive episode. In a manic or hypomanic episode, someone may love someone one minute and then respond to them in an angry and irritable manner the next. An individual who's sliding into a depressive episode may appear to devalue or lessen the importance of the person who's trying to help them because they're nonresponsive or communicating a sense of worthlessness and lack of appreciation for their efforts.

BPD is also perplexing because it's associated with multiple psychological, social, and biological issues. Biologically, when looking at pictures that depict frightening or adverse images, such as fearsome animals, reptiles, or insects or bodily deformity, BPD patients have been found to have greater amygdala (an almond-shaped mass in your brain involved in experiencing emotions) and occipital lobe (the visual processing center of your brain) activity when compared to those who don't have BPD (Koenigsberg et al. 2009). This neurological activity produces a heightened response, often making it challenging to calm down and return to baseline, after being activated. Being activated can include frustrating instances, arguments with loved ones, or intense abandonment fears. These biological differences and the associated challenges add to difficulties that often lead to misdiagnosis, frustration, and confusion by all involved in the treatment but also by those who are concerned for your well-being.

Many times, due to the multiple and overlapping issues associated with BPD, mental health providers often assess symptoms in an unstructured way, meaning no formal assessment procedures or approaches are used. When mental health providers don't use structured measures, such as a systematic and consistent approach to interviewing and diagnosing individuals, there is more than a 50 percent chance of missing co-occurring conditions (Zimmerman and Mattia 1999). This delays accurately identifying a condition, which subsequently slows efficacious and targeted treatment. Due to these unstructured practices, the average time between the onset of symptoms and formal diagnosis is more than seven years (Mantere et al. 2004). Over this time, your BPD symptoms may worsen as you go from therapist to therapist and continue to erode your self-concept and relationships as you struggle to find solid footing in your life.

When Your Symptoms Start to Show

Approximately 75 percent of all mental health disorders begin to show symptoms before age thirty, with the peak period of onset for depression, bipolar disorder, and BPD being between the ages of thirteen and twenty-five (Chanen, Berk, and Thompson 2016; Chanen and McCutcheon 2013). Due to this wide onset period, BPD is further confused and problematic as most symptoms aren't fully formed (for example, some symptoms may have a shorter duration or not be prominent enough to meet full criteria). Also, when BPD occurs early in life, inherent and universal issues of puberty and early adulthood complicate the issue.

BPD can be diagnosed in people as young as sixteen (for more information, consult Kaess, Brunner, and Chanen 2014), but this diagnosis must meet very strict criteria. This is because many beliefs, behaviors, and patterns aren't fully formed during the teenage years, and diagnosing someone with a personality disorder who doesn't have one can be severely detrimental to their development. Perhaps you experienced this as well.

All this complexity can lead to you feeling isolated and cast out due to feeling different and perceiving others as not having the same challenges that you did when your symptoms started to show.

Is It Traits or the Full Disorder?

Most people aren't going to meet enough criteria to be accurately diagnosed with a full personality disorder, BPD included. This means that either you don't have enough symptoms or they're not frequent or severe enough to qualify for the full personality disorder, in this case, BPD. If you don't qualify for the full disorder, but you have some symptoms related to BPD, you're more likely to accurately meet criteria for what's called "BPD traits." If you're confused, let's clarify.

- **Traits** are symptoms that aren't severe enough, don't occur often enough, and don't cause socioeconomic dysfunction (described below) to meet criteria for BPD.

- A **disorder** occurs when symptoms are severe, occur frequently enough to fit a maladaptive response pattern, and cause socioeconomic dysfunction.

Knowing whether you have traits or the full disorder is important for prognosis, which is helpful for anticipating the length of time you're likely to be in treatment and the degree of disruption in your life and the lives of those with whom you share it.

You're Not Alone

Many individuals with BPD feel that they're all alone with this disorder, but BPD is actually more common than you realize. In the United States, approximately eighteen million—or nearly 6 percent—of adults have been diagnosed with BPD (Grant et al. 2008). Outside of the United States, the prevalence of BPD is estimated to range between 1.4 percent and 5.9 percent of the general population (Samuels et al. 2002; Coid et al. 2006; Lenzenweger et al. 2007; Grant et al. 2008; Trull et al. 2010). Though this isn't a rare disorder, it's one that continues to be misunderstood.

It was once believed that females met the criteria for BPD more often than males by as much as three to one, but in actuality, it's nearly equal for both genders (53 percent women, 47 percent men; Grant et al. 2008). This erroneous belief in the gender disproportion is alive and well today and adds to the confusion, misdiagnosis, and stigma of BPD.

It's important to know that the experiences of many people have shown that BPD is a treatable disorder. Researchers and clinicians have found this to be true for several decades, but the stigma of BPD being untreatable remains intractable (Gunderson and Hoffman 2016; Linehan 1993). Let's take a deeper look at the various stigmas out there.

The Stigma of BPD

If you were diagnosed with BPD, you may have felt overwhelmed with a tidal wave of thoughts and emotions that include varying degrees of confusion and terror. If so, know that this isn't an uncommon response to hearing this diagnosis. You may have also felt a sense of liberation that at least you know there's a name for what's been going on inside of you and causing problems in your life for so long.

At the same time, when you research BPD, you may notice that the stigma is prominent and provides a sharp sting. You likely found the following descriptors: "treatment-resistant," "difficult," "overly sensitive," "antagonistic," "manipulative," and many more. Seeing this may have brought you back to, or even encouraged, that all too familiar sense of hopelessness and despair.

After learning of the intensity and pervasiveness of the BPD stigma, you may not even tell your mental health or medical provider you've been diagnosed with the disorder, or think you have it, because you've encountered, or are afraid to encounter, those who refuse to treat or associate with you because of it.

There is little debate that the stigma associated with BPD adversely impacts perception, accurate diagnosis, management, and treatment availability for this disorder. The stigma of BPD is unwarranted as the effectiveness of treatment for BPD is well documented, typically involving two to three hours per week for one or more years with a trained mental health professional using an efficacious intervention. These interventions include:

- dialectical behavior therapy (DBT; Linehan 1993)

- mentalization-based therapy (Bateman and Fonagy 2016)

- transference-focused psychotherapy (Doering et al. 2010; Levy et al. 2006)

A general psychiatric management approach that includes meeting at least once a week and focuses on interpersonal relationships along with family intervention and medication has also been found to be effective (APA 2001; Gunderson 2009). Another common experience you may have run into is the belief that you're intentionally acting, thinking, and responding the way you do on purpose and that BPD isn't a real disorder. Let's address that fallacy now.

BPD Is a Real Disorder

You may have been told "to just stop it," "you're being dramatic," or other dismissive statements of blame for your BPD-related beliefs, behaviors, and reactions. These declarations assume that BPD is a choice and that the issues that drive destructive behaviors are willful and planned, but the reality is that they're not. BPD isn't a choice, nor is it a choice to destroy your life or the lives of others. It's a disorder that develops out of an attempt to manage years of anguish and disappointment. Sadly, it often comes with the lack of a supportive compass that shows the way to the resources that build a sense of self that's caring, hopeful, and balanced. Knowing the symptoms and the causes are a critical part of this process.

Pathways and Causes of BPD

There are many theories as to how someone gets on the path to developing and ultimately meeting a diagnosis for BPD or having BPD traits. Knowing that BPD isn't a simple disorder, mental health providers and clients aren't surprised that there's no simple explanation for its origin. Researchers have worked to isolate BPD's possible origin, by looking at genetics, abuse, and family environment, and knowing this can give perspective into how you may have developed traits or the full disorder.

The Genetics of BPD

Many individuals with BPD see themselves as products of their genetics. Many say, "My mom has it, my dad has it, or my sister has it. It runs in our family, so I have it." Let's explore how true this really is based upon the data. People who have a relative with BPD are five times more likely to be diagnosed with the disorder (Gunderson 1994). More recently, studies have shown that when an individual qualifies for a BPD diagnosis, there is a 46 percent chance that another close family member (mom, dad, sibling, or other first-degree relative) will qualify as well (Skoglund et al. 2019). As you know, BPD is a cluster of traits, so let's look at the traits that make up BPD to get a better idea of its complicated makeup.

Some of the traits that make up BPD include impulsivity, neuroticism, affective instability, depression, anxiety, and interpersonal relationship disturbance. These traits have a strong genetic connection and are often used to discriminate between BPD and other mental health disorders (Few et al. 2016; Skodol et al. 2002; Witt et al. 2017). In addition, other BPD-specific traits with strong genetic components include rapid mood fluctuations, submissiveness, insecure attachment, cognitive dysregulation, and identity problems and show up in 44 to 53 percent (Skodol et al. 2002) of people with BPD. There are no studies that show 100 percent genetic cause for BPD. This means that there are other factors at work, and the experience of abuse is one of those factors.

BPD and Abuse

Before diving into the evidence, it's important to remember that abuse isn't a universal factor across all individuals who develop BPD; this is a common myth we'll debunk now.

- Sexual abuse has been found to have occurred between 36.5 and 68 percent of those who develop BPD (Elzy 2011; Kuo et al. 2015; Menon et al. 2016).

- The severity, age when abuse first began (the younger, the more debilitating), and types of abuse (physical, sexual, and/or emotional) also contribute to the degree of impairment related to BPD symptoms (Ibrahim, Cosgrave, and Woolgar 2018; MacIntosh, Godbout, and Dubash 2015).

- Multiple instances of trauma, as opposed to a singular event, appear to have a greater relationship to the development of BPD (Kuo et al. 2015).

Abuse certainly confuses how you see others and yourself. It complicates not only understanding your traits and their expressions, but it also increases the probability of developing BPD traits or the full disorder. By seeking out resources, like this book, that help you identify how you see yourself, others, and your world, you empower yourself to overcome the pain of the past and embrace a new future with the knowledge that you define yourself and your life trajectory, and those who mistreated you do not. These people may or may not have been a part of your family environment.

BPD and Family Environment

The family environment is a powerful thing that shaped, and continues to reinforce, many of the views, values, and scripts you've been living by. Family environments have been found to contribute to the development of BPD when a combination of experiences were present to varying degrees, including (Dahl 1985; Fruzzetti, Shenk, and Hoffman 2005; Giffin 2008; Robertson, Kimbrel, and Nelson-Gray 2013; Tackett et al. 2009; Zanarini et al. 2000):

- neglect

- conflict

- hostility

- chaotic unpredictability

- parental mental illness

- insecure bonding with parents who provide a combination of neglect and overprotective responses

- disrupted attachments to others that impair trust and sense of safety

- having multiple caregivers

- parental neglect, alcohol, and drug abuse

- emotional instability in the home

There is no specific combination of these experiences or particular level of severity that equals the development of BPD traits or the full disorder. However, Marsha Linehan's (1993) biosocial theory model proposed three invalidating family types that consider the experiences mentioned above, which contribute to the development of BPD traits and the full disorder.

The biosocial theory considers the long-term impact of adverse interactions between a biologically vulnerable child (such as those identified in the previous genetics section) and their environment. These invalidating family types reject the expression of emotional experiences and produce an environment that irregularly reinforces extreme expressions of emotion. In addition, they concurrently send a message to the child that such emotional displays are unjustified, that emotions should not be expressed, and that the child will go without parental support. As a result, the child doesn't learn how to understand, identify, manage, or tolerate emotional responses and instead learns to fluctuate between emotional "stuffing" (holding emotion inside) and extreme emotional expression. This may describe some or all of what it was like for you growing up. Let's build your insight into which of Linehan's family types you fit into so you can gain the knowledge and understanding that will help you move forward in your process of growth beyond BPD.

The three emotionally invalidating family types that are related to the development of BPD (Linehan 1993) are *chaotic, perfect,* and *typical* and are described in the table on the next page. I also included an additional family type, called *ideal,* which was not identified by Linehan because she identified negative environments that are likely origins for BPD. *Ideal* is a noninvalidating family type option. The ideal family environment is a consideration, as not all individuals who develop BPD have a singular family environment that's all negative, and it also provides something for you to strive for in creating your own family environment.

Family Types

Chaotic	Caretakers in my home environment abused drugs and alcohol, had issues with mental illness and financial problems, were mostly absent, and gave me little of their time and attention. My needs were mostly disregarded and invalidated.
Perfect	Caretakers in my home environment minimized my negative emotions (anger, sadness, fear, and so on) and would ridicule, make fun of, or disregard them when displayed to make it seem as if we had a perfect, flawless family image. I had intense difficulty controlling these emotions as they were often seen as my fault and as a character flaw within me.
Typical	Caretakers in my home environment would intensely and routinely try to control my thoughts and emotions and never pay attention to controlling and appropriately expressing their own emotions. Boundaries between myself and others were inflexible and rigid, and only high achievement and mastery of skills were seen as successes. Emotional control was of the utmost importance, though I received no help or support in controlling emotions.
Ideal	Caretakers in my home environment would be patient and listen to my thoughts, emotions, and concerns. I was encouraged to follow my passions and hopes. When I encountered obstacles and emotionally painful circumstances, I was given time to express my feelings openly without ridicule or blame. My caretakers could be trusted that they wanted the best for me.

Consider This: Your Family Environment

On a new page in your journal, write "My Family Environment." Read each description above, and if it fits your family environment, write it under the heading. It's possible that you may write down more than one or all of them. Look for keywords or situations that support your identified family environment and write them down as well. The word "caretakers" refers to anyone who looked after you while you were growing up.

Since we're talking about a complex disorder, BPD, that came out of complex environments, it's not uncommon for more than one of these environments to be present. If this is the case for you, under the family type, write down who in your life encouraged these types of environments. For example, if your aunt created a "perfect" invalidating environment, write her name below "Perfect." If your dad created a "chaotic" invalidating environment, write "Dad" under "Chaotic."

This exercise is designed to help you identify what type of environment you grew up in and who fostered it. This insight provides the framework to do it differently in your own home with those with whom you share a family environment. It will also help you recognize patterns of your past that may be causing and, directly or indirectly, supporting and encouraging your BPD and co-occurring conditions. As you go through this book, you're probably going to find that this foundational information keeps coming up. This is a normal and expected part of the growth process. See this for what it is and remember, "That was then, this is now," and continue to explore and learn about yourself as you continue this journey.

A cyclical pattern was likely created from these invalidating family environments that led to great harm and put you on a trajectory to develop BPD or BPD traits. Here is an outline of this developmental pattern and process.

- It began with one or several of the invalidating and dysfunctional family environments you identified previously, which fed your difficulty managing your emotions and finally drove you to act out emotionally.

- This resulted in you applying more stress and pressure on yourself to adapt to your maladaptive family rules and expectations while adaptive and healthy skills weren't taught to you, so you internalized these maladaptive coping skills and responses in order to survive.

- The development of destructive and unhealthy default (automatic and instinctive) behaviors and patterns gave rise to the development of your BPD or traits.

- You may have encountered corrective experiences and people— those who tried to help you learn adaptive and healthy strategies to grow beyond your borderline disorder and traits and attain greater control over yourself and your environment.

- When you tried using your adaptive and healthy strategies, you likely encountered pressure to go back to the old maladaptive emotional actions and reactions. This is typically an unconscious attempt by those in your family to maintain the family's "maladaptive homeostasis," which is a balanced state of "normal" or usual functioning—however painful or damaging it is.

- Due to this pressure, and sense of guilt, you go back to those maladaptive family rules and expectations so you aren't the cause of the homeostasis disruption.

The cycle likely continued throughout your growth and development, and as you moved into adulthood, you came to rely on these maladaptive default behaviors and patterns to get through life. Although they're not healthy, they are likely all you knew until you encountered a corrective experience. A corrective experience can be treatment or learning skills to lessen, manage, and ultimately change the old maladaptive patterns into healthy and adaptive ones. This book is a step in that direction.

There isn't a single pathway or trajectory to BPD, and it's often a combination of genetics, abuse, and family environment.

A Combo Makes BPD

Now that we've covered the big three theories related to what likely put you on the path to BPD, its complexity becomes even more apparent. The combination of the three and their varying degrees over time caused you to create a pattern of perception and behaviors to manage your world to the best of your ability. BPD is, in many ways, an intricate maladaptive management tool you devised along the way in an effort to survive your early family environment and your life today. The problem is that it's a tool that reinforces those old family values, scripts, and rules that cause you pain and that leads to great turmoil in your life.

Building knowledge, enhancing your understanding of yourself and your world, and then learning the skills to control BPD are what will empower you to make the changes to unlearn and forego those old views, values, scripts, and rules and grow beyond your BPD. Identifying the symptoms of BPD that you possess and experience is a critical first step.

Your BPD Symptoms

Symptoms identify the diagnosis. The prevalence and intensity of each symptom must be considered to help you build insight to determine whether BPD is a possible disorder that fits for you. This book isn't going to give you a diagnosis; only a qualified mental health or medical provider should do that. What this book will do is provide you with a greater understanding of your symptoms and traits as they relate to BPD and the co-occurring conditions. This will help you seek the treatment you need to make changes to how to you see yourself, others, and your world to help you grow beyond your BPD.

Degrees of BPD

All disorders exist on a spectrum, and BPD is no different. The spectrum runs from absent to extreme. All symptoms for all disorders fall along this spectrum. The combination of the severity of symptoms is used to identify the overall severity level of the disorder, as assessed by a trained mental health or medical provider. For example, if you fall within the extreme severity level of BPD, you're likely to experience the following:

- You harm yourself (for example cutting, burning, banging your head) often.

- You almost always have intense rage and anger episodes that last for thirty minutes to hours.

- You have been admitted as an inpatient for BPD symptoms (listed below) often.

- You often experience episodes of detachment when stressed.

- You have short-lived but intense depressive episodes.

- You do not know who you are or what you believe in.

- You see others as heroes one minute and then zeroes the next.

- You desperately want to be close to someone but engage in intense efforts to push them away.

In comparison, if you were at the moderate level of severity, which constitutes the majority of those diagnosed with BPD, you'd likely experience the following:

- You may or may not harm yourself; if you do, it tends to not be too severe or frequent.

- Your anger and rage episodes don't occur often, and their intensity rises and falls quickly.

- You may or may not have been an inpatient for BPD symptoms, and if so, it was no more than twice.

- You've not experienced detachment when under intense stress.

- You have short-lived but intense depressive episodes (similar in moderate and severe cases).

- You do not know who you are or what you believe in (similar in moderate and severe cases).

- You see others as heroes one minute, and then zeroes the next (similar in moderate and severe cases).

- You desperately want to be close to someone but engage in efforts to push them away but not as intensely.

These two lists illustrate the varying degrees of symptom intensity and frequency. Notice that some of the symptoms don't really change from the moderate to extreme level, whereas others change quite a bit. This is a big part of why BPD is such a complex disorder, even without the consideration of co-occurring conditions. If you'd like more information to help you determine your BPD severity, consult *The Borderline Personality Disorder Workbook* (Fox 2019).

Going forward, it's important to remember that all the disorders we'll examine in this book fall along a spectrum with one common symptom. This is the one symptom that must be present to meet criteria for BPD, and all other disorders, and we're going to call this the "universal symptom" and explore it now.

The Universal Symptom

Socioeconomic dysfunction is the universal criterion necessary to fully qualify for any mental health disorder. Socioeconomic dysfunction is an enduring pattern of impairment that leads to the inability to have stable social interactions, including platonic, familial, and romantic interactions, and economic stability. Economic stability is a broad term that, in this case, includes work or career as well as academic pursuits that add to your ability to take care of yourself and your responsibilities. As you read each symptom that constitutes BPD, think about whether it disrupts your ability to function socially and economically or academically. Think about how that symptom affects your socioeconomic functioning. Using the following exercise, consider how the universal symptom and other symptoms of BPD pertain to you.

Consider This: Your BPD Symptoms

To help you increase your insight and identify your BPD symptoms, let's look at what they are and how often they're present in your life. On a new page in your journal, write "My BPD Symptoms" at the top and write the numbers 1 to 27 on the left side of the page. As you read each BPD-related symptom, put a *T* to indicate the symptom is true and something you experience often or an *F* if the symptom is false and something you don't experience often. Be sure to read the directions and take note of the time components, as these are critical to determining whether symptoms are situationally bound or occur across multiple contexts. Symptoms that occur across multiple contexts are related to mental health disorders, whereas those that are situationally dependent are due to the circumstance or location.

Only consider the presence of these symptoms and issues when you're not using drugs or alcohol or taking medication and they are unrelated to a medical condition. This list isn't meant to be used for clinical diagnosis but to help you build insight into your symptoms and issues so you can better manage them and seek appropriate mental health assistance. *Mark the following symptoms as true if they occur often and are part of a longstanding pattern that impacts you, others, and your world.*

1. I engage in behaviors out of desperation to prevent actual, possible, or perceived abandonment.

2. I have erratic and volatile relationships with others that go from seeing that person as a "hero" to seeing them as a "zero."

3. I feel uncertain about who I am and what I believe.

4. I engage in behaviors or activities that are harmful, such as reckless spending, excessive gambling, promiscuity, binge-eating, or drug or alcohol abuse.

5. I make suicidal threats and attempts.*

6. I engage in behaviors of self-harm, such as cutting myself, banging my head, or burning myself.*

7. I experience depressive spirals, agitation episodes, or intense anxiety that's overwhelming but lasts no more than a few days.

8. My depressive spirals tend to be caused by fear of abandonment that resolve when that person returns or is able to calm me down.

9. I have a feeling of hollowness, as though I have a hole inside that can never be filled.

10. I experience overwhelming feelings of annoyance, displeasure, or hostility and difficulty controlling these feelings.

11. I engage in behaviors and statements to keep loved ones close but then engage in behaviors to repel them.

12. My mood can be attributed to an identifiable stressor, such as an argument with a loved one, feeling unheard or dismissed, or feeling ignored.

13. I'm highly defensive to feedback.

14. I'm intensely afraid that others are going to let me down, which would "ruin me."

15. I'm guarded when meeting someone new or someone who wants to help me.

16. When under intense stress, I fear that others mean to do me harm.

17. When under intense stress, I have difficulty focusing my attention.

18. When under intense stress, I feel like I'm in a daydream-like state.

19. When under intense stress, my memory and recall are impaired.

20. When under intense stress, I feel as if my thoughts and feelings are unreal or don't belong to me.

21. When under intense stress, I feel detached from my environment and the objects and other people in it.

22. I have blank periods in my memory or feel that I've "lost time."

23. I disconnect from who I am.

24. I've felt or been told that I have another identity that I'm not fully aware of.

25. I lose touch with my feelings or feel emotionally disconnected.

26. I lose control of my body movements.

27. My symptoms cause socioeconomic dysfunction.

These symptoms are related to thoughts of or intent for self-harm or suicide. Please turn to the introduction and refer to the section titled "Suicidal Ideation or Intent" for resources that can help.

Review your responses and take notice of the symptoms you marked as true. These ratings are the significant symptoms that increase the likelihood that BPD could be an accurate diagnosis for you. Remember, this is an insight-building exercise, not a diagnostic one, and that only a qualified mental health or medical provider can give you a diagnosis.

The last criterion is the universal symptom, and if you marked it as true for you, this means that the other symptoms you marked as true significantly disrupt your ability to keep a job, stay in school, or maintain a relationship. If you marked socioeconomic dysfunction as false for you, this means your symptoms are more likely to be traits as opposed to the full disorder.

Listing and reviewing your symptoms this way can be a very powerful experience, as BPD can be overwhelming when seen as a whole. When understood as a combination of symptoms and issues, your BPD is more manageable and your efforts are more impactful and focused as they target particular symptoms. This leads to greater symptom reduction and overall control of your BPD.

In this chapter, we covered the critical components of BPD and what makes it a disorder. This sets the foundation for moving forward and building an understanding of BPD and the co-occurring conditions. This chapter was designed to provide you with knowledge of the following:

- what personality is and the five factors that are used to identify and describe individual differences

- the prevalence and stigma of BPD that add to its misunderstanding and confusion

- the key concepts that have been found to be related to the origin of BPD

- the symptoms associated to BPD

- the fact that BPD is an actual disorder that includes the universal criterion of socioeconomic dysfunction

The confusion surrounding BPD lies in perpetuated outdated misinformation. As reliable and valid treatments and resources have been created, individuals with BPD have become success stories. You have the power to be one of those success stories. Regretfully, these success stories aren't as ubiquitous as the darker tales of BPD's past, but it's books like this one and people like you who seek out the knowledge and want to learn about the proven treatability of the disorder that contribute to the success stories. By doing this work, you're helping yourself, as well as others with BPD, to perpetuate realistic and accurate knowledge about BPD and the true potential for success in treatment. The remainder of this book will help you see and understand BPD in a new, more accurate, and clearer way while providing you with the knowledge, skills, and abilities to manage it effectively. Let your success story begin.

CHAPTER 2

Pure and Complex BPD with Co-Occurring Conditions

"If you leave me, I'll disappear."

—Martin, 33

Martin has been married for the last twelve years and works in product development for an international engineering firm. He and his wife, Paula, have separated two times in the past, after Paula finding out that Martin had been cheating on her with someone from his office. When they last separated, Martin "broke down," cried profusely, called her continuously, bought her a brand-new Mercedes, and threatened to commit suicide because "without you, I will just disappear. You're my perfect fit. I can't exist without you." Paula eventually agreed to go back with Martin if he would seek treatment and genuinely commit to the relationship.

Once Martin moved back into the house, he put off making the appointment with the therapist, making excuses as to why he couldn't go. When Paula asked why Martin appeared to be avoiding therapy, he would yell at her, call her names, and write her faults on sticky notes and leave them on the refrigerator or bathroom mirror to remind her to "fix yourself" before passing judgment on him.

At work, Martin continued to have problems for not being productive due to socializing with young female interns. To try to get the attention of the interns, Martin would dress in trendy clothes, have the latest model phone, show up at popular bars and restaurants they would frequent, and change his political and personal views to be liked by them. When the interns didn't give him the attention he felt he needed, he would be overcome with panic, doubt, and fear about his manliness and sex appeal. This would be followed by him being in bed for days, having crying spells, and refusing to go to work or to speak to Paula or anyone else. Paula would tell his employer that Martin had a chronic medical condition that caused him to be incapacitated, and they reluctantly understood and accepted that he'd be out of work for extended periods four to five times a year.

After these periods, he would be "fine" for a while. He would be kind to Paula, attentive at work, appropriately social though flirtatious with the interns, and responsive when people needed help or there was a new project at work. Martin appeared to maintain this level of functioning unless he encountered a disappointment or rejection from the interns or other women. This would send him back into a downward spiral. During his most recent spiral, he told Paula how empty he felt inside, how she wasn't doing enough to provide a full life for him, and that he'd be better off ending his life. He then pulled a gun out of a brown paper bag and laid it on his lap. Paula immediately called 9-1-1, and Martin was taken and admitted to the hospital.

While undergoing treatment, Martin had frequent intense anger outbursts and crying spells. He refused to attend group therapy and would only participate in individual therapy with a female therapist. Martin remained in the hospital for thirty days and was diagnosed with alcohol use disorder, cocaine use disorder, bipolar disorder, and eventually borderline personality disorder.

The Symptoms Identify the Diagnosis

The story of Martin illustrates the challenge often seen in those with borderline personality disorder (BPD) and co-occurring, or comorbid, conditions. The clinical picture can be so full of symptoms that it's not uncommon for all involved to get overwhelmed. In Martin's case, and perhaps in yours, when all your symptoms overload your ability to control your emotions and behaviors, your probability of treatment dropout and misdiagnosis increases. It took Martin being admitted as an inpatient for an extended period for him to finally receive and accept treatment. In doing this, he was able to reach a level of stability he hadn't achieved before. You may have been on a similar roller coaster with your BPD and co-occurring conditions.

This doesn't mean that you and everyone else who has BPD and co-occurring conditions needs to be admitted to the hospital. But Martin's symptoms, behaviors, and threat to himself and others was so extreme that removal from his environment and placement into a safe and structured setting was needed. Once removed from his environment, he could detox from alcohol and cocaine, and he was given medications to stabilize his mood. Once under control, a pattern of thoughts, feelings, and behaviors emerged that led his treatment team to identify BPD.

One reason his BPD remained is because there is no medication for personality or personality disorders. Medication helps to lessen or control what's called *surface structure content*, but it can't do that for *core content*. Surface structure content are the behaviors or symptoms that rise to the surface as a result of the core content. Let's break it down below.

> **Core content** makes up the internal part of yourself that represents how you think and feel about yourself, others, and your world. Core content can include a sense of worthlessness, abandonment, emptiness, vulnerability, or feeling invisible, for example, but it's not always negative. We all have positive core content as well, such as determination, integrity, resolve, and independence, to name a few. Identifying core content is a critical step in managing surface structure content and controlling and lessening your BPD.

> **Surface structure content** includes depression, anxiety, panic, anger, and other emotions, but it also includes behaviors, such as acting out aggressively toward yourself or others, promiscuity, idealization and devaluation, negative self-talk, and giving up right before success is achieved.

Martin's Journey, Continued

During Martin's intake, it became evident that he had a history of manic episodes. These included five or more days of staying out all night, not sleeping for days, meeting countless new people, spending his and Paula's savings on drinks and cocaine, having unprotected sex with strangers, working intensely but not completing anything, and repeatedly calling the interns asking them to hang out with him at all hours. While at the hospital, he was put on a mood stabilizer, and over the course of the next few days, his symptoms began to remit.

By the end of the second week at the hospital, Martin was doing well and showing improvement. However, he continued to be flirtatious with young nurses, exhibited low frustration tolerance, and was highly sensitive to slights. At this time, his BPD hadn't been identified. His morning therapy sessions typically began at 8:00 a.m. sharp. One day at 8:05 a.m., he was still waiting in the reception area when his therapist hurriedly walked in holding a Starbucks cup. Before she could apologize for being late and open her office door, Martin began yelling at her, calling her names, and telling her to "fix yourself and get your life together." He refused to meet with her, calling her incompetent and blaming her for making her coffee more important than her patients. Martin eventually finished yelling at her, stomped back to his room, and laid on his bed crying profusely. He never heard her explanation that the cup was from yesterday and she was just going to throw it away. She wasn't late because coffee was more important, but he left before she could explain.

The therapist and Martin repaired their relationship. She was able to use that instance to explore his core content, identify his surface structure behaviors, and help him learn adaptive strategies to control his maladaptive (unhealthy) patterns. This was a change in the treatment trajectory, as she initially believed substance use and bipolar disorder were central issues. It wasn't until those conditions were stabilized that she could accurately see that there was much more work to be done.

As treatment progressed, it was challenging for both, but ultimately successful. Martin learned that he would become hypersexual, flirtatious, or emotionally volatile when triggered or discussing issues pertaining to his core content of emptiness, abandonment, and feeling invisible. He also learned that he had positive core content of resolve to achieve his goals. This insight helped him learn that his surface structure behaviors of flirtatiousness with young women, infidelity, blaming others, anger outbursts, self-loathing, and substance abuse weren't all associated with bipolar disorder. These were also being driven by his core content of emptiness, abandonment, feeling invisible, and resolve to do well that stemmed from many of his early experiences with his parents and the death of his sister when he was nine.

The death of his sister caused his parents' relationship to dissolve and his parents to emotionally neglect him as he grew up, and he secretly wished he had died instead of his sister. These issues and his core content were foundational to his BPD and drove his maladaptive patterns outside of his bipolar symptoms.

Martin continued treatment with his therapist after he left the inpatient facility. He remained compliant on his medication, and though he had some setbacks, with continuous treatment, he was able to manage his maladaptive patterns and use adaptive and healthy ones to support Paula in their marriage and return to work.

The Heart of the Problem

Martin's journey is an example of the complexity involved when someone has not only a personality disorder but also other comorbid mental health conditions. The problem is that many mental health providers are trained to recognize and work with surface structure content, such as depression, anxiety, trauma, and others. The addition of a personality disorder intensifies surface structure content and, in many cases, causes it to appear intractable, due to the intensity of negative core content. Mental health providers aren't typically trained in identifying and working with core content, and therefore, you and your mental health provider may find yourselves continually trying to lessen the impact of your issues with little positive outcome. When there is minimal identifiable change, you both feel frustrated, stuck, trapped, annoyed, and hopeless, and you're more likely to prematurely terminate treatment, or get dismissed. Identifying and working to manage and control core content are paramount to long-term change.

Consider This: Is It Core or Surface Content?

When you recognize your core and surface content, you become empowered to take greater control over your thoughts, feelings, and emotions. By doing this, you're better able to replace maladaptive patterns with adaptive and healthy ones.

Below is a mixed list of core and surface content for you to identify. On a new page in your journal, draw a line down the center. At the top of the left column, write "Core Content," and at the top of the right column, write "Surface Content." Read each word, and if you think it's core content, write it in the "Core Content" column. If you think it's surface content, write it in the "Surface Content" column. Use the box below to check your answers.

emptiness	integrity
shame	self-harm
dissociation	promiscuity
acting out	grandiosity
abandonment	worthlessness

This is a very important exercise as it builds your insight into your thoughts, feelings, and behaviors. Recognizing what drives your urges to respond helps you see that you're not powerless in an uncontrollable cycle of stimulus and response. There's a driving factor, and knowing the difference between your core and surface content will help you control it.

Answers:
C=emptiness, S=shame, S=dissociation, S=acting out, C=abandonment,
C=integrity, S=self-harm, S=promiscuity, S=grandiosity, C=worthlessness

The story of Martin and the identification of his core and surface content laid the groundwork for understanding the complexity associated with BPD. If you have or know someone who has BPD, you're probably not surprised to learn that BPD is a complex disorder, but often individuals are unsure what makes it a complex disorder. Let's take a look.

Pure and Complex BPD

Pure BPD and complex BPD are terms you may not have heard before. This is due to the lack of use of the word "pure" in reference to a personality disorder because it's typically used in research and not clinical work, though it should be. The word "complex" to identify a personality disorder hasn't been used before, but it's highly applicable and serves a great purpose for you, others, and clinicians. However, "complex" is used in reference to a nonpersonality-related disorder, complex post-traumatic stress disorder (C-PTSD; Hermann 1992a). Let's briefly go over it now to give some context. PTSD is a condition that develops out of a degree of exposure to actual or threatened death, serious injury, or sexual violence related to a specific event or series of events. C-PTSD is a broader diagnosis that includes the components of PTSD as well as the *adverse psychological impact* due to sustained and multiple forms of trauma, such as sustained child abuse or domestic violence. The complex type takes into account all the facets of the noncomplex disorder, PTSD, but considers the additional adverse psychological impact that causes the disorder to be more challenging to identify, to distinguish from other disorders, and to treat. We won't go into depth about PTSD and C-PTSD here; to learn more, see chapter 11. Applying a similar lens to BPD is of great use, but we first have to understand the terms.

Pure BPD signifies that all symptoms and behaviors can be linked to BPD *only*.

Complex BPD (CBPD) signifies that the symptoms and behaviors can be attributed to BPD and other mental health co-occurring conditions.

For instance, all symptoms and behaviors can't be linked to BPD alone but also to other mental health conditions, such as bipolar disorder.

Using a term like "CBPD" opens the door to taking into account all the facets of pure BPD while adding the consideration of other disorders to account for the presentation of symptoms beyond only BPD. This distinction helps not only with identification of the origin of symptoms but also with planning treatment trajectories as you go through this book and beyond.

Understanding Pure BPD

As stated above, pure BPD is when your core content (underlying issues) and surface content (thoughts, feelings, behaviors, images in your mind) are related to BPD *only*. A good example of this is Pam from chapter 1. Her thoughts, emotions, behaviors, and patterns could be traced back to BPD alone, to pure BPD. No other diagnoses were identified or are present. Pam encountered problems with treatment, was misdiagnosed, and experienced many issues and concerns that are common in those with BPD. However, when BPD was addressed, explored, and treated, the condition decreased in severity to manageable levels, and she could learn adaptive over maladaptive patterns of functioning.

The presence of pure BPD in no way means that quick and simple fixes can be applied and that the difficulties you encounter don't cause significant life challenges, because they certainly do. The twenty-seven symptoms and issues that define pure BPD, which you identified in chapter 1, often have a substantial, disruptive impact on your life.

Your symptoms and conditions don't form an orderly line as if they're waiting their turn at Disneyworld. Instead, it's a melee for dominance and control over the internal whirlwind of pain, fear, emptiness, worthlessness, and so on. This makes up the underlying negative core content that manifests in continual maladaptive attempts to find peace, stability, hope, and help. Your pure BPD symptoms and issues can be overwhelming, but when co-occurring conditions exist, they add to the confusion and complication of the clinical picture, and this is what we're calling complex BPD.

Understanding Complex BPD

You've probably done a lot of research on BPD to better understand why you do the things you do, feel the way you feel, and respond the way you respond. You're likely familiar with many aspects of BPD, but what you may not know is that most articles and books are referring to what we're calling complex BPD (CBPD) in this book. These articles and books note the presence of co-occurring conditions but see them as supplemental or secondary concerns. This is a mistake and needs to stop. BPD and co-occurring conditions need to be seen as creating a complete condition that impacts you, and others, uniformly. CBPD does this by expanding clinical considerations to include the combination of BPD symptoms and behaviors with co-occurring conditions.

For pure BPD, we looked at Pam. She certainly struggled with many issues in her life, and it took a long time for her to find a therapist and a method that were able to help her overcome her issues related to pure BPD. When we look at Martin's case, we see a much more complicated picture. Martin's journey is more clinically complicated by the presence of added symptoms that meet the qualifications for additional disorders. CBPD further disrupts building insight and makes it even more arduous to learn adaptive strategies because when one condition is identified and managed, others arise. It's like a mental health whack-a-mole (an arcade game where the player uses a mallet to whack mechanical moles that randomly pop out of their holes; as one goes down, another pops up). This isn't making light of the condition in any way but an example to illustrate when conditions like substance use and bipolar disorder are identified and then controlled, other symptoms pop up that complicate the clinical picture. The presence of this issue may be more common than you realize.

Approximately 3 to 15 percent of all individuals diagnosed with BPD *don't* have a co-occurring, or comorbid, condition; this is pure BPD (Fyer et al. 1988; Lenzenweger et al. 2007; Pfohl et al. 1986). Consider the other side of this coin: anywhere between 85 and 97 percent of all individuals with BPD have at least one comorbid condition. If CBPD is so prevalent, why have clients, researchers, and clinicians missed it for so long? The answer to that question is in the cycle of symptom dismissal.

The Cycle of Symptom Dismissal

The concept of pure BPD and CBPD is perplexing to clients and mental health providers because when the personality disorder is identified, in this case BPD, you, other clients, individuals with BPD, and mental health providers begin to lose sight of the comorbid conditions and symptoms. They begin to ascribe all surface structure content to BPD, not considering the possibility that it may be derived from the comorbid conditions as well. They forget about the presence of CBPD. For example, when symptoms unrelated to the personality disorder begin to surface, the mental health provider, as well as friends, family, coworkers, and even the client, say, "That's because of BPD," and they get dismissed when they shouldn't be.

When this happens, a cycle of symptom dismissal has begun. It begins with the presence of additional symptoms being explained away as all or part of BPD, when they're actually related to the comorbid conditions. Over time, your symptoms remain "explained away" and unattended to or minimized, increasing the likelihood of worsening symptoms. Due to this, your functioning and self-control continue to lessen until they reach a breaking point, such as self-harm gestures, inpatient treatment, incarceration, and so on. At this breaking point, more intensive treatment may be needed, such as an increase or change in medication or frequency of group and individual therapy. Hopefully, your symptoms decrease to a level you can control, but without accurate identification, they only decrease for a finite period until they resurface again later. This cycle continues because many falsely believe that a BPD diagnosis equals pure BPD and that *all* symptoms are attributed to that diagnosis, which removes the consideration of comorbid conditions. This results in a failure to see what's genuinely present because we don't see what we're not looking for.

To lessen the cycle of symptom dismissal, all of us who work with and live with this disorder need to be more aware of the probability of comorbid conditions. This includes knowing which ones are most likely to be prevalent and develop a strategy for identifying and working with them. Let's get started and examine the comorbid conditions we're going to explore in this book that make up CBPD.

CBPD's Comorbid Conditions

We've laid a strong foundation for the identification and distinction of pure BPD and CBPD. Now, we'll examine the more prevalent comorbid conditions: bipolar disorder, depression, psychosis, attention deficit/hyperactivity disorder (ADHD), and PTSD and C-PTSD. These disorders present unique challenges to not only you or your loved one with BPD, but to those who know, interact, and work with people with BPD.

These comorbid conditions create barriers to accurate insight and diagnosis, making successful treatment more evasive. Each comorbid condition mixed with BPD causes unique manifestations that are as varied as you and others with CBPD. However, there are common components, traits, and behaviors that can be identified to determine what's core content and what's surface content, which provides for more accurate self-understanding, insight building, diagnosis, and treatment. For example, in Martin's case, his infidelity appeared to be related to hypersexuality during his manic phases, but in actuality, it was driven by BPD core content of emptiness. Medication and managing his mania didn't lessen his drive to fill his emptiness through sexual conquests with young interns. Failure to identify this would likely have resulted in his medication being reevaluated and it being determined that his manic-like behavior wasn't well controlled, followed by an increase or change in medication, which then would have increased the probability of side effects. The increase in side effects would raise the likelihood of him becoming noncompliant with his medication, which would likely lead to a resurgence of bipolar symptoms.

This sequence is regretfully not unique, and you may relate to, or have experienced, a similar situation. It doesn't have to be this way, but you have to know which conditions you're contending with to build your knowledge and insight and target your skills and abilities to manage them more effectively.

Your Comorbid Conditions

In chapter 1, you identified your symptoms and issues related to pure BPD, but that was only part of completing your clinical picture. The exercise below is designed to help you determine which co-occurring conditions may be present and direct you to the related chapter or chapters.

Consider This: Your Conditions Compass

Below are the prevalent comorbid conditions covered in this book followed by central symptoms that will help guide you to specific chapters for you to learn more. On a new page in your journal, write the name of each condition identified below followed by the number of symptoms listed below. For example, bipolar disorder has ten symptoms, so write numbers 1 through 10 down the left side of page. As you read each symptom, put a *T* to indicate the symptom is true and something you experience often, or an *F* if the symptom is false and something you don't experience often. Be sure to read the directions and take note of the time components, as these are critical to determining whether symptoms are situationally bound or occur across multiple contexts. Symptoms that occur across multiple contexts are related to mental health disorders, whereas those that are situationally dependent are likely due to the circumstance or location.

Only consider the presence of these symptoms and issues when you're not using drugs or alcohol or taking medication and when they are unrelated to a medical condition. Let's start with bipolar disorder symptoms.

Bipolar Disorder

Bipolar disorder is made up of manic/hypomanic symptoms and major depressive disorder symptoms. When you're trying to determine whether bipolar disorder is a possible CBPD condition to explore further, we want to consider both ends of the polar extremes (high-highs = manic/hypomanic symptoms and low-lows = depression symptoms).

Manic/Hypomanic

When considering symptoms 1 through 5, they must've occurred for four consecutive days or more.

1. I've been unusually exhilarated and elated to the point it causes problems in my life.

2. I feel like there's nothing I can't do and no one can stop me, which is outside the norm for me.

3. I do more, have lofty goals, and come up with amazing, one-of-a-kind ideas that are going to change my life and the world.

4. I'm unusually more irritable and angrier, which is accompanied by a decrease in ability to control my behavior.

5. I have little or no need for sleep, and I'm not tired due to lack of sleep.

Depression

When considering symptoms 6 through 10, they must've occurred for two consecutive weeks or more.

6. I have feelings of sadness and dysphoria most of the day, nearly every day.

7. I lose interest in activities I usually enjoy.

8. I have difficulty motivating myself to engage with others and complete personal hygiene and important daily tasks.

9. I feel intensely insignificant, desperate, and inept.

10. I see my future as desolate with no hope for change.

If you identified three or more symptoms from numbers 1 through 5 and three or more symptoms from numbers 6 through 10 as true for you, please read chapters 3 and 4.

Depression

These symptoms are the same as those listed above, as major depressive disorder is part of bipolar disorder, but it can also be its own condition. When considering these symptoms, they must've occurred for two consecutive weeks or more.

1. I have feelings of sadness and dysphoria most of the day, nearly every day.
2. I lose interest in activities I usually enjoy.
3. I have difficulty motivating myself to engage with others and complete personal hygiene and important daily tasks.
4. I feel intensely insignificant, desperate, and inept.
5. I see my future as desolate with no hope for change.

If you identified three or more symptoms as true for you, please read chapters 5 and 6.

Psychosis

When considering these symptoms, they must've been present for at least one day.

1. I've fixated on beliefs though there was clear evidence that showed they were false.
2. I've seen, heard, felt, tasted, or smelled something that others say isn't there.
3. I've lost touch with my reality and felt outside myself.
4. I've experienced "lost time": losing sense of the passage of time. (This does not include being engrossed in an activity or project.)
5. I've felt as though others were out to get me, without clear evidence to prove it.
6. I've felt as though I had special powers.

7. I've believed someone was in love with me, without clear evidence to prove it.

8. I was convinced a major catastrophe was going to happen to me or those I love, without clear evidence to prove it.

9. I was convinced I had, or would get, a life-threatening disease or illness, without clear evidence to prove it.

If you identified four or more symptoms as true for you, please read chapters 7 and 8.

Attention Deficit/Hyperactivity Disorder

When considering these symptoms, they must've been present for more days than not over a period of six months or more.

1. I have great difficulty focusing my attention on things I enjoy and things I don't.

2. It is hard for me to focus my attention when people are talking to me.

3. I make careless mistakes due to rushing through things or overlooking details.

4. It's very hard to organize things I need to do and follow through and get them done.

5. It's very difficult for me to sit still due to restlessness, feeling energized, and an uncontrollable urge to move and keep moving.

6. I interrupt others or cause disruption because I can't wait my turn and feel an intense urge to "get it out" (my thoughts, things I feel compelled to say).

If you identified three or more symptoms as true for you, please read chapters 9 and 10.

Post-Traumatic Stress Disorder

When considering these symptoms, they must've been present for at least one month.

1. I've learned of, directly experienced, or witnessed death, serious injury, or sexual assault.

2. I have intense memories, dreams, or experiences that remind me of a traumatic event where I thought I was going to die or someone else was going to die who was close to me.

3. I avoid situations, people, or places that remind me of past traumatic events.

4. Following the traumatic event, my memory and emotions are poor and difficult to control.

5. Following the traumatic event, I'm jumpy, easily agitated, irritable, and reckless, and I have trouble concentrating.

If you identified three or more symptoms as true for you, please read chapters 11 and 12.

Complex Post-Traumatic Stress Disorder

When considering these symptoms, they must've been present for at least one month and are the direct result of experiencing a traumatic event.

1. I feel related guilt and shame.

2. I have difficulty controlling my emotions.

3. I feel a sense of detachment from myself and my surroundings.

4. I have physical complaints, such as headaches, stomachaches, dizziness, chest pains, and so on.

5. I'm distant from friends and family, and my relationships have "taken a turn for the worst."

If you identified three or more symptoms as true for you, please read chapters 11 and 12.

Now that you've identified which conditions are most salient for you, you can use this information to help you choose which chapters to focus on going forward. Of course, you don't have to focus only on those chapters that make up your CBPD. You can read the others to help you better distinguish the symptoms and comorbid conditions you believe you don't have. There are two chapters related to each co-occurring condition. The first describes the condition and has a symptoms and issues list. The second walks you through building skills to manage your symptoms and issues pertaining to CBPD made up of the specific co-occurring condition and BPD.

Remember, the lists in this book aren't to be used to self-diagnose, but to help you build insight into your symptoms and behaviors so you can seek out appropriate mental health assistance. *Knowledge is empowerment.* Empowerment will help you manage and control your pure BPD and CBPD so you can replace maladaptive patterns with adaptive and healthy ones. You may want to bring the information and insight you gain from this book into your treatment sessions, as not only content for discussion, but also to help identify trajectories for treatment. We have a chapter for that, chapter 14, to help you.

In this chapter, we identified and differentiated pure BPD and CBPD. You should now have a solid foundation of knowledge about BPD that will help you go forward and better distinguish the symptoms, issues, and behaviors that have been problematic for you for so long. This chapter hopefully provided you with a clear understanding of the following:

- core and surface content and how it relates to mental health, specifically BPD

- the similarities and differences between pure BPD and CBPD

- the problematic cyclical pattern that's created by dismissing symptoms

- the co-occurring conditions that complicate your clinical picture, making it difficult to accurately determine which disorders are present

- the symptoms and issues that make up several comorbid conditions often seen in those with CBPD

As you journey through this book and embrace its knowledge, you open yourself to the adaptive strategies and skills to live your life differently, engage with others more effectively, and have more authentic and less chaotic relationships. At times, you may want to abandon this journey, but I encourage you to stick with it. Letting go of the old and embracing the new is scary for all of us, but it's an important part of life. One of my favorite quotes is by author Mandy Hale (2013), "It's okay to be scared. Being scared means you're about to do something really, really brave," and I commend you for it.

CHAPTER 3

The Turbulent Highs and Crashing Lows of Bipolar Disorder

"I'll be on top of Mount Everest only to plummet to the depths of hell."
—Wendy, 20

Wendy has a long history of depressive and manic episodes. She had her first depressive episode when she was fifteen years old. It was around this time that her first boyfriend broke up with her because she didn't want to go out to parties or watch him play football. Also, around this time, she stopped going to track practice, distanced herself from her friends, and would stay in her room in bed when not forced to go to school by her parents. After six weeks, she started to have more energy, she would get up in the morning and eat breakfast, and her grades improved. She reconnected with most of her friends and was able to get back onto the track team. Her mood maintained for the next two years.

Wendy's second depressive episode was more intense. She would cry uncontrollably, couldn't get out of bed, and didn't care how or what her parents did to try to get her out of bed to go to school. She just didn't have the energy. Her parents took her to her primary care doctor, who diagnosed her with depression. This caused her mother to break down into tears and she said, "I was hoping it would skip her." She then proceeded to recall how she, her sister, her mother, and her grandmother had all been diagnosed with depression. The doctor prescribed Wendy an antidepressant. About a week later, Wendy was highly irritable and pushy, making demands for things she wanted and would become hostile if she wasn't responded to immediately. She hardly slept and would talk and text her friends all hours of the night. Her parents initially dismissed this behavior as her returning to being "a typical seventeen-year-old girl," though she hadn't acted like this before. Because Wendy felt "so great," she stopped taking her antidepressant. After several days, her depressive episode returned with a vengeance, and all her symptoms were amplified. Her parents soon discovered she wasn't taking her antidepressant and began making sure she was taking it by giving it to her each morning, but Wendy only pretended to take it as she no longer wanted to try to get better. She felt her world and life were hopeless. After a month and a half, she started to have more energy and feel "more like myself," and she was able to graduate high school and attend college.

While away at college, she made friends, attended classes, got good grades, and functioned well. In the middle of her first year, she suddenly felt powerful, as if she had the answers to every question. She wasn't sleeping, she was meeting many new people, she was barely eating, she would talk nonstop, she relentlessly worked on her English paper, and she would have unprotected sex with people she hardly knew. Her friends, not knowing her history, thought she was being obnoxious at first and, then over several days, noticed that she wouldn't stop talking, was very flirtatious, and became unusually demanding and easily frustrated. Her dorm mate thought she was doing drugs and notified the counseling center and their English professor. When staff tried to intervene, Wendy became very upset, crying loudly and accusing them of trying to contain her brilliance out of jealousy, and ran out of the dorm. With staff in pursuit, she looked back over her shoulder and didn't see the car coming around the corner, which hit her, causing her to roll over the hood and onto the pavement.

Wendy was sent to the hospital for the injuries, scratches, and a fractured wrist, but she said she felt fine, couldn't feel a thing, which proved her bones were made of titanium. Her mood and energy level stayed elevated, and her mood rapidly changed from angry to sad and then back to angry while in the emergency room. The staff called a mental health specialist to evaluate her. She met with a psychologist who identified the manic episode, spoke with her parents, chronicled her history, and diagnosed her with bipolar I disorder. Her medication was changed to a mood stabilizer, and she began therapy to learn about mood fluctuations and management. Her parents were also educated about bipolar disorder signs, symptoms, and various intervention strategies. At this time, Wendy has a good prognosis to manage her disorder.

The Symptoms Identify the Diagnosis

You may relate to Wendy's experience, as it's a common one. Her change in mood first appears as depression, which is overlooked because she has a decrease in functioning, but it's not to the level of severe socioeconomic (socio-academic in her case) dysfunction. Her depression remits, but when it returns, it does so more intensely, causing significant dysfunction. She hadn't had a manic episode yet, so treating her depression appears appropriate. Notice that only medication is prescribed, no therapy. This is also an all-too-common occurrence. Therapy could've provided a continual resource to teach her the skills to identify and monitor her mood fluctuations.

The medication drives the exposition of manic-like symptoms (irritability, demanding, not sleeping). These are referred to as manic-like because they don't meet the threshold for a full manic or hypomanic episode yet (these will be described below). This is something else you may have experienced. In many instances, individuals stop their medication when in the manic phase of bipolar disorder. If you've been in this situation, you may have felt so great and so energized you didn't want it to stop, but as you know, it always does. During a manic phase, there's also a high degree of impaired insight that further complicates the issue, and stopping your medication can lead to a severe rebound of depressive symptoms. This rebound is a bouncing back of symptoms with increased intensity, like they did in Wendy's case.

Wendy's parents noticed the severe impairment and tried to take an active role in helping her. However, her parents failed to notice the manic-like symptoms, and they didn't know she should be reevaluated. Her parents weren't educated on symptoms, on how to handle them, and on what to do when new symptoms appear. At that time, she was unmedicated and saw no need for it, and her family and friends weren't aware she was noncompliant or of the effects of not being compliant. The manic-like episode then turned into a severe depressive episode. Fortunately, she was able to get through the next severe depressive episode and stabilize for an extended period.

Wendy's manic episode in college was so severe that it required the intervention from others. It was while she was in the hospital that the doctors were able to accurately identify the disorder and provide education and treatment. This story may frustrate you, and it's easy to point the finger at her parents and others who maybe *should've* been more attentive to her issues and concerns. Remember, you're reading this from the "outside-in" perspective, and mental illness is a challenge to identify and treat, particularly when you are the one trying to get help and identify resources; this is the "inside-out" perspective. Wendy's parents didn't know the signs and symptoms, as her mother was familiar with depression but not mania. Her doctor didn't tell them to be aware of other symptoms, suggest therapy, or provide other needed instructions. This is very common, and it requires that you and your loved ones be educated and vigilant about identified disorders and possible comorbid conditions and hence, the importance and value of books like this.

Wendy's experience is a best-case scenario for such a severe and multifaceted disorder. The reality is that bipolar disorder rarely occurs alone. In the story of Wendy, only bipolar disorder is present; however, approximately 95 percent of individuals with bipolar disorder also meet criteria for three or more other psychiatric diagnoses (Kessler 1999). One of the most challenging of these is BPD, as this negatively influences not only the presentation of mood symptoms but also the prevalence and likelihood of bipolar disorder remissions (Bieling, et al. 2003; Tamam, Ozpoyraz, and Karatas 2004). This is why you and those closest to you need to learn about the disorder and comorbid conditions in order to lessen the confusion of these complex disorders.

When Your Bipolar and Borderline Symptoms Overlap

You may have wondered whether your symptoms are caused by bipolar disorder or by BPD. This is a common question that isn't perplexing only to you but also to many psychologists, psychiatrists, and other specialists in the field. If you take your time, tease it out, as you're doing in this chapter, you can lessen the confusion and arrive at very helpful answers that you can use to manage your symptoms.

Research has shown that bipolar disorder and BPD are comorbid in approximately 27.6 percent of cases (Gunderson et al. 2006). Due to the high degree of prevalence, it's important to rule out or confirm the presence of one, the other, or both to ensure that accurate management and treatment are in place. When bipolar disorder and BPD make up your CBPD, you and your family, friends, coworkers, and treating professionals are tasked with a number of significant challenges due to similarities in symptoms as well as learning how to recognize when they present.

Irritable mood, racing thoughts and ideas, rapid speech, engaging in risk-taking behaviors, and impulsivity are symptoms of BPD but are also exhibited when individuals are in the manic phase of bipolar disorder. During the depressive phase of bipolar disorder, the individual experiences a decline in energy, prolonged sadness, a decrease in activity, poor concentration and decision-making, excessive worry and anxiety, feelings of guilt, and possible suicidal ideation, intent, or gestures. These are common symptoms seen in those with BPD as well. The average age of the initial manic or hypomanic episode is approximately eighteen, and the first BPD symptoms are likely to occur in early adulthood, which begins at age eighteen (APA 2013). Noting the similarity in symptoms and age of onset, it's no wonder there's so much confusion that impacts the interventions.

If you've been diagnosed with bipolar disorder when it's actually BPD, the approach to treatment and therapeutic expectations are going to be vastly different and likely miss the mark of an effective intervention. In this case, it can mean that you're given a medication that has limited impact on symptoms or causes side effects, and therapy may not be the central focus, like in Wendy's case. If therapy is pursued, the treatment trajectory and goals will be different and are *unlikely* to include therapeutic strategies from effective treatments for BPD, such as dialectical behavior therapy (DBT) or transference-focused psychotherapy.

In the opposite case, if you've been diagnosed with BPD, but it's actually bipolar disorder, you may not receive mood-stabilizing medication or interventions that pinpoint specific areas of concern, such as impairment in cognitive functioning (Porter, Inder, et al. 2020). Also, your mental health provider may be ill prepared to manage and confront your mood fluctuations and subsequent behavioral changes often seen in those with a bipolar disorder diagnosis. You may be misperceived as "treatment resistant," meaning that you've not been complying with treatment goals purposefully. The truth is that the mood episodes that accompany your bipolar disorder can be only minimally managed without proper medication intervention. This may have led you and your mental health provider to feel perplexed, frustrated, and hopeless, leaving you afraid of your own thoughts, emotions, and behaviors. Regretfully, this often leads to terminating treatment prematurely.

Let's take another look at Wendy's story to see how the presentation changes when she meets criteria for CBPD that's made up of bipolar disorder and BPD.

Wendy's Complex Journey

At age twenty, Wendy was seen at the college counseling center following release from an inpatient treatment program where she was diagnosed with bipolar disorder. She recalled for her therapist how she had been diagnosed with many different disorders since age fifteen, when her first boyfriend broke up with her and she felt depressed. It was after the breakup that she felt the full intensity of the emptiness in her stomach. The emptiness had been there for a long time, but she was previously able to fill it with school activities and hanging out with friends. Those things quit working, and she slipped deeper into her "inner void."

Eventually, "I crawled out, and I felt like my old self, but I started to look around and see who had stolen my boyfriend." Her friend Jessica was flirtatious with him, and Wendy just knew he was going to sleep with her. In the hall, she saw Jessica flirting with him, and she explained, "I just freaked. I ran up to her and slammed her books on the floor and got in her face. I told her to close her legs and leave him alone!" Jessica started crying, but Wendy kept verbally and physically pushing her until Jessica pushed back, and it escalated into a physical fight. She had been in trouble before, but this was the first time for a fight. Also, Wendy had recently become more promiscuous, and her old friends started to become distant, but she met new friends who were doing the same, which encouraged her to continue down this destructive path. She desperately wanted to fit into this new crowd to give her a sense of acceptance and definition.

Her second depressive episode got the attention of her parents, and she learned about her maternal family history of depression. Wendy became so angry with her mother for hiding this secret. She lost trust in her because if this was being hidden, she wondered what other secrets were hidden too. This left her with no parent she could trust. She never had much trust in her dad and felt like she hardly knew him because he was always working. "Instead of confiding in them, I did so with my friends and sex partners. This made me feel whole and connected," she explained. While taking antidepressants, she found that she was even more driven to get what she wanted. She could see her desires and taste her success. She felt energized, limitless, invincible, and as if she didn't need the medication any longer. At this time, she was also being aggressive and demanding, hardly sleeping, and talking and texting her friends all hours of the night. Soon, the inner void pulled her into her depression again. For the next six weeks, her sense of not knowing herself, the pain from the subterfuge of her mother, the indifference from her father, and the uncertainty of her future exacerbated and held her down in such a way that she felt as though she was "wrapped in a thousand-pound, cold, wet, smothering blanket."

She slowly came out of her depression, but the pain from her mom, emotional abandonment from her dad, and uncertainty of who she was and what she was going to do with her life remained, and she felt like it was going to follow her everywhere she went. Her parents demanded that she go to college, and she reluctantly agreed, feeling like it was hopeless because she had no real intelligence or skills to get through college and would rather get a job and marry some guy so she could have a baby to give it the love she never had.

While in college, she was directionless in her classes, not knowing what she was interested in or who she wanted to be. She had an anger episode after her boyfriend, whom she met a week earlier, didn't call her back right after she left him a message. During her anger episode, she yelled, punched the wall, and curled up and cried on her bed because she knew he was with someone else, that he had abandoned her, and that he was probably laughing about her behind her back with another woman. When he finally did call her back, she yelled and screamed at him that he didn't care about her and that he was probably cheating on her or was certainly going to the next chance he got.

After this relationship ended, she became very promiscuous, and her moods ranged from sad to angry to giddy. She would often argue with her dorm mate when she would say how worried she was about her. Wendy interpreted the concern as off-handed offensive remarks and as being talked down to and belittled. She then had short periods of sadness but not like before. She was unmedicated and in the middle of her freshman year when she suddenly felt a swell of energy like she had years before. She became even more sexually adventurous with multiple partners, her agitation and paranoia grew in intensity, and she kept talking incessantly and becoming even more demanding and easily frustrated. When her dorm mate reported her behavior to the counseling center and their English professor, Wendy became aggressive, accusing her of jealousy and wanting to ruin her life. She was hit by a car while fleeing from the counseling center and was taken to the emergency room, where she met with the psychologist who diagnosed her with bipolar disorder.

Wendy was given a mood stabilizer at first, which lessened some of her agitation and expansive mood, but her paranoia and hostility remained. She initially refused to participate in therapy and was making threats to harm herself if she wasn't released. She was disruptive on the unit, argumentative with the other patients, and often voiced her dissent over how she was being treated. She would continually state how no one cared about her and how others were pushing her to the point where she'd explode into violence. Her medications were changed in type and dosage with little reduction in symptoms.

Over the course of the next thirty days, she started to participate in treatment, and she remained compliant with her medication. In therapy, her BPD symptoms became apparent: unstable self-image, feelings of excessive self-criticism, chronic feelings of emptiness, uncertainty in goals and aspirations, impaired ability to recognize the feelings and needs of others, tendency to feel insulted, and the long history of intense, unstable, and conflicted close relationships marked by mistrust, neediness, and anxious preoccupation with real or imagined abandonment.

Through the course of ongoing therapy and routine visits with a psychiatrist, Wendy learned a lot about herself and her experiences. She's purposefully not in a relationship now, and she's working through her feelings of alienation from the people in her life. She remains compliant on her medication and has good insight into its purpose and importance. She continues to have low-level symptoms of depression that last for a few hours to one day. She has accepted her diagnoses of bipolar disorder and BPD, and she's determined to be a success story by learning about the signs and symptoms of her CBPD and how to manage it.

There is a vast difference between the two parts of Wendy's case study. The first is difficult but comparatively less chaotic and complex. In the second part, the perplexity and intensity of symptoms confuses the clinical picture. It initially appears that all symptoms are attributed to the manic episode, but once those are managed, other problems remain. The socioeconomic (or socio-academic) dysfunction continues, and the implementation of treatment is much more difficult due to the pathology that remains. If the psychologist and other treatment providers had been aware of the prevalence of comorbidity between bipolar disorder and BPD, she could've been assessed for these at intake. Once identified, treatment could've been provided to attenuate the BPD symptoms while simultaneously addressing the bipolar mood fluctuations. Wendy's story illustrates the importance of being aware of CBPD and how it broadens the scope of these disorders, resulting in improved diagnosis and treatment. Knowledge is empowerment, and you can use it to help you discern between these two disorders, just as we're going to do now.

Making the Bipolar Disorder and BPD Distinction

As you learned through Wendy's story, making the distinction between bipolar disorder and BPD isn't easy. Experts often cite the confusion and the problems that arise in trying to determine whether it's one, the other, or both. Bipolar disorder is made up of symptoms that are polar opposite of extremes of mood, hence the use of the term "bipolar." At the high end of this extreme is the manic episode, whereas at the low end is the major depressive episode.

To add further confusion is the presence of what are called hypomanic episodes. Hypomanic and manic episodes have immense overlap in symptoms and are differentiated by severity and the length of time symptoms are present. Mania and hypomania involve behavior and mood symptoms outside those typically seen in the individual. During a manic episode, the individual can't successfully participate in required daily activities and may need hospitalization due to delusions or hallucinations, and there is a high likelihood of impaired insight into behavior and emotions. During a hypomanic episode, family and friends notice a difference in behavior and mood. The individual may have impaired insight and may be able to fulfill some daily activities. Impairment is present, but task completion is possible and, in some cases, even likely. For example, you may quickly get up for work, rapidly get ready, and buzz around your house doing this and that because you're so full of energy, but you get too excited and distracted to actually leave for work as new and stimulating tasks keep popping up.

Timing is a critical component for distinguishing a manic from a hypomanic episode. For a manic episode, the symptoms must last for one week or longer, and during a hypomanic episode, they are present for four consecutive days or more (APA 2013). It's important to be aware that if a hypomanic episode goes untreated, it can lead to a manic episode. Being aware of the difference between manic and hypomanic episodes is of great value in understanding the degrees of mania, but going forward, I'll use the term "manic" or "mania" to include both manic and hypomanic symptoms.

A central component of the distinction between bipolar disorder and BPD is the timing and severity of symptoms. In bipolar disorder, the symptoms must be present for the specified amount of time: four or more days in a row and are outside usual behavior. For example, Wendy's symptoms of mania include her not sleeping, texting her friends, being promiscuous, feeling incredibly powerful and that she has every answer, and relentlessly working on her English paper for a week. These aren't symptoms associated with her BPD. Wendy has an anger episode due to her boyfriend not calling her back right after she left him a message. During her anger episode, she yells, punches the wall, and curls up and cries on her bed because she believes he's with another woman, has abandoned her, and is probably laughing behind her back with this other woman. When he finally does call her back, she yells and screams at him that he doesn't care about her and that he was probably cheating on her. These are symptoms of BPD (the inappropriate, intense anger, or difficulty controlling anger), not bipolar disorder.

Another critical differentiator is the presence of a stressor(s) and the related core content that it activates prior to a mood episode, such as feeling abandoned, empty, rejected, and so on, which are seen in those with BPD but not in those with bipolar disorder. Let's use the same instance of Wendy's boyfriend not calling her back. The stressor is him not calling her back, which activates her core content of abandonment and emptiness, which drives her surface content maladaptive pattern to cope with these feelings by having an anger episode that includes yelling, punching the wall, and curling up and crying on her bed. If he had called her back right away or picked up, she would've been less likely to have had her abandonment and emptiness core content activated (see chapter 2 for more on core and surface content issues and BPD) and the subsequent anger episode.

When an identifiable stressor(s) can't be identified and you behave in a way that's outside your usual behavior, such as displaying euphoria or grandiosity, for a period of four or more days, it's important to know that it is an indicator of a manic episode, not BPD acting out. For example, during her manic episode, Wendy is more excited, joyful, and energetic than usual; isn't sleeping for more than a few hours a day; is meeting many new people and having sex with them; and is texting and calling her friends all hours of the day and night. When you examine her behavior over time, you can't find an identifiable stressor for her behavior. This is because her behaviors are linked to her manic episode and not her BPD.

Periods of stability in mood and behavior are likely if you have bipolar disorder when you're not experiencing a manic or depressive episode. If you have BPD, you're likely to have periods of instability that are frequently peppered throughout your history. Also, if you have bipolar disorder, you're at an increased likelihood of having deep, meaningful, longstanding, and less turbulent relationships as compared to if you had BPD. This is because those with BPD often have relationship disruptions due to angry and impulsive outbursts, paranoia, and idealization and devaluation of their partner, whereas those with bipolar disorder are less likely to.

Bipolar disorder is much more responsive to medication than BPD, and medication's lack of efficacy on core content can be seen as a discriminator. This distinction is based upon the effectiveness of medication on bipolar disorder, as it significantly reduces not only the severity of manic and depressive episodes but also lengthens the period of stability when taken as directed. Medication has limited impact on BPD. Medication only addresses surface content, such as depression, anxiety, impulsiveness, and so on. It doesn't attenuate the severity of core content, such as feelings of emptiness, low self-worth, or abandonment. Due to these differences in response to medication, if you have BPD, it's likely that you would be prescribed medications from different classes (for example, antipsychotics, antianxiety, antidepressants, mood stabilizers, and anticonvulsants) to attempt to lessen the intensity of core content, but medications are unable to do this (Starcevic and Janca 2018). For example, there is no medication for emptiness or abandonment fears. Many argue that these issues manifest as depression and anxiety, so treating these psychological issues is treating the core content. However, due to your BPD, you are likely to continue to report reduced efficacy of your medications to manage your BPD symptoms, often feeling continued emptiness and fear that your loved one is going to abandon you. This is because your core content issues drive surface content symptoms.

Consider This: Identifying Mania, Depression, and BPD Symptoms

Symptoms identify the diagnosis, but many times these overlap, leading to misdiagnosis and time spent treating the wrong disorder. Knowledge and awareness of symptoms can help you better identify which diagnoses are present, which are absent, or if they're occurring together, creating CBPD.

On a new page in your journal, make two columns. Write "Manic Symptoms" at the top of the column on the left, and write "Depressive Symptoms" at the top of the column on the right. Number from 1 to 11 down the left side of the page and number from 1 to 16 down the left side of the column on the right. As you read each symptom, put a *T* to indicate the symptom is true and something you experience often, or an *F* if the symptom is false and something you don't experience often. Be sure to read the directions and take note of the time components, as these are critical to determining whether symptoms are situationally bound or occur across multiple contexts. Symptoms that occur across multiple contexts are likely related to mental health disorders, whereas those that are situationally dependent are likely due to the circumstance or location.

Only consider the presence of these symptoms and issues when you're not using drugs or alcohol or taking medication and they are unrelated to a medical condition. This list isn't meant to be used for clinical diagnosis but to help you build insight into your symptoms and issues so you can better manage them and seek out appropriate mental health assistance. Let's start with manic symptoms.

Manic Symptoms

You've experienced the following for four or more days in a row.

1. My mood is unusually higher and more irritable than usual.

2. I'm intensely goal focused and full of energy to the point it creates problems.

3. I feel like I'm on top of the world, can do anything, and deserve all that's great and special.

4. I'm sleeping less than three hours a night without feeling tired or worn out.

5. I'm more talkative than usual or feel pressured to keep talking.

6. I'm long-winded and ramble, rapidly changing thoughts or ideas that are loosely connected to one another.

7. I'm easily distracted by insignificant details or things going on in my environment.

8. I'm unusually intense and goal directed at school or work, by an activity, or with sex.

9. I experience anxious restlessness that causes me to feel the intense need to move constantly.

10. I intensely participate in activities with a high likelihood of painful outcomes, such as spending sprees, promiscuity, or bad business or employment decisions.

11. These symptoms cause socioeconomic dysfunction.

Depressive Symptoms

You've experienced the following symptoms for at least two consecutive weeks.

1. I feel sad, hopeless, and helpless most of the day, nearly every day.

2. Other people have noticed that my mood is sullen and that I appear sad.

3. My interest in things I usually enjoy is significantly decreased or absent.

4. I lose weight due to not eating and having no appetite.

5. I gain weight due to overeating.

6. I'm unable to sleep well.

7. I oversleep on a consistent basis (hypersomnia).

8. I experience uneasiness that has caused me to feel a strong need to move constantly.

9. I persistently have low energy or feel very tired.

10. My depressive symptoms don't lessen even when situations resolve or others return to my life.

11. I feel worthless or guilty for no identifiable reason or for something I've done.

12. It's hard for me to focus my attention or make a decision.

13. I think about death or ending my life.*

14. I have a specific plan to end my life.*

15. I engage in actions to end my life.*

16. These symptoms cause socioeconomic dysfunction.

These are symptoms related to thoughts or intent for self-harm or suicide. Please turn to the introduction and refer to the section titled "Suicidal Ideation or Intent" for resources that can help.

Take a moment to go over your BPD symptoms from chapter 1 to help you clarify the separation of bipolar disorder symptoms from BPD. Look over your manic and depressive symptoms ratings and mark or circle the ones you indicated as true for you. These ratings are the significant symptoms that increase the likelihood of bipolar disorder being an accurate diagnosis. Remember, this is an insight-building exercise, not a diagnostic one, and only a qualified mental health or medical provider can give you a diagnosis.

The last criterion is the universal symptom, and if you identified it as true for you, you're indicating that the other symptoms also identified as true significantly disrupt how you live your life. This increases the likelihood of meeting criteria for the full disorder. However, if you marked the universal symptom as false, you may have symptoms related to bipolar disorder, but they're not to the level of causing continuous disruption in your life. This still merits exploration, and you may benefit from reading the next chapter to learn management skills.

Listing your symptoms can be a very powerful experience because BPD and comorbid conditions can be overwhelming when seen as a whole. When understood as a combination of particular symptoms and issues, your CBPD is more manageable and your efforts more impactful and focused as they target particular symptoms. This leads to greater symptom reduction and overall control of your CBPD.

As you went through the chapter and exercise, you may have found that you have many symptoms consistent with mania, depression, *and* BPD. This alludes to the presence of your CBPD being made up of bipolar disorder and BPD. The following chapter will help you take this knowledge and apply it to learn strategies to manage your CBPD.

In this chapter, we explored the intersection and distinction of bipolar disorder and BPD. This type of CBPD baffles not only clients but seasoned professionals as well. This chapter hopefully lessened the confusion inherently associated with CBPD that's made up of bipolar disorder and BPD. This chapter was designed to provide you with a clear understanding of the following:

- the bipolar disorder and BPD symptoms that make up this type of CBPD

- the distinction and overlap of both disorders that cause confusion between bipolar disorder and BPD

- the similarities and differences between manic and hypomanic symptoms

- your own manic, depressive, and BPD symptoms and issues to help you gain greater understanding of your mood episodes and fluctuations

The information you learned from this chapter can be applied to the skills and abilities you'll learn in the next chapter. Knowledge is essential to change, but using this knowledge to take action against that which holds you back, like your CBPD, is critical.

CHAPTER 4

Activities to Maintain Your
Mood Stability

In this chapter we're going to go over how to build insight and manage your symptoms to strengthen your knowledge, skills, and abilities to lessen and have more control over the negative impact of your CBPD.

The previous chapter hopefully provided you with the knowledge and insight regarding your symptoms. Now, we're going to take that information and use it to build a strategy to help you enhance your self-efficacy and self-control. The first step to managing this type of CBPD is to stabilize the bipolar episodes. Due to bipolar disorder having biological underpinnings, medication is going to be very important to control manic and depressive episodes. Effective medication management and compliance are critical to lessening the bipolar episodes that exacerbate BPD symptoms. Having unmedicated bipolar episodes that co-occur with BPD is like periodically throwing gas on a fire that's burning down your house in the hopes that the flames will just go out one day and cause no more damage. Regretfully, this just doesn't happen. We have to develop and use the tools to prevent the house from catching fire to begin with.

Early-Warning Signs

Once medication is on board, identifying early-warning signs of mood fluctuations is the next step. You may have experienced an increase in energy, loss of interest in people or activities, impaired concentration, irritability, poor sleep, and other things when your symptoms first appeared, but you didn't know what was going on. Being aware of symptom presentation is a critical component. In Wendy's situation, she knows she's moving into a manic phase when she experiences insomnia and has trouble focusing on what her friends and family are saying. She keeps a mood journal and uses an app on her phone to help track her moods and behaviors. This gives her invaluable insight, and she keeps up with it daily. When she experiences these early-identifiable symptoms, she reaches out to her mental health provider, psychiatrist or primary care physician, or her friends and parents for help. She also has agreements with friends and family that when they see her early-warning signs, they'll tell her.

Consider This: Your Early-Warning Signs

On a new page in your journal, write "Early-Warning Signs" at the top. Review the early-warning signs listed below and write down which ones are indicators to you that you're moving into a manic or depressive episode. Remember, these are changes in mood, manic or depressive, that aren't connected to a trigger (a trigger is a thought, feeling, action, or reaction to something that drives you to respond using adaptive or maladaptive strategies).

elevated or irritable mood	depressed mood
increased self-esteem or self-confidence	unable to concentrate or make decisions
insomnia or decreased need for sleep	hypersomnia or sleeping too much
racing thoughts	fatigue or loss of energy
talking more than usual	feeling sluggish or weary
easily distracted	feeling worthless or guilty
increased goal-directed activity (cleaning or spending excessively)	loss of interest or pleasure in activities that you used to enjoy
highly driven to engage in pleasurable activities	thoughts of suicide or death*

*These symptoms are related to thoughts of or intent for self-harm or suicide. Please turn to the introduction and refer to the section titled "Suicidal Ideation or Intent" for resources that can help.

Increasing your awareness of early-warning signs is a critical first step to gaining greater control over your bipolar mood episodes. Let's take this information and move forward to develop a plan for when you feel your early-warning signs arise.

An additional step to monitoring and managing bipolar mood episodes includes planning early interventions. These are clear and detailed steps for you, and trusted others, to take when early-warning signs are present. *Preparation is very important.* You don't want to wait until your mood episode takes over to try to manage it. This is equivalent to waiting until you're in a house fire to start trying to put it out. By that time, it's way too late. Common early action plans include:

- using mindfulness and relaxation strategies

- calling your mental health provider

- giving a trusted person your credit card if spending is an issue

- giving friends and family intervention steps that detail how to intervene when these symptoms become present

These are great things to have written down in detail so you and your loved ones can access this list to help you when you need it.

Consider This: Your Early-Intervention Plan

In this exercise, you're going to be as descriptive as you can in detailing what you and others are to do to help you. You may not know all the answers right now, and that's okay. You can use any of the strategies in this chapter or any of the others to help you. Do some research online on what others do to help control their symptoms or ask your mental health provider for suggestions. Be as detailed as possible and make sure you share it with trusted others in your social support network.

On a new page in your journal, write "Early-Intervention Plan" at the top. Below that write each step and leave enough space to put your responses. You can even have each step on its own page. Do whatever works for you. Let's go through the exercise now:

Step 1. What I will do first when I feel my early-warning signs. Some suggestions are to practice mindfulness, use grounding techniques (see chapter 8), express your thoughts and fears in writing, exercise, don't isolate, and make sure you're compliant with prescribed medication. Remember, you're identifying your early-warning signs, and you want to engage in behaviors to try to prevent the warning signs from exacerbating.

Step 2. What I want my trusted other to *do* to help me. Some suggestions are to verify you've been compliant with your medication; limit access to your impulsive "go-to's," which may include food, drugs, alcohol, social media, and so on; take a walk with a friend or family member; do mindfulness or grounding techniques together; and call your doctor or 9-1-1 when... (add specific details here).

Step 3. What I want my trusted other to *say* to me to help me. Some suggestions are to listen to your fears, let you know you're not alone, be optimistic, and help you remember the good times.

Your early-intervention plan is very helpful for you and your loved ones because it gives them a road map on how to help you best. The expectation can't be that they're responsible for your moods or controlling your moods. The idea here is to outline how you can help yourself but also how to get assistance from others to help you amplify your ability to manage your moods. It is possible, it can be done, and you can do it!

Tracking Your Mood Episodes

The next step to managing your CBPD is to track your mood episodes. This is critical for identifying and using alternative adaptive and healthy responses. Doing this will help you determine whether the changes are related to bipolar disorder or BPD. The first step is to determine whether the activating event is related to a trigger. Next, write down which of your core content was activated, and then write down the thoughts, feelings, and mental images that occurred as a result of this activation. The fourth step is to identify the urge you feel to respond and then to note how you responded or planned to respond. Lastly, write down an alternative healthy and adaptive response. To help you work through this, download the "Daily Mood Tracking Worksheet" at http://www.newharbinger.com/48558.

Using this worksheet regularly will empower you by building insight into your mood fluctuations and help you determine whether they're related to your bipolar disorder or BPD symptoms. If your responses, urges, thoughts, feelings, and mental images are related to core content activation, they're BPD symptom responses. If they're not, they're likely related to bipolar disorder mood fluctuations.

Your Cognitive Biases

Another area that adds significant difficulty in processing and functioning for individuals with this type of CBPD is cognitive biases. Research shows that individuals with bipolar disorder and BPD are impaired by a tendency toward cognitive biases (Lahera et al. 2012; Peckham, Johnson, and Gotlib 2016; Baer et al. 2012). There are hundreds of cognitive biases, but here we're going to review cognitive biases pertaining to attention, memory, distorted beliefs, and interpretation. The following chart lists the biases, their definitions, and examples. Review each of the cognitive biases below and complete the exercise that follows in your journal.

Cognitive Bias	Example
Attentional bias: Tendency to focus awareness on certain information over other information.	When I'm angry, I focus more on things in my environment that are related to anger as opposed to those that are pleasant or calming.
Memory bias: Tendency to recall memories that are similar to the current emotional state.	During depressive episodes, I'm more likely to recall instances of sadness and loss, compared to when I'm not feeling depressed.

Cognitive Bias	Example
Distorted beliefs bias: Tendency to rely on beliefs that are based in emotion and are not supported by observable and identifiable facts.	Distorted beliefs are when I feel like I "just know" there's an unpredictable and severe consequence right around the corner even though there's no justifiable evidence of it.
Interpretation bias: Tendency to inaccurately attribute an ambiguous stimulus to a mistaken perception.	While feeling socially anxious, I interpret my partner's yawn as a sign of boredom with me and the relationship, rather than exhaustion.

As you went through the chart, were you able to identify which cognitive biases you use? Recognizing your biases is important, but breaking them down into how they manifest in your life is empowering. Making it personal helps to get a feel for the impact and intensity of distortion these cognitive biases can cause.

Consider This... In your journal, write "My Cognitive Biases" at the top of the page. On the left side of the page, write each cognitive bias listed above, but leave enough space to write out how the cognitive bias is expressed in your life, just like the example. When in a manic or depressive phase or when having a BPD depressive, agitated, or euphoric mood, the biases you use are heavily influenced by those phases and moods. Having the insight into which ones you're most likely to experience not only helps you identify the mood you're in at the time but also empowers you to use cognitive restructuring to combat it, which adds to a more authentic and realistic view to the perception of your world.

Restructuring Your Cognitions

Cognitive restructuring is a skill where you identify and challenge irrational or maladaptive thoughts, such as the biases listed above. There are six steps to cognitive restructuring. In your journal, write "Restructuring My

Cognitions" at the top. You're going to list each of the six steps outlined below, leaving enough space to write your responses.

1. The upsetting event. Be as specific as you can in describing this event. For example, *My boss calling everyone else into the office for performance reviews, and I'm last.*

2. My mood. Before you identify your mood, take three slow, deep breaths in through your nose and out through your mouth. This is to help you gain control over your mood and lessen the distortion of being emotionally overwhelmed. Write down your moods, whether they're mad, sad, glad, afraid, agitated, and so on. For example, *I feel angry, disgusted, worried, and afraid.*

3. My thoughts and images. Identify the thoughts and images that popped into your head when the event occurred. For example, *I know he hates me, and he's going to fire me. I imagine going into his office and him firing me, and I'm homeless forever.*

4. Bias betrayal. Using the cognitive biases chart above and the information from your journal after you did the "My Cognitive Biases" exercise, identify which biases are in place and whether they connect to steps 2 and 3. For example, *The distorted beliefs bias and the interpretation bias are at work, causing the distortion in my thoughts and images, and I know this adds to feeling angry, disgusted, and afraid. I worry about being discarded.*

5. Challenge to do it differently. Now that you've enhanced your awareness of the event and all the related aspects, it's time to challenge them and reassess them using identifiable and observable information. For example, *My boss often says he likes my work. I've worked for him for nine years, and other performance reviews have been good or great. He's calling me in last because my last name starts with Z, and he's going alphabetically.*

6. Reexamination. Reassess your thoughts, feelings, and images after you did steps 2, 3, and 4 and challenged the distortion in step 5. For example, *My boss doesn't have it in for me. I'm good at my job and valued* *by him. I feel less angry, disgusted, worried, and afraid. I see the situation accurately, and I'm better able to control my thoughts, feelings, and actions.*

After this activity, do you feel more in control? Has your negative mood decreased? After going through this process, most people feel more grounded and relaxed. They've challenged their cognitive distortion and supported or refuted the inaccuracies.

Cognitive restructuring is a powerful process to do whenever you feel yourself being pushed and pulled by overwhelming thoughts, feelings, and images associated with your CBPD phases and moods.

In this chapter, you learned the skills to enhance control, empower yourself with choice, and make changes to manage this multifaceted type of CBPD. This chapter hopefully provided you with a clear understanding of the following:

- your early-warning signs

- your early-intervention plan

- how to use the "Daily Mood Tracking Worksheet" to increase insight into your mood fluctuations

- your cognitive biases and how to restructure them to have a more authentic and realistic view of yourself and your world

The turbulent highs and crashing lows of bipolar disorder that co-occur with your BPD symptoms make up your CBPD. The skills and abilities you learned through this chapter, and will learn throughout the rest of this book, will empower you to take control of your thoughts, feelings, behaviors, and patterns to manage your life. Every wonderful success starts with the initial steps of acquiring knowledge and then putting it into practice to get you to your goal. You have the knowledge to step outside your CBPD and into your new self-empowered life. Use these skills daily, build them up as adaptive habits, and the positive change you're seeking will emerge.

CHAPTER 5

Your Sins and Sorrows in Depression

"Nothing matters when you're alone in the dark."

—Ray, 35

Ray is entering treatment for the first time after being found by his wife, Maria, unresponsive after she returned home from a funeral for her uncle. When she arrived, Ray was lying in bed facing the ceiling. As she walked into the room, she was hit by the intense smell of urine, feces, and body odor as he hadn't gotten out of bed for several days to eat, go to the restroom, or take a shower. He looked at her face that showed horror and shock and said, "Just let me wither, as nothing matters when you're alone in the dark." She immediately called 9-1-1, and he was taken to the hospital.

While he was at the hospital, he answered questions with one-word responses and broke down crying. He would trail off into statements of despair, such as, "I feel like I have no batteries to get up, look up, think, or imagine anything. No one cares anyway, and we're all doomed to either kill each other or live out this life until we're finally allowed to leave through death or old age." He presented with a rapid heartbeat and breathing and reported feeling dizzy when not lying down, and his skin was extremely dry. Ray had been in bed for the last five days and was severely dehydrated. He was admitted to the hospital to be stabilized.

After twenty-four hours, Ray's medical condition improved, but his psychological symptoms remained. A psychiatrist came to see him to assess his situation. He again answered using one-word responses, had a fatalistic outlook on his life and everyone else he knew, reported continued fatigue that didn't go away with rest and sleep, and would cry for no identifiable reason. He was offered an antidepressant, which he refused because he saw no point in medication "to change who I really am." Due to not being an imminent harm to himself or others, he was discharged, and Maria took him home. Before being discharged, he was given the contact information for a psychologist to follow up with in the next few days. His wife made sure he went.

At the first session, Ray only gave one-word responses. The psychologist attempted to ask him how he was doing, but Ray would only talk about how the world was "dark and doomed" and how hopeless he felt, followed by him breaking down crying. At the next session, Ray agreed to allow Maria to sit in. When Ray wouldn't respond to the psychologist's questions, she would answer, which provided a much clearer picture of Ray's current and historical issues.

Maria and Ray met in high school. They fell in love and had great plans to leave El Paso and move to New York, where he could sell his art and she could focus on school to become a teacher. They graduated high school, and Maria became pregnant before they could make their big move. They needed to stay in El Paso to get family support. Ray got a job at a security company, and Maria stayed home with their daughter, Jenni. Ray was doing well at the security company and was given a promotion after working there for three years; he had to be twenty-one to be a supervisor. About six months after his twenty-first birthday, he started to "not be himself." He would get angry easily and isolate himself, appeared sad most of the time, completely stopped painting, and would sketch images of dark skies and people falling into deep dark holes.

His moods would come and go for years but didn't worsen until his thirtieth birthday, when Maria found him crying in his car before work. She asked him what was wrong, and he said he felt guilty bringing Jenni into a world so corrupt, evil, and empty. He said he couldn't make up his mind whether he should divorce Maria or not because she deserved someone better who wasn't "an empty vessel." Ray told her that it would be better if he wasn't here but would never take his life because of his daughter, as it would leave no one else to protect her.

Over the years, his symptoms worsened, and Ray continually refused to see a doctor or a mental health provider. He started leaving work early because he was too tired and felt overwhelmed by the responsibilities of his job. He then stopped going in at all and would sit in his car across the street, watching his coworkers and thinking how much better their lives were than his. He was eventually fired and felt that this was proof of his inherent failure as a person, a father, and a husband. When Maria's uncle passed away, Ray was indifferent. A part of him was sad, but another larger part was numb. When she left, he slipped into bed, not having the energy to get up, giving in fully to his despair, and stared at the ceiling until he was found by Maria.

After being released from the hospital into Maria's care and with her encouragement, Ray agreed to take medication for his mood. Maria monitored the medication and continued to track his food and liquid intake. Over the next several weeks, Ray's symptoms lessened, and he remained in treatment and started opening up, revealing that his mother, father, and grandparents on both sides had depression. He had an uncle who completed suicide when he was young, and he remembered the pain it caused his father and didn't want to do that to Maria or Jenni. As treatment continued, Ray felt energetic, and his ability to think was improving. He was able to use the strategies he learned to manage the pull into his "depressive hole." He was eventually able to get his job back at the security company and began painting again. Fourteen months after starting treatment, remaining compliant with his medication and using his adaptive strategies, he sold his first painting.

Ray continued to do well, and with his depression stabilized, he built up the courage to submit his paintings for an exhibit in Santa Fe, New Mexico. Waiting to hear about his acceptance into the upcoming show, Ray would check the mail every day. He couldn't wait. This was going to be major exposure for his art. When he finally got the letter, he quickly opened it, his heart racing with excitement as the El Paso sun beat down on his face. The letter said that the gallery was declining his submission and that they were going to put another artist in his place. Ray was breathless and felt the tight grip of his depression rising. He began thinking, *They know I'm a fraud. My art isn't good enough to be in a show. I'm just a security company manager with a hobby, and that's all I'll be. Jenni and Maria will be embarrassed to know me, they'll leave me, and I'll be alone, lost, and end up lifeless in bed withering.*

Ray took control of his feelings, thoughts, and mental images linked to his depression that were building inside of him. He said to himself, *Okay, I'm getting overwhelmed, and my depression just went from a 1 (low level) to a 6 (moderate level). I need to define my feelings. I'm sad, disappointed, afraid. I think no one will ever like my art. I see myself dying in bed alone.* He pushed back against these default depressive feelings, thoughts, and images. He then said to himself, *I've sold my art before. They invited me to submit to the art show. I'm getting more and more recognition every day. I also don't know why they replaced me. I'm going to find out, but no matter what the reason, I choose my worth. My art is unique and powerful, that's what the* New York Times *critic said, and that's what I believe.* Ray did a quick self-assessment, *I'm now at a 3 and will talk this over with Maria and Jenni and let them know about my disappointment, but these things happen, and it's nothing I did.*

Ray continued to use his strategies to manage his depression and to keep control of it. Over the next few years, with his doctor's awareness and guidance, Ray lessened his medication and adopted a healthy lifestyle of eating well, exercising, self-monitoring his depression, and using his strategies. He sold more paintings and was eventually featured at the art gallery that had once rejected him.

The Symptoms Identify the Diagnosis

Was there anything about Ray's experience that mimics your own? Ray's depression was longstanding and worsened over the years due to not seeking treatment. It's important to know that it's not Ray's fault and that depression isn't a passive illness, but a very active one. It's an insidious disorder that works against you, convinces you to let go of hope, drives you to embrace despair, and distorts your belief in getting control of it and mastering it.

Ray's symptoms were initially mild to moderate and didn't cause socio-economic dysfunction (see chapter 1 to learn more about socioeconomic dysfunction), and they remained that way for years. After his twenty-first birthday, his depression exacerbated. He started getting angry easily, isolated himself, appeared sad most of the time, completely stopped painting, and sketched images of dark skies and people falling into deep dark holes. He didn't seek treatment at that time, and his depression was recurrent; Ray's symptoms would "come and go for years." Recurrent means that the depression comes and goes in episodes, which is more common than occurring once (a single episode) and lasting for one long continuous major depressive episode (APA 2013).

His depressive symptoms remained unchecked until his thirtieth birthday when they became severe and started to cause socioeconomic dysfunction. By then, the depression took root, influencing his perceptions of self and others, causing him to cry before work, leading him to see the world as a "corrupt, evil, and empty" place, and leading to uncertainty whether he should end his marriage because of his low sense of self-worth. As you can see, all these things were worsening, but Ray continued to refuse to see a mental health provider or someone who could help him. Regretfully, this isn't uncommon; perhaps you've been in Ray's situation. Many individuals don't seek treatment for depression until it reaches a level of high or extreme severity, and even then, they tend to go for treatment for something other than depression (Roberts et al. 2020). This is because depression makes you think hope is a scary thing, so you shy away from it. The reality is that hope is a critical part of remitting symptoms and managing it.

Due to Ray's depression, he lost his job, felt emotionally numb, and was overwhelmed by depression. It'd finally taken over his life to such a degree that he didn't have the energy to even use the restroom and only had enough energy to cry. When he was taken to the emergency room for treatment, he was dehydrated, which was treated, but he still refused treatment for depression and was sent home with contact information for help. Fortunately, Maria called and set up the appointment. With no attenuation in symptoms, because Ray didn't participate in treatment. Maria took a guiding hand and participated in therapy with him. She monitored his food and liquid intake and medication compliance, and his symptoms remitted. With his symptoms attenuated, Ray participated in therapy, learned the skills he needed to monitor and manage his condition, began to embrace hope to get better, and was able to get control over his depression and put his life back on track.

As you read Ray's story, you may have noticed the shift from him making his choices and controlling his life to his wife having to do that for him. This is a common occurrence when depression goes unchecked and worsens. Ray and Maria had been together a long time, and he was stead-fastly resistant to treatment until it reached the extreme severity level. Ray's story doesn't say why, and the "why" is irrelevant, as untreated depression is like an untreated infection; over time it'll worsen until it takes over your functioning and in some cases your life. Also like an infection, it can be treated, contained, and managed over time.

Ray continued treatment, learned to monitor his moods, and built insight into his early signs and symptoms. Just because Ray is in treatment and doing well doesn't mean his depression isn't going to try to make a comeback into his life. We saw this at the end of the story. The depression could've taken hold, but he used his adaptive strategies to manage it, and he was open and honest with those who support him about what happened, how he felt, and the strategies he used to go forward. He actively pushed back on the insidious nature of the depression and was able to control it, and you can too.

Only major depressive disorder was present, and we see how Ray strug-gled with symptoms, managing those symptoms without assistance, and how severe it got before he willingly participated in treatment. Major depres-sive disorder is common around the world. It has a lifetime prevalence rate of 16.2 percent in the United States (Kessler et al. 2003), and worldwide is expected to be the leading cause of death and disease complication by 2030 (World Health Organization 2008). Certainly, major depressive disorder is complicated all on its own, but when comorbid with a personality disorder, like BPD, it's even more problematic. When you initially presented to therapy, did you report another presenting concern (for example, relationship or work stress) or depressive symptoms? Not reporting depressive symptoms is very common as you may not have known it was major depressive disorder, and you certainly may not have known about BPD because it's often identified later. These disorders are difficult to diagnose and treat due to symptom overlap. This is why it's so important to learn about comorbid conditions in order to lessen the confusion of these complex disorders.

Your Depressive-Borderline Complexity

Major depressive disorder occurs in 83 percent of individuals with BPD (Zanarini et al. 1998) and can be a deadly co-occurrence. The combination of major depressive disorder and BPD has been found to increase the frequency and severity of suicide attempts (Soloff et al. 2000). The increased risk of CBPD due to the presence of these two conditions illustrates the need for accurate identification and treatment.

Major depressive disorder symptoms are very similar to the depressive symptoms that are part of BPD. They often include:

- consistent low mood

- low energy and volition

- decreased interest in activities you once enjoyed (anhedonia)

- disrupted sleep patterns (insomnia or hypersomnia)

- weight gain or loss

- a sense of worthlessness

- difficulty concentrating and focusing your attention

- increased suicidal ideation or self-harm behaviors

- impaired social, academic, or occupational functioning

- intense guilt and shame

Research shows that your outlook and interpretation of yourself, others, and circumstances are a critical factor in the prediction of major depressive disorder episodes (Bonde 2008; Charles et al. 2013; Greaney et al. 2019). Major depression tends to cause greater emotional reactions to perceived environmental stressors, which increases the likelihood of experiencing a depressive disorder episode. This fits with the confusion related to your BPD: you're at a higher likelihood of perceiving and experiencing stressful events in a more intense way, which prompts a BPD symptomatic, sometimes depressive, response.

Depression can occur in a single episode or be recurrent. Recurrent episodes are more common, and the presence of a single episode increases the probability of having another in the future (APA 2013). A single episode is when you experience consistent and unabating depressive symptoms, such as those listed above, and it continues without a lessening of symptoms or a return to "normal" functioning (before depressive symptoms began). You don't have to have all the symptoms listed above, but the more you have and the longer they're present, the greater the probability you're experiencing a major depressive episode that qualifies for major depressive disorder. Recurrent episodes are much more likely to be present, such as in the story of Ray, as his depression ebbed and flowed. It's not one long steady depressive occurrence, but depression comes and goes in episodes.

It's important to distinguish whether the depressive features are related to fear of separation followed by impulsive suicidal ideation, gestures, or self-harm behaviors (Gunderson 2009) or not. In some cases, depressive symptoms are a means to express feelings you're unable to verbally convey, such as hopelessness, anger, frustration, hatred, powerlessness, or disappointment. These maladaptive expressions are often directed at a specific person or situation and tend to be minimally attenuated by medication. Working through the situation or processing the issue with your therapist in treatment tends to produce the greatest reduction in symptoms. In a case like this, the root must be discerned. Is your suicidality and self-harm a byproduct of the maladaptive need to communicate pain and to acquire a sympathetic, or possibly a relationship restorative, response (a BPD component), or is it grounded in despair and hopelessness (a depressive component)? This is a critical determination to make because it guides symptoms and disorder identification as well as future treatment.

If you believe you have major depression only, you're likely to receive an antidepressant, and you may participate in individual therapy. Interestingly, studies have continually shown that therapy is as effective, or more effective, than medication to treat depression (Cuijpers et al. 2013; De Maat et al. 2006; Imel et al. 2008). As illustrated in Ray's story, Ray went for an extended period without treatment, which permitted his depressive symptoms to worsen. When he did receive treatment, he was prescribed an antidepressant and was *also* provided treatment where he learned skills to manage his symptoms.

In situations where you're assessed and diagnosed with major depressive disorder, but your BPD goes unidentified, the treatment approach and outcome are very different, and there is a low probability of success. Depression is often resistant to medication when it co-occurs with BPD (Gunderson 2009). In treatment, you and your therapist are likely to continually encounter obstacles of sullen mood, a tendency to report passive and active suicidal ideation and intent with co-occurring nonlethal self-harm gestures, and an affective instability that includes intense sadness, hopelessness, or worthlessness for a distinct period of time. Additional symptoms are often misconstrued as having depressive origins and include frequent temper outbursts, agitation, and irritability that mimics depression with anxious distress. You also may report feelings of emptiness and stress-related paranoia with severe dissociative symptoms that look like depression with psychotic features. This can easily send you and your therapist into a tailspin that often concludes with you terminating treatment early and leaving you feeling a greater sense of loss and hopelessness about your mood and your life. This doesn't have to be the case. You can push back against your CBPD by continuing to go through this chapter and this book.

If your CBPD is composed of major depressive disorder and BPD, focusing on the depressive symptoms alone is unlikely to attenuate the condition because these symptoms are driven by BPD pathology and *not* depressive symptomatology. When the BPD is addressed and begins to attenuate, the depression does as well. This is a very different approach and a very different clinical presentation that all clinicians need to be aware of because missing it could lead to misdiagnosis, early termination of treatment, and greater episodes of lethal self-harm or worse.

Let's take another look at Ray's story to see how the presentation changes when he meets criteria for CBPD that's made up of major depressive disorder and BPD.

Ray's Complex Journey

Ray was taken by ambulance to the emergency room for extreme dehydration after not eating and drinking for five days. He smelled of urine, feces, and body odor due to not using the restroom properly or attending to his hygiene. Physicians and nurses started an IV, which he attempted to reject, but he was too weak to physically prevent them from starting it.

While at the hospital, Ray refused to answer any questions, appeared angry and agitated, and broke down crying. He shouted about the listlessness, exhaustion, and hopelessness that consumed him.

After twenty-four hours, Ray's medical condition improved, but his psychological symptoms remained, and he refused to speak to the psychiatrist. When he found out that he was going to be discharged, Ray began to speak to staff and the psychiatrist, but his mood and outlook remained negative. He was offered an antidepressant, which he refused, saying, "You want to change who I really am. Nice try, it's not going to work. They don't make medication that strong."

He remained in the hospital for an additional twenty-four hours to assess whether he needed psychiatric hospitalization due to his hopeless and helpless outlook. During this additional time in the hospital, Ray classified his relationship with his wife as "rocky and challenging" due to her being at work so much and her trying to poison his daughter against him. He reported continued and longstanding fatigue, low frustration tolerance, and restlessness.

Ray was eventually discharged, and Maria took him home. They were given the number for a psychologist for Ray to follow up with in a few days. Ray initially refused to call because he saw no point and felt it was a tactic by Maria to take away his parental rights and leave him. Over the next few days, Ray's agitation and sadness worsened and during an argument, he punched the wall and broke a kitchen cabinet door. With the broken cabinet door in front of him, he began crying and fell to the floor. "Just leave me already. You know I'm no good. Take Jenni and leave and let me die already of a broken heart," he said. The next day, Maria called the psychologist and set up an appointment for her and Ray; she didn't want him to go and refuse to speak like he had in the hospital and to therapists before that.

Once in the psychologist's office, Ray said, "You've got to do something, Doc. This has gotta stop." Ray recalled his history growing up and with Maria. Ray described his father's verbal and physical abuse, his father's alcohol problem, and how he would leave for days at a time, leaving him and his family without food, sometimes for days. Ray's mom finally had to get a job, which meant that Ray had to take care of his three brothers and sister. He learned at a young age that he was a "good enough artist" that people would pay him to paint murals or make cards with unique designs that gave the family extra money. He struggled in school, often got into trouble for acting out, and was sent to the school counselor multiple times. The counselor thought he had attention deficit/hyperactivity disorder (ADHD) and told his mom, but they couldn't afford treatment, so he never went.

In high school, he met Maria. She was a good student, and she motivated him to try to do well and keep up with his art. They graduated high school, and Maria became pregnant, before they could make their big move to New York. Ray had trouble keeping a job due to constant fatigue, sadness, irritability, lack of motivation, and hopelessness. Also at this time, Maria had a high-risk pregnancy brought on by stress at home and at work, so they needed to stay in El Paso to get family support.

Ray got a job at a security company, and Maria stayed home with their daughter, Jenni. Ray was given a promotion after working there for three years. When he was first promoted, he had some altercations with other employees and once with his boss. Ray would often charm his way back into "their good graces" by drawing them something or making them laugh. Maria often said, "He can be very sexy and charming when he wants to be."

Six months after his twenty-first birthday, he became more easily agitated and angry, would isolate himself, appeared sad more often, stopped painting, and would sketch images of dark skies and people falling into deep dark holes. He would tell Maria how empty he felt, knowing that one day she was going to find someone who was a better artist, smarter, nicer, and worthy of sharing her life. Ray would often cry in his car before work, and one day Maria found him with a pill bottle and asked him what was wrong. He told her of the guilt he felt about being worthless, of feeling empty inside, and that he thought it'd be better if he were dead.

Maria convinced Ray to go with her to the emergency room, where he was admitted. Ray was an inpatient for three days. During that time, he was diagnosed with major depressive disorder and impulse control disorder. His symptoms were feelings of sadness, helplessness, and hopelessness that lasted for more than two weeks; becoming tearful easily; restlessness and irritability; complaints of constantly being tired and insomnia; a negative outlook on himself and the world; and generalized guilt. Ray was given an antidepressant and a mood-stabilizing medication, and he participated in individual and group therapy. He did well in individual therapy but was often disruptive in group therapy, arguing with the other members and trying to be the "group clown." At the time of his discharge, his depressive symptoms appeared moderately controlled, but many symptoms remained. He continued to report feeling empty and lost in life, fearing abandonment, idealizing then devaluating Maria and the hospital staff, experiencing intense anger following minor slights, and feeling paranoia about Maria tricking him so she could steal Jenni away.

Ray was eventually fired from the security company for missing too many days of work. This intensified his depression, and he stopped taking his medication. Maria's uncle then passed away, and she went to the funeral. The loss of Maria's uncle only seemed to prove to Ray that the world was corrupt, evil, and empty because he died while trying to help someone on the side of the road and was hit by another car driving by. While away consoling her family, Maria called multiple times but never heard back from Ray. This wasn't uncommon, as Ray would often not text or call back. After five days, Maria arrived back home, found Ray in bed, and called 9-1-1.

Ray resumed his medication and over the next several weeks, his depressive symptoms and acting out in frustration lessened, but his feelings of emptiness, abandonment, idealization and devaluation, intense anger, and paranoia remained. He believed that he was inherently bad and would berate himself and focus largely on things in his environment that proved he was no good, as opposed to seeing any moments of success. As treatment continued, Ray would have depressive episodes, but they followed an iden-tifiable trigger, tended to last between a few hours to one day, and would remit after the prompting event ended or went away. The psychologist was able to identify these and followed the symptoms and behavioral presenta-tion to diagnose Ray with BPD as well. This became a turning point for treatment because it changed the trajectory and focus from depression to the underlying core content issues related to Ray's BPD.

Over the next three years, Ray learned that his depression was the result of his inability to communicate his intense fear of loss of Maria and Jenni, which would spark his emptiness and abandonment related to his experiences growing up, which only Maria could fix when she was idealized and caused when she was devalued. Ray learned that he had CBPD that was made up of major depressive disorder and BPD. He was able to identify the root of his BPD, learn and apply skills to manage his actions and reac-tions, work with Maria on their marriage and how they interacted, manage his moods, and interact with others more effectively.

Ray's complex story shows the increased complexity when BPD is comorbid with major depressive disorder. The first part of his story is cer-tainly difficult, as extreme major depression often is, but when BPD is added to the clinical picture, it becomes even more challenging to distinguish whether the symptoms are related to depression, BPD, or both. Fortunately, Maria was there to help Ray and support him through the process. Without external support, Ray's treatment would've been significantly more difficult, with many more setbacks, but not impossible. You may not have reliable significant others, but it doesn't mean you can't have stability and treatment successes like Ray. If you don't have a reliable and healthy person you can count on, you must set up a schedule and contact list of the individuals or services in your area or online that can provide help when you need it. If you're not sure what services are available in your area, ask your physician or mental health provider, and if you don't have either one of those, do a search online for resources you think you'll need in times of stress and difficulty.

In Ray's story, once his BPD was identified, the course and focus of therapy changed to building core content identification and surface content management skills (see chapter 2 for more on core and surface content issues and BPD), which subsequently lessened the depressive as well as other symptoms. The accurate identification of one, the other, or both is critical to good self-management, treatment, and prognosis. The problem is that making the distinction isn't always easy. Now that we've learned the complexity of the combination, let's focus on the distinction.

Discerning Between Your Major Depression and BPD

You may have been treated for major depression that was part of your surface content, but when symptoms didn't remit, you were considered treatment resistant. In actuality, it was your CBPD that disrupted the progress. Only part of the picture was being addressed. Perhaps you went through multiple therapists and services to try to gain knowledge, skills, and abilities to manage your issues and related maladaptive patterns but had little success. You may have started to believe that you're ultimately untreatable and doomed. The lack of progress in treatment and symptom attenuation isn't due to resistance or reluctance but to confusion regarding the full clinical picture. Telling the difference between major depression and BPD will help you gain the knowledge, recognize the skills, and acquire the abilities to build insight and strategies to manage maladaptive patterns and symptoms more effectively.

The central component to distinguish major depressive disorder from a BPD depressive episode is timing. Depressive symptoms must be present for two consecutive weeks or more (APA 2013). In contrast, a BPD depressive episode tends to include intense depression, sadness, irritability, or anxiety that typically lasts for a few hours, but in rare cases may last for more than a few days (APA 2013). Knowing how long the symptoms are present helps to discern whether the episode is indicative of major depressive disorder or a BPD depressive reaction.

Stressor or trigger presentation is another important facet to consider. You can experience the same depressive symptoms, but if they're subsequent to an identifiable trigger or stressor, such as loss of a relationship or perceived abandonment, they're likely related to BPD and not major depression. Once the issue pertaining to your identifiable trigger or stressor is restored, for example, after you reconcile with your loved one and no longer feel rejected, your depressive symptoms are likely decrease or remit completely. Recall from Ray's story that there was no identifiable stressor or trigger for his depressive episodes, they appeared to come and go, and they were recurrent. Ray met criteria for CBPD that's made up of major depressive disorder and BPD. If Ray had had depressive reactions due to Maria going to the funeral, for example, and then when she returned, his depressive symptoms lessened significantly or went away, that would be a strong indicator of a BPD depressive episode and not one that fits major depressive disorder.

There are additional identifiers that can help you discriminate between major depressive disorder and a BPD depressive reaction. Individuals with BPD tend to have symptoms that begin at an earlier age, are more likely to have co-occurring social phobia and substance abuse, and have higher rates of suicide attempts and self-mutilation (Joyce et al. 2003). Two forms of rumination—depressive and anger—have been found to be specific factors related to BPD and could be used to discern between BPD and major depression (Baer and Sauer 2011; Selby et al. 2009). Depressive rumination is when you continually engage in negative appraisals of yourself and your emotions, behaviors, situations, life stressors, and ability to cope, whereas anger rumination is when you repeatedly focus your attention on your angry mood and the cause of your anger. In these instances, you perseverate on depressive or angry thoughts, feelings, and images, and you find it difficult to let go. As you ruminate, you become more agitated and depressed, likely sparking a BPD symptomatic response.

Consider This: Identifying Your Depressive and BPD Symptoms

Symptoms identify the diagnosis, but many times these overlap, leading to misdiagnosis and time spent treating the wrong disorder. Knowledge and awareness of symptoms can help you better identify which diagnoses are present, which diagnoses are absent, or if they're occurring together, creating CBPD.

On a new page in your journal, write "My Depressive Symptoms" at the top of the page and number from 1 to 16 down the left side of the page. As you read each symptom listed below, put a *T* to indicate the symptom is true and something you experience often or an *F* if the symptom is false and something you don't experience often. Be sure to read the directions and take note of the time components, as these are critical to determining whether symptoms are situationally bound or occur across multiple contexts. Symptoms that occur across multiple contexts are likely related to mental health disorders, whereas those that are situationally dependent are likely due to the circumstance or location.

Only consider the presence of these symptoms and issues when you're not using drugs or alcohol or taking medication and when they are unrelated to a medical condition. This list isn't meant to be used for clinical diagnosis but to help you build insight into your symptoms and issues so you can better manage them and seek out appropriate mental health assistance.

Depressive Symptoms

You've experienced the following symptoms for at least two consecutive weeks.

1. I feel sad, hopeless, and helpless most of the day, nearly every day.

2. Other people have noticed that my mood is sullen and that I appear sad.

3. My interest in things I usually enjoy is significantly decreased or absent.

4. I lose weight due to not eating and having no appetite.

5. I gain weight due to overeating.

6. I'm unable to sleep well.

7. I oversleep on a consistent basis (hypersomnia).

8. I experience uneasiness that has caused me to feel a strong need to move constantly.

9. I persistently have low energy or feel very tired.

10. My depressive symptoms don't lessen even when situations resolve or others return to my life.

11. I feel worthless or guilty for no identifiable reason or for something I've done.

12. It's hard for me to focus my attention or make a decision.

13. I think about death or ending my life.*

14. I have a specific plan to end my life.*

15. I engage in actions to end my life.*

16. These symptoms cause socioeconomic dysfunction.

These symptoms related to thoughts or intent for self-harm or suicide. Please turn to the introduction and refer to the section titled "Suicidal Ideation or Intent" for resources that can help.

Take a moment to go over your BPD symptoms from chapter 1 to help you clarify the separation of major depressive disorder symptoms from BPD. Look over your depressive symptoms ratings and mark or circle the ones you indicated as true for you. These ratings are the significant symptoms that increase the likelihood of major depressive disorder being an accurate diagnosis. Remember, this is an insight-building exercise, not a diagnostic one, and only a qualified mental health or medical provider can give you a diagnosis.

The last criterion is the universal symptom, and if you identified it as true for you, you're indicating that the other symptoms also identified as true significantly disrupt how you live your life. This increases the likelihood of meeting criteria for the full disorder. However, if you marked the universal symptom as false, you may have symptoms related to major depressive disorder, but they're not at the level of causing continuous disruption in your life. This still merits exploration, and you may benefit from reading the next chapter to learn management skills.

Listing your symptoms can be a very powerful experience, as BPD and comorbid conditions can be overwhelming when seen as a whole. When understood as a combination of particular symptoms and issues, your CBPD is more manageable and your efforts more impactful and focused as they target particular symptoms. This leads to greater symptom reduction and overall control of your CBPD.

In this chapter, we explored the similarities and differences between major depressive disorder and BPD that form this type of CBPD. This chapter hopefully provided you with the knowledge to learn skills and abilities to help you control your CBPD instead of it controlling you. This chapter was designed to provide you with a clear understanding of the following:

- the similarities and differences associated with major depressive disorder and BPD symptoms that make up this type of CBPD

- how to lessen the confusion between depressive periods often seen in those with BPD and major depressive episodes

- your depressive symptoms and issues so you gain greater understanding of your mood episodes and fluctuations and how they compare with your BPD to develop a greater understanding of your CBPD

Your CBPD has been distorting your view of yourself, others, and your world long enough. Along with the knowledge you've acquired here and the skills you'll learn in the next chapter, you'll be able to empower yourself with the adaptive abilities to do it differently and to start on the path of a new and powerful you.

CHAPTER 6

Activities to Push Back on Your Depression

The most important aspect of working with and managing CBPD made up of depression and BPD is identifying your BPD core content issues first. If the focus is on the depressive symptoms or surface content issues, your BPD core content issues will continually drive depressive responses. The treatment steps below will help you build insight and gain skills to manage both disorders that make up this type of CBPD.

The Core of Your Depression

Core content is a powerful thing, and it's in all of us. Your core content influences how you see yourself, others, and your world. Your core content was created over time, as you grew up, and came out of your positive and negative experiences. Sometimes, your core content is directly related to an individual, usually a parent or caregiver, but other times, it can be associated with events or situations. Identifying your core content can be a challenging task because it's often protected by what are called defense mechanisms. Defense mechanisms are usually perceived as unhealthy, but actually, there are healthy and unhealthy ones.

Before we get into identifying your core content, use the "Consider This" activity below to identify some common defense mechanisms that may get in your way. This activity is designed to empower you with knowledge to lessen your defenses and give you greater access to your core content.

Consider This: Defending Against
Your Defense Mechanisms

Below is a list of common defense mechanisms used by those with BPD. This isn't an exhaustive list, and if you want to learn more, see *The Borderline Personality Disorder Workbook* (Fox 2019). In your journal, write "My Defense Mechanisms" at the top of a new page and list which ones you use most often. You can also indicate with whom and in what situations you tend to use them for added insight.

Defense Mechanism	Definition
Acting out	This involves acting on impulse to avoid a feeling, belief, thought, or image rather than waiting for a more appropriate time to deal with it. Acting out can be verbal and/or physical.
Humor	This involves openly expressing feelings and thoughts in an amusing or comedic way without causing others pain or discomfort.
Passive aggression	This involves indirectly expressing your irritation or anger by failing on purpose, procrastinating, faking an illness, and so on to cause others difficulty, anger, or frustration.
Rationalization	This involves generating various explanations to justify your actions or the situation you're in while denying your feelings.
Splitting self and others	This involves seeing yourself or others as all good or all bad as opposed to a mixture of positive and negative attributes. The shifts can be rapid and intense.
Suppression	This involves making the choice to avoid thinking about something negative or delaying the impulse to respond.

Building your awareness of your defense mechanisms helps you lessen their influence in keeping you separated from your core content.

Your Core Content

With knowledge of your defense mechanisms in place, let's identify your core content. To do this, think about an early experience that's significant for you. This may be of a person who let you down, helped you, left you, or did something to hurt you. As you think about this, be aware that your defense mechanisms are likely going to try to prevent you from recognizing core content or may distort it. You're only going to briefly think of this incident, so resist the urge to dwell on it. That's not what we're doing here; we're only looking through a store window; we're not going inside. It may be difficult to acknowledge your core content, but growth happens in the light, and putting a light on your core content is a critical first step to controlling its influence.

With this early experience in mind, identify an associated feeling, thought, or image. Does this cause a fear of abandonment; a sense of worthlessness or emptiness; or a feeling of safety, vulnerability, isolation, or exclusion or lack thereof, for example? This is your core content. On a new page in your journal, write "My Core Content" at the top and underneath, write your core content.

This process can sometimes be confusing, so I'll provide an example that helped Ray identify his core content of emptiness and abandonment. The feelings of emptiness and abandonment that Ray attributed to Maria and Jenni came from growing up with his father's verbal and physical abuse and alcoholism and how he'd leave Ray and his family for days at a time, sometimes without food. This core content was a driving force for Ray's surface content of depressive symptoms as well as his BPD symptoms of agitation, emptiness, and paranoia. Now that you've identified your core content, let's make the connection between it and your depression.

Your Depression-Colored Glasses

When your core content is activated, it drives your surface content expression of depressive symptoms, potentially leading to a major depressive episode. When your depression reaches a certain level, you put on your depression-colored glasses, which helps the depression stay active and in place. However, when you know the root of your core content, you can better recognize the connection, which empowers you to challenge your core content, leading to a reduction in depressive symptoms and, ideally, the severity of the major depressive episode.

CBPD made up of depression combined with BPD drives a powerful sense of helplessness that's connected to your core content. This helplessness can become so overwhelming that you feel blocked, trapped, and disconnected from your personal power to control your thoughts, feelings, and behaviors. Let's examine the areas your depression-colored glasses may distort:

- motivations: fear motivation, incentive motivation, inspiration motivation

- thoughts

- feelings

- actions

- events

- situations

Your depression-colored glasses probably tend to make you see and feel a drain in your motivation, making you believe you don't have the energy to meet your needs or the needs of others. They can also distort your perceived internal and external motivations. Internal motivation is the degree of personal satisfaction you get from doing something for yourself or someone else. Your CBPD makes you see only the negative and causes you to believe that there is no satisfaction to be gained in fighting back against your CBPD as nothing will come from it and you're doomed.

When wearing depression-colored glasses, external motivations are affected similarly to your internal motivations. Let's look at three common internal motivations: fear, incentive, and inspiration:

- **Fear motivation** includes acting in a way that's directed by the fear associated with the consequence. These glasses only show you the dreadful outcomes and what you have to lose, which activates your core content, draining your ability to push back against your CBPD symptomatology.

- **Incentive motivation** is behavior that's driven by an external reward, such as money, sex, or gratitude. This level of motivation is impacted by you downplaying the reward or only seeing the negative side of it, such as not enough money, no one wants to have sex with you, or no one is going to be thankful for what you do, so why do it.

- **Inspiration motivation** is from words, emotions, and actions put out by others. In this case, your CBPD causes you to discredit and distrust sources of inspiration and drives you to see them as ploys to trick you or take advantage of you. This leads you to believe there is no sincerity in someone's inspiring words or deeds or that you couldn't be inspiring or have a positive impact on yourself or someone else.

When your core content is activated, it influences your surface content depression that distorts your thoughts, feelings, and actions. It does this by muddying your clearheadedness, which adds to your confusion and promotes the negative feelings of helplessness, hopelessness, worthlessness, emptiness, and abandonment. This can cause a significant and perpetual sense of confusion to see your goals, to see yourself and others clearly, and to evaluate events and situations accurately.

Misperceiving events and situations often leads to CBPD symptom expression, such as impulsive risk-taking behaviors, self-harm, and isolation, to name a few, and this makes it harder to determine the best course of action. When you're led by your core content and depression-colored glasses, you see threat, fear, abandonment, and worthlessness in most, if not all, events and situations.

Consider This: Discarding Your Distortions

On a new page in your journal, write "Discarding My Distortions" at the top. Draw a line down the center of the page. On the left side write, "Depression-Colored Glasses Distortion Areas." Below that, write each distortion area listed above (motivations, thoughts, feelings, actions, events, situations), leaving enough space to write your responses. Describe the distortions you see using your depression-colored glasses, being as detailed as possible. On the right side of the page, write, "Seeing with Clarity." Below that, write something that challenges these distortions. You can also download the worksheet "Discarding My Distortions" at http://www.newharbinger.com/48558.

For example, under "motivation," Ray wrote, "I see no purpose, no one helping me, and no change coming in my future." Under "seeing with clarity," he wrote, "Maria and Jenni are continually supportive of me. My art is well received and respected. I have the skills to make the changes I need in my life."

Remember, your core content feeds your CBPD. It's been with you for a while, and it doesn't want to go away, but it's time. You may feel overwhelmed, confused, or even a rush of other CBPD symptoms while doing this. This is expected, as your core content is being challenged and isn't used to seeing the world without the maladaptive depression-colored glasses. Seeing with clarity is a powerful skill, but it is just that, "a skill," and all skills are built with time and perseverance. You may be wondering, *Can I do this?* The answer is: *Yes, you can do this!*

Your depression-colored glasses are fed by a cycle that justifies your core content, leading to surface content expression of CBPD symptomatology that keeps it powerful and in place. The more you feed your CBPD core content and engage in the maladaptive patterns that reinforce it, the longer you're tethered to it. To prevent this, you need to learn to see with clarity, like you just did, but also you have to learn to push back on your CBPD.

Discredit Your Depression

We've examined how your core content and your major depression, when combined with BPD, creates your CBPD. This type of CBPD may often feel like it's too strong, like it's more than you can handle, but that's part of the trickery of your depression-colored glasses. Your CBPD wants you to feel powerless, it wants you to feel helpless, but you're not. Not even close!

In many cases, your depression-colored glasses feel as though they're almost glued to your head by beliefs, behaviors, patterns, and images. You've believed the distortion and walked down that avenue of thinking you had no recourse, but hopefully you're starting to see and feel that you do. The "Consider This" activity below was designed to help you directly challenge your distortion areas, loosening the glue that kept them in place, but your CBPD is no one-trick pony, and it has many avenues to take you down. We've got to beat it at its own game, and now that we've hit the specific distortion, let's debunk the general. The first step to debunking your depression is to pull apart the trickery, expose it, and then replace it with adaptive and healthy messages.

Consider This: Debunking Your Depression

To debunk your depression, you must first see it for what it is, a distortion. Your depression doesn't want you to see the reality or have hope because in many ways it's a living thing. Living things want to survive, even if it means poisoning the host, and that's you. Your depression feeds on your sorrows and perceived sins by filling your head with fear, doubt, powerlessness, and helplessness often put there by your core content. To undo this, you must call it out. Using a new page in your journal, write "Debunking My Depression" at the top, and then create three columns with the following headers: "Depression Message," "Debunk Data," and "Healthy/Adaptive Message." You can also download the worksheet "Debunking My Depression" at http://www.newharbinger.com /48558.

Let's walk through this exercise: write your depression message, identify data in your life that proves it's wrong, and then overlay that with a more accurate and adaptive message. Here's an example from Ray's journal.

Depression Message: I'm a fraud of an artist, and Maria and Jenni are going to leave me.

Debunk Data: I've sold my art to prominent galleries, and I got an awesome write-up in the *New York Times*.

Healthy/Adaptive Message: I'm a good artist, I've been recognized as such, and Maria and Jenni believe in me.

Now that you've identified your healthy and adaptive message, I want you to say this to yourself on a regular basis. The more you say it, the more powerful it becomes. We adapt to what our brain tells us. If you tell yourself you're a fraud of an artist, you'll believe it over time, but if you tell yourself you're a good artist and add clear data to support that, you'll believe that, too.

Your adaptive and healthy messages are an important part of managing and controlling your CBPD and getting those depression-colored glasses off once and for all. The next step is to take this insight, engage in behavior change, and build habits that encourage your empowerment.

Consider This: Empowerment Habits

Below is a list of empowerment habits to help you feel better about yourself. These habits can be paired with your healthy and adaptive messages to further empower you to resist the pull of your depression-based CBPD. Do these on a routine basis to make them habits, and over time, you'll do them as default responses when your core content is activated.

On a new page in your journal, write "Empowerment Habits" at the top. Below it, write your healthy/adaptive messages from the previous exercise. Below these messages, list the empowerment habits that will help you strengthen these messages. There are twenty listed below but come up with some of your own as well. Empowerment habits make your healthy/adaptive messages come to life, and that's exactly what we're to do with this activity.

going to the beach or park

going out to eat

going shopping

painting or drawing

putting on makeup or perfume

eating healthier

exercising

doing mindfulness or praying

doing something for others

getting together with friends

playing a game with others

cleaning the house or doing chores

gardening or planting

writing positive things in your journal

singing or listening to music

reading a book or magazine

watching a funny movie or show

taking a bath or shower

eating something sweet as a treat

doing word puzzles or playing cards

Now that you've identified your empowerment habits, I want you to do them multiple times per day and throughout the week, as often as you can. You're going to do these things so they become a part of your routine. Your depression-colored glasses became a part of your life, so much so that you started putting them on as soon as you got up in the morning. They became your default view of yourself and your world and became depression-stabilizing habits. To break them, you must overlay them not only with healthy and adaptive messages but also with empowerment habits.

In this chapter, you've worked to build a lot of insight into your CBPD and learned exercises to push back your depression that was created and encouraged by your core content. The key to strengthening these gains is to build them into daily habits and behaviors. You likely feel a degree of safety and comfort in your depression-based CBPD, and it's normal to have that. It's also normal to be afraid to do it differently. However, you picked up this book to do it differently. It's never easy, but it's important and empowering. You've come this far, and I want to encourage you to go a little further and build a strategy that promotes moving forward beyond your CBPD and opening your life to all the positives that are out there for you. Positive change isn't always easy, but it's often very rewarding.

Do It Differently

To minimize your depression-based CBPD, you must have a strategy, a plan where it all comes together so you're ready for the good times and the bad. There are many benefits to doing it differently without depression-based CBPD in your life. These include better relationships with loved ones, friends, and partners; more employment opportunities and better pay; a greater sense of freedom; better sex; deeper friendships and intimacy with others; greater passion and drive to achieve; and increased likelihood of achieving goals and aspirations. You'll also find that people seek you out more often to spend time with you. These benefits are based upon what individuals often report when they have greater control over their depressive-CBPD thoughts, feelings, behaviors, images, and patterns and use healthy and adaptive strategies to get their needs met. It's time to put your plan together to do it differently.

Consider This: Doing It Differently Plan

Use the following steps to outline your plan for doing it differently and living life with less interference from your CBPD. At the top of a new page in your journal, write "My Doing It Differently Plan." Use the prompts below to help you outline and create your plan. Be as descriptive as you can, and the more detail you can add, the easier it will be for you to follow through. Once you've written out your plan, implement it into your daily life. You may need to update it from time to time as this isn't a one-and-done deal. It takes practice, perseverance, courage, and strength—all the things you possess to do it differently. I know you have this because you've made it this far in the book, and that's a great and empowering accomplishment.

My Doing It Differently Plan

1. My core content is:

2. My core content activates and encourages my CBPD when:

3. My CBPD shows up in my life (CBPD messages and behaviors) when:

4. I push back on my depression-based CBPD by thinking, feeling, and doing (healthy and adaptive messages and empowerment behaviors):

5. I can put these empowerment habits into practice when, where, and by doing:

6. The benefits of doing it differently are:

Reread your plan multiple times. It's not uncommon for your depression-colored glasses to try to distort the perception of your ability to do things differently. Resist this, and remind yourself it's a distortion and not the truth of clarity.

Having your plan in place is a powerful thing. Including your core content into your plan provides a deeper level of impact so you can push back on your depression-based CBPD. Use this plan daily, build it into your life, and strengthen your healthy and adaptive skills to overcome your CBPD.

In this chapter, you took the knowledge from the previous chapter and applied it to learning the skills and abilities to enhance your self-control and overcome your CBPD. This chapter provided you with a clear understanding of the following:

- your core content that's associated with your depression-based CBPD

- common defense mechanisms and how to defeat them to access your core content

- the knowledge, skills, and abilities to push back on your depression-based CBPD

- a plan to do it differently to turn insight and awareness into action to continue to grow beyond your CBPD

Depression can seem like cinderblock shoes that get heavier with each step. Adding BPD symptoms and issues makes it feel as though your heavy shoes are walking on shaky ground that's about to collapse at any minute. These two sensations create this type of CBPD. Using the tools in this chapter daily will help you create a stable surface for you to chip away and break free from your cinderblock shoes, walk tall and proud, and be in greater control of your life and what's ahead of you.

CHAPTER 7

When Your Reality Is Challenged Through Psychosis

"No one listens to the words except me."

—Annalise, 35

Annalise is a divorced attorney living in a large metropolitan city. Local sheriff deputies took her to the emergency room due to odd behavior, reported hallucinations, and suicidal intent. She presented as seductive and aggressive, and she reported male voices outside her head, telling her others are undermining her because they know what she's thinking and can predict how she'll behave and the only solution is to kill herself.

While being interviewed in the emergency room, Annalise's mood would become angry, and she was insistent, saying that she didn't like to talk about her problems and that her therapist wouldn't believe her because "no one listens to the words except me." The voices were telling her to kill herself and that her therapist refused to help her in any way. Annalise was admitted to the hospital and given an antipsychotic medication. The next morning, Annalise was calm and alert but groggy and signed a release to allow the psychiatrist to contact and talk with her partner, Carmon. Carmon agreed to come to the hospital to be interviewed.

Carmon provided much-needed background information about Annalise. She stated that Annalise has always been reliable, compassionate, and caring with others. She often took cases pro bono to help those in need. She graduated from a well-renowned law school and worked at a private firm for many years until she started her own practice that was going well and was busy. She was also working as an adjunct professor at a local law school. A year ago, Annalise started having generalized worry that she couldn't control about their relationship, her practice, and her status in the legal profession. She was feeling restless, easily fatigued, and irritable as well as experiencing muscle tension and chronic insomnia. Her anxiety seemed to grow as time went on, but she continued to take more and more cases.

Approximately four months prior, Annalise had started therapy following a panic attack just before she had to appear in court. Carmon reported that therapy seemed to be helping "somewhat," but Annalise never practiced what she learned in therapy because she felt she didn't have time, and then everything seemed to "pile on top of her until she broke." Medication was discussed at the time, but Annalise declined due to concern about potential side effects and how it may impact her functioning at work, saying, "The last thing I need is for something to slow me down."

Just before being brought to the emergency room, Annalise was up all night preparing a case, and Carmon heard her arguing loudly with someone. Carmon went to check on her and saw Annalise was arguing, but she wasn't on the phone, and no one was there. She seemed to be getting more upset, and when she noticed Carmon, she focused her attention on her and tried to seduce her but was still talking to someone else. Carmon called the emergency line for Annalise's therapist, who told her to call for help so she could be taken to the emergency room. Carmon called 9-1-1. When Annalise heard her on the phone, she began screaming how the only way out is to kill herself and that the voices knew her soul wanted out of its flesh entrapment. When paramedics arrived, she was yelling at them and refused to go with them and became combative. The local sheriffs were called, who subdued Annalise and brought her to the emergency room.

In the hospital, Annalise's psychotic symptoms were responsive to the medication and not evident by early afternoon the following day. She was oriented to where she was, who she was, and the date and time. She stated that she remembered the voices but wasn't hearing them and denied past and present thoughts, plan, or intent to hurt herself beyond what the voices were telling her to do the day before. Carmon agreed to stay in close proximity to her for the next few days to make sure she kept follow-up appointments with her therapist and remained compliant on her medication.

At the follow-up meeting with her therapist, they reviewed the two days leading up to her psychotic episode. Annalise reported that she had taken on two new cases, Carmon's birthday was coming up, she wanted it to be special, so she was planning for that, and the clerk had called her about two of her cases being moved up per the judge's calendar, which conflicted with another high-profile case she had. Annalise said that her sleep remained disrupted (a long-lasting symptom from her anxiety) and she couldn't focus on what she was reading because the words just didn't stick in her mind. She started to feel as if someone were watching her and then whispering to her. She said, "It seemed to take over. It was loud, like a stereo turned up, but I didn't have the volume button. I couldn't control it. It told me I didn't have to read, that it would read to me. It said no one helps me, that you're a liar (the therapist), and that killing myself was the only relief for my soul that was encased in its flesh entrapment." Annalise had good insight. She recognized the oddity of the experience and the content. This motivated her to increase the priority of taking care of her mental health.

Annalise remained in treatment and continued to build and use her skills to manage her anxiety, workload, and relationship expectations. She never had another psychotic episode or showed signs of psychotic symptoms. She continued to take the antipsychotic medication for another three months and then slowly weaned off it under her doctor's supervision. Annalise had been diagnosed with generalized anxiety disorder with panic attacks prior to her psychotic episode. Following the episode, she was given an additional diagnosis of brief psychotic disorder with marked stressors (this means that the psychotic symptoms are due to events that would greatly stress out just about anyone), in full remission.

The Symptoms Identify the Diagnosis

Let's unpack what led up to Annalise qualifying for her diagnoses. Annalise has a high-stress job and continues to take on responsibilities. As her stress builds, her functioning decreases. She experiences anxiety, which exacerbates because it's ignored. She then experiences a panic attack, which drives her to begin treatment even though she's loosely engaged in the process and remains highly focused on her work and responsibilities. She starts therapy and learns anxiety-management skills but doesn't practice them due to feeling like she doesn't have the time. Her therapy sessions are only "somewhat" helpful as she gains benefit from talking about her anxiety and how to manage it, but its benefits are limited due to her not practicing outside of session.

Medication isn't prescribed for her anxiety because Annalise is concerned about the potential side effects of headaches, confusion, fatigue, and others. Not all anxiety requires medication, and Annalise has a right to decline it. Her anxiety meets the criteria for generalized anxiety disorder because it's excessive worry that lasts for at least six months. She had been feeling restless, was easily fatigued and irritable, and reported muscle tension and chronic insomnia. Her anxiety was causing socioeconomic dysfunction (see chapter 1 for more information), and her symptoms aren't accounted for by drug abuse or medication because she didn't use illegal drugs and wasn't taking any medication. Also, her symptoms weren't associated with a medical condition or another mental health issue. Annalise's struggle to manage taking care of responsibilities and her own mental health may speak to you as you read her story. She, and you, aren't alone in trying to balance "the world first and me second," but as it did for Annalise, that approach increases the probability of symptoms worsening.

Her anxiety symptoms exacerbate to the point where she has a brief psychotic episode, which is when Carmon called the sheriff for help. At that point, medication became essential. Her psychosis was of a short duration, lasting at least one day but less than one month, and consisted of an auditory paranoia-based command hallucination telling her that others are going to sabotage her achievements and successes, that the voice knows everything she's going to do while giving an extreme command on how to rectify it: suicide. Her psychosis wasn't caused by another disorder, like major depression, bipolar disorder, medication, or substance use. Her symptoms fit the criteria for brief psychotic disorder. Because it was the result of significant stressors and then remitted when treated, she was given the specifiers of "with marked stressors and in full remission."

Perhaps Annalise's anxiety doesn't seem that different from yours because as the pressure of the world increases, your responsibilities intensify and your self-neglect becomes chronic. Anxiety often precedes and accompanies paranoia and psychosis and is a psychosis risk factor (Baer, Shah, and Lepage 2019; Hartley, Barrowclough, and Haddock 2013). This means that monitoring and controlling the impacts of anxiety are critical and that failure to do so can result in psychotic symptoms. Psychosis is certainly challenging enough, but things get even more so when BPD co-occurs.

Psychosis and the Borderline Complexity

The link between psychotic symptoms and BPD is longstanding and inherent to its very name. BPD is so named due to it once being believed that individuals with this disorder were "on the border" of psychosis (Stern 1938). You won't be surprised to learn that psychotic symptoms, such as auditory hallucinations, significantly worsen functioning and treatment outcome of those with BPD (Slotema et al. 2017). Hallucinations, a central component of brief psychotic disorder and other psychotic disorders, have been estimated to occur in 26 to 54 percent of individuals diagnosed with BPD (Kingdon et al. 2010; Niemantsverdriet et al. 2017). Delusions, another key component of psychotic disorders, have been estimated to occur in 17 to 29 percent of those with BPD (Kingdon et al. 2010; Pearse et al. 2014). When your CBPD is made up of paranoid fears, dissociation, or psychotic symptoms, the identification, treatment, and ability to care for yourself becomes much more challenging.

BPD is a complex disorder, and the addition of psychotic symptoms certainly adds to it. Psychotic symptoms can manifest in a variety of ways:

- the experience of intense fear that others or organizations mean to do you harm

- difficulty focusing your attention, feeling as though you're in a daydreaming-like state

- impaired memory and recall

- feeling as if your thoughts and feelings are unreal or don't belong to you

- feeling disconnected from your environment and the objects and other people in it

To fully understand psychotic symptoms as they relate to BPD, we have to explore these psychotic-like symptoms, also known as quasi-psychotic symptoms.

When You're Fearful and Detached

The symptoms bulleted above aren't psychotic symptoms but are associated with suspiciousness and fear related to the motives or intent of those in your life. This may be a very common experience for you and one that tends to follow an anxiety-provoking experience that revolves around fatalistic beliefs of impending doom and abandonment. These thoughts and fears are typically unsubstantiated and attenuate when the stress-inducing situation subsides.

Dissociation is also not a psychotic symptom, but a cognitive disturbance; it falls under the category of unusual perceptual experiences. Dissociation can be defined as a disrupted, nonpsychotic thought disturbance that includes impaired attention, recurrent illusions (sensing the presence of a force or person who isn't actually there), a daydreaming-like state, disturbance in memory, depersonalization (a state in which your thoughts and feelings seem unreal or not belonging to you), and derealization (feeling detached from your environment and the objects and other people in it). Dissociation is often seen as a defense mechanism designed to protect yourself from overwhelming emotions and memories related to traumatic events (Terr 1991). Research has shown that individuals with BPD have higher rates of dissociation compared to those with other mental health disorders except those with dissociative disorders (for example, dissociative identity disorder) or post-traumatic stress disorder (PTSD) (Scalabrini et al. 2017).

These symptoms are often misconstrued and confused with psychosis and quasi-psychotic symptoms. Let's clear that up now.

Psychotic and Quasi-Psychotic Symptoms

Psychosis is essentially an impairment in reality testing, which manifests as the inability to differentiate self from others, to differentiate internal from external stimuli and circumstances, and to maintain emotional control within social contexts (Kernberg and Caligor 2005). Reality testing is the unbiased and unimpaired evaluation of emotions and thoughts; you see, think, and feel things in yourself and the world around you as they actually are. Impaired reality testing is a central criterion to all psychotic disorders, from a brief psychotic disorder to schizophrenia; this is when you see, think, and feel things that aren't there, such as hallucinations and intense irrational fears. You're likely to have intact reality testing if you have BPD, but if you've experienced intense stress, which impairs your reality testing, it can lead to quasi-psychotic symptoms.

Psychotic symptoms seen in individuals with BPD, in our case CBPD, are often referred to as quasi-psychotic symptoms. They're called this because of the identifiable presence of hallucinations and delusions that occur for less than two days and are uncommon compared to the symptoms seen in individuals with full-fledged psychotic disorders. If your CBPD is made up of quasi-psychotic symptoms and BPD, you may exhibit paranoia and suspiciousness that aren't odd or bizarre in nature and that may center around an identified individual, such as a spouse or parent, whom you fear may leave you, abandon you, or cheat on you. In contrast, those with a psychotic disorder have longstanding symptoms that significantly impair their functioning and are unusual or stereotypical. In the story, Annalise's symptoms are bizarre because her voices are telling her, "The only way out is to kill yourself," and they knew her soul wanted out of its "flesh entrapment."

The presence of psychotic or quasi-psychotic symptoms adds to the intricacy of CBPD and impairs your perception of yourself, others, and your world while decreasing your ability to function successfully when experiencing these symptoms. Let's take another look at Annalise's story to see how the presentation changes when she meets criteria for CBPD that's made up of psychotic symptoms and BPD.

Annalise's Complex Journey

Annalise was taken to the emergency room by local sheriff deputies as a result of aggressive behavior, reported hallucinations, suicidal intent, and refusal to cooperate with paramedics to come to the hospital willingly. Her behavior was initially seductive with hospital staff but then became aggressive when she realized she wasn't going to be released as she demanded. While being interviewed by the psychiatrist, she would intermittently look off toward an empty corner of the room as if being called out to. When asked about this, she would say, "It's none of your business." After talking to the psychiatrist for some time, she reluctantly told him about the male voice coming from the corner of the room, telling her how he was planning to undermine her because he knew what she was thinking and was able to predict how she was going to behave, and that the only solution was to kill herself.

Annalise screamed at the psychiatrist and the medical staff that she was an attorney and was planning to sue each of them if she was remanded to the inpatient unit. She refused to take the medication when initially offered and hit it out of the nurse's hand. More attempts were made for her to take the medication voluntarily, but she became more combative and was eventually given an injection of an antipsychotic medication. The next morning, Annalise was calm and alert but groggy and signed a release to allow the psychiatrist to contact and talk with her partner, Carmon. The psychiatrist called Carmon, and she was asked to come to the hospital to be interviewed about Annalise and provide background information.

Carmon stated that Annalise had a long history of difficulty getting along with others and making decisions, was prone to anxious and depressive episodes when she perceives even the slightest disrespect, but at times was very compassionate and caring with others, including taking pro bono cases to help those in need. She graduated from a well-renowned law school, worked at a private firm for many years, but was asked to leave due to problems with coworkers and her supervising attorney. She then started her own practice, and she was consistently busy. She was also working as an adjunct professor at a local law school but was having problems with the students and would often become overinvolved in their lives. She would give them advice on their personal life or allow them to help her at the law office with case law and filing documents. Whenever a student would make a mistake, she would fly into a rage and humiliate them, then feel intense guilt and shame over her behavior, and then try to make it up to them in some way. Students started to complain, and the school was looking into canceling her teaching agreement.

Annalise started having intense anxiety that she couldn't control about a year prior. This was different from her previous anxious and depressive episodes, as those would include her "blanking out" for a few seconds to several minutes, but they ended soon after Carmon got home or she could be "talked down or out of it," and she would be fine for the next few days or a week until she was triggered again. This anxiety was continuous and centered on their relationship, her practice, and her status in the legal profession. She was often more restless than usual, easily agitated and chronically fatigued, and fixated on whether Carmon was going to leave her. Her anxiety got so bad that she developed chronic insomnia, only sleeping two to three hours a night. Although her anxiety seemed to worsen, she continued to take more and more cases.

After her first panic attack, Annalise started treatment again. She had been to several therapists starting in high school when she had attempted suicide with her mother's Xanax. She would often quit therapy when she felt the therapist was asking too many questions, was too stupid, or didn't know enough to understand her, or when she just felt that she got whatever she needed at the time. Carmon reported that the therapy seemed to be helping "somewhat," but Annalise was very resistant to questions that encouraged her to look into her past and link it with her present thoughts and behaviors. The psychologist taught her some techniques, but she never used them, saying she didn't have the time or didn't see the point. The psychologist discussed medication, but Annalise refused and saw this as offensive and labeling her as weak and not smart enough to control herself.

Carmon explained how her symptoms and behavior kept getting worse and how Annalise kept pushing herself and blocked everyone out of her life up until the night she called 9-1-1 when the sheriff had to bring her to the hospital. Annalise's psychotic symptoms were responsive to the medication and weren't evident by early afternoon the following day. She was very tearful and expressed intense guilt over having her psychotic symptoms and felt as if she'd let Carmon down by not being "stronger" and more in control. She encouraged Carmon to leave her, questioned why she would stay with someone so "broken" when she was so ideal, but then said that she couldn't see her life without her and maybe Carmon was more broken than she was. This fluctuation in devaluing Carmon had happened often in their relationship. She reassured her of how much she loved her, but Annalise continued to encourage her to just leave her like everyone else but then begged her to stay.

When Annalise was released from the hospital, Carmon agreed to stay close to her for the next few days to make sure she kept her follow-up appointments with her therapist and to help ensure her compliance with medication.

At the follow-up meeting with her therapist, they reviewed the previous two days leading up to her psychotic episode. Annalise was tearful and conflicted and felt as if she were "losing her mind"; that her psychotic break only justified her brokenness and how empty, lost, and worthless she is; and that she knew this was going to be the last straw for Carmon, who was going to leave her any day. The therapist took note of these symptoms and her history and concluded that BPD was present. With this knowledge, the therapist went back over the anxiety-reduction techniques, but this time focused on Annalise's drive to be a better version of herself, wanting to be a better partner, attorney, and professor. He focused on getting her intrinsically motivated to face and work through her issues. This approach included grounding techniques (discussed in chapter 8) to help better assess her internal experiences and accurately interpret others and her environment. The therapist knew that she needed to be grounded and have the skills to control any quasi-psychotic symptoms or dissociation that may appear as they explored the root of her issues. Annalise and her therapist worked to identify and resolve underlying and past issues that were influencing her current behavior and mental health issues (core and surface content is discussed below). Therapy also focused on assertiveness skills with others and how to manage moments of agitation, loss, fear, doubt, emptiness, and abandonment.

Annalise remained in treatment for the next three years. She progressed very well, but like all treatment, she had some setbacks and regressions but never had another psychotic episode. She continued to take the antipsychotic medication for another nine months until she slowly weaned off it under her doctor's supervision. She was offered medication for her anxiety but refused due to fear of possible side effects. Annalise had been diagnosed with generalized anxiety disorder with panic attacks prior to her psychotic episode. Following the episode, she was given an additional diagnosis of brief psychotic disorder with marked stressors, in full remission. Her therapist recognized the intense efforts to avoid abandonment, the unstable and intense relationships with Carmon and her students, the depressive and anxious episodes that resolved when Camron returned or she talked her through it, chronic feelings of emptiness, inappropriate intense anger with poor ability to control it, and socioeconomic dysfunction related to these symptoms and diagnosed her with BPD as well.

When psychotic or quasi-psychotic symptoms co-occur with your BPD, your functioning and self-control are impaired to a greater degree. When we compare the two parts of Annalise's story, we see the added complexity when BPD features are present. These features cause greater instability in her relationships and make it more difficult to get her mental health issues under control, and her fear, anger, emptiness, and poor impulse control are intensified as well as the distorted perception of herself and others.

In the second story, you may have noticed that Annalise remains on her medication for a longer period and the approach to treatment is very different. This is because the addition of BPD changes the intensity of symptoms, tends to increase the likelihood of medication nonadherence, and the time in treatment is longer as deeper issues (core content) are driving many of Annalise's presenting problems (surface content); see chapter 2 for more on core and surface content issues and BPD. Annalise refuses antianxiety medication due to fear of side effects. Many of Annalise's anxiety episodes, prior to her generalized anxiety disorder and panic attacks, were driven by her core content, her underlying issues, that were causing her anxiety response, her surface content. Had the therapist only focused on her anxiety episodes and not identified the core content and BPD, the therapeutic process would've been erratic and had a greater probability of premature termination.

Fortunately, in both cases, Annalise had a partner she could rely on. If this wasn't the case, it would've been much more difficult for her to make the gains she did. She would've had a greater likelihood of being medication noncompliant, which could've led to another psychotic episode, or she could've had a resurgence of BPD symptoms due to not having continued support to help her maintain her mental stability. You may not have a reliable significant other or person you can count on, but this doesn't mean you can't have stability and treatment successes like Annalise. If you don't have a reliable and healthy person you can count on, you must set up a schedule of the things you need to do to maintain your mental stability as well as create a contact list of the individuals and services in your area or online that can provide help when you need it. If you're not sure what services are available in your area, ask your physician or your mental health provider, and if you don't have either one of those, do a search online for resources you think you'll need in times of stress and difficulty. There are resources out there; don't let your BPD distort your hope.

The accurate identification of which disorders are present and the reason those symptoms are being exhibited are critical to good self-management, treatment, and prognosis. The challenge is to know the difference between these symptoms because this increases the probability of success and long-term change.

Is It Psychosis or BPD?

Psychotic and quasi-psychotic symptoms that are comorbid with BPD can significantly impair your ability to function and to receive the correct treatment. Making the distinction between them is central to not only seeking appropriate help but also to building insight into your issues and concerns.

When you encounter extreme stress, momentary paranoid ideation or dissociative symptoms may occur. Your paranoid ideation is likely to center around issues of abandonment and manifest as unjustified suspiciousness or ideas of reference; this is often referred to as nondelusional paranoia. Paranoia seen in those with a psychotic disorder is different, as it tends to adhere to the idea that one is being conspired against, cheated, spied on, followed, poisoned or drugged, slandered, harassed, or blocked from the pursuit and attainment of long-term goals. These individuals tend to be resistant to outside evidence to the contrary, and the paranoia is sustained over time. For you, and others with BPD, the nondelusional paranoia that's usually abandonment-focused remits when the person related to the feared abandonment returns.

Timing is critical, as it is in all disorders, as the nondelusional paranoid ideation in those with BPD tends to last from minutes to hours. To qualify as a psychotic symptom, symptoms must be present most of the time for one month or longer according to the DSM-5 (APA 2013). The amount of time these symptoms occur is a clear and significant factor to distinguish between nondelusional paranoia and psychotic paranoid ideation.

Under intense stress, you may experience dissociative symptoms, also referred to as unusual perceptual experiences that often include impaired attention, a daydreaming-like state, disturbance in memory, depersonalization, and derealization. The severity is generally not enough to merit another diagnosis. Just like nondelusional paranoia, these symptoms typically manifest as a response to a real or perceived abandonment and remit when the individual returns. However, research has shown that dissociative symptoms identified in individuals with BPD aren't always short-lived (Korzekwa et al. 2009; Ross, Ferrell, and Schroeder 2014; Zanarini et al. 2000) and in some cases may be associated with dissociative identity disorder, which should be ruled out.

Dissociative identity disorder (DID) is made up of discrete personality identities and is a severe form of dissociation. There are often repeated breaks in the recall of everyday events and important personal information, which aren't limited to traumatic events and aren't related to ordinary forgetting. It's estimated that 10 to 24 percent of individuals with BPD also meet criteria for DID (Korzekwa et al. 2009; Ross 2007; Şar et al. 2006). When these two disorders are comorbid, clinical symptoms are more severe than when they occur separately (Ross, Ferrell, and Schroeder 2014). You may be wondering whether you have DID comorbid with your BPD, and there's a way to tell. An individual with BPD tends to display rapidly changing, poorly controlled emotions in response to the environment; is usually able to recall their behaviors associated with different emotions; and doesn't feel that they're so unusual as to be disbelieved (Brand and Loewenstein 2010). An individual with DID tends to have greater severity of amnesia, identity confusion, and identity alteration (changes in identity accompanied by shifts in behavior that are evident to others) than those with BPD (Boon and Draijer 1993).

Making the distinction between stress-related nondelusional paranoia, dissociative symptoms, and DID helps you see your symptoms more clearly and can be used as a guide to move forward to help you manage them more effectively. Let's explore the distinction between psychotic and quasi-psychotic symptoms since they may coexist as part of your BPD.

Psychotic and Quasi-Psychotic Symptoms

If your CBPD is made up of psychotic or quasi-psychotic symptoms, you're likely to experience:

- difficulty staying on topic and being easily distracted by internal and external stimuli

- speaking in poorly connected sentences (for example, "I went to get something to eat, but my shoes weren't at the beach")

- feeling as though others are putting ideas, images, or other content into your head

- repeating noises and words you hear instead of verbally expressing your thoughts

- a longer course of treatment

- treatment interruptions

Similar to the paranoid ideation and dissociative symptoms we explored earlier, psychotic and quasi-psychotic symptoms are likely to be in response to extreme stress.

Odd thinking has been identified as an indicator of nonpsychotic thought patterns found in those with BPD. Odd thinking includes:

- intense suspiciousness

- believing you can read someone else's mind

- believing you can tell the future

- holding on to an idea or belief to such an extreme that you're preoccupied with it and it dominates your life

Odd thinking, as it relates to your BPD, doesn't cross the threshold into psychosis, but deviates from the unimpaired or "normal" cognitive processes. This is why it's considered a quasi-psychotic symptom.

Making the distinction between psychosis and quasi-psychotic symptoms as they relate to your CBPD is likely to be a matter of degrees as opposed to a simple question of presence or absence. For example, you may experience delusions in the form of biases that include jumping to conclusions and distorted attribution of harmful intent by others. These rarely rise to the level of delusions seen in those with psychosis, such as paranoia, grandiosity, or somatization, which tend to be longer lasting and not to remit when your stress reduces or when the object you feared was going to abandon you returns.

Consider This: Identifying Psychosis and BPD Symptoms

Symptoms identify the diagnosis, but many times they overlap, leading to misdiagnosis and time spent treating the wrong disorder. Knowledge and awareness of symptoms can help you better identify which diagnoses are present, which are absent, or if they're occurring together, creating CBPD.

On a new page in your journal, write "My Psychotic or Quasi-Psychotic Symptoms" at the top and number from 1 to 15 down the left side of the page. As you read each symptom listed below, put a *T* to indicate the symptom is true and something you experience often or an *F* if the symptom is false and something you don't experience often. Be sure to read the directions and take note of the time components, as these are critical to determining whether symptoms are situationally bound or occur across multiple contexts. Symptoms that occur across multiple contexts are likely related to mental health disorders, whereas those that are situationally dependent are likely due to the circumstance or location.

Only consider the presence of these symptoms and issues when you're not using drugs or alcohol or taking medication and when they are unrelated to a medical condition. This list isn't meant to be used for clinical diagnosis but to help you build insight into your symptoms and issues so you can better manage them and seek out appropriate mental health assistance.

Psychotic or Quasi-Psychotic Symptoms

When considering these symptoms, they must've been present for at least one day.

1. I hear sounds or voices that others say aren't there.

2. I see things that others say aren't there.

3. I feel things on my body that others say aren't there.

4. I smell things that others can't.

5. I taste things that aren't there.

6. People or organizations are out to do harm to me and disrupt my plans.

7. I feel that I have the power to influence others' thoughts, feelings, and actions.

8. My thoughts are cloudy, confused, or disrupted by too much information or sensations.

9. I have thoughts that others say are unfounded or unusual.

10. I hold on to beliefs regardless of what others tell me or show me.

11. I stay away from others due to intense distrust of their motives or my social discomfort.

12. I feel like I'm under the control of a special power.

13. I've been told that my behavior is unusual and inappropriate for the circumstance I'm in.

14. One or more of my parents, siblings, or children have been diagnosed with a type of psychotic disorder.

15. These symptoms cause socioeconomic dysfunction.

Take a moment to go over your BPD symptoms from chapter 1 to help you clarify the separation of psychotic or quasi-psychotic symptoms from BPD. Look over your symptoms ratings and mark or circle the ones you indicated as true for you. These ratings are the significant symptoms that increase the likelihood of the presence of psychosis being an accurate comorbid condition. Remember, this is an insight-building exercise, not a diagnostic one, and only a qualified mental health or medical provider can give you a diagnosis.

The last criterion is the universal symptom, and if you identified it as true for you, you're indicating that the other symptoms also identified as true significantly disrupt how you live your life. This increases the likelihood of meeting criteria for the full disorder. However, if you marked the universal symptom as false, you may have psychotic or quasi-psychotic symptoms but they're not to the level of causing continuous disruption in your life. This still merits exploration, and you may benefit from reading the next chapter to learn management skills.

Listing out your symptoms can be a very powerful experience, as BPD and comorbid conditions can be overwhelming when seen as a whole. When understood as a combination of particular symptoms and issues, your CBPD is more manageable and your efforts more impactful and focused as they target particular symptoms. This leads to greater symptom reduction and overall control of your CBPD.

As you've gone through this chapter, many concepts and issues may have struck you, and you may have thought, *Hey, that's me. I experience that!* That is a sign that you're not alone in your fight against CBPD. The more you learn about your symptoms and issues, the better able you are to identify and use appropriate interventions to lessen the adverse impact of your symptoms but also to empower yourself with choice.

In this chapter, we explored CBPD when it's made up of psychotic or quasi-psychotic symptoms and BPD. This chapter was designed to provide you with a clear understanding of the following:

- psychotic and quasi-psychotic symptoms as they relate to your CBPD

- how psychotic symptoms complicate the understanding and presentation of your CBPD symptoms

- stress-related paranoia and dissociation and the differences between them

- psychotic and quasi-psychotic symptoms and the differences between them

- how to tell the difference between psychotic and BPD-related quasi-psychotic symptoms

Psychotic and quasi-psychotic symptoms are frightening. They challenge your reality and add to the false belief that you're unable to master and control your CBPD symptoms due to the sensation of losing a grip on your thoughts, feelings, behaviors, and life. You've learned that you have recourse when you're under intense stress now that you're armed with the knowledge and insight provided by working through this chapter and, overall, through this book. This can serve as that first step to recognizing your concerns and issues related to psychotic or quasi-psychotic symptoms. Empowered with this knowledge and insight, you're ready to learn how to manage and control these symptoms in the next chapter.

CHAPTER 8

Activities to Ground You in the Present

CBPD that's made up of psychotic or quasi-psychotic and BPD symptoms is distressing, but the symptoms are equally troubling to family, friends, and treatment providers and pose a unique challenge for management and treatment. There are four areas of focus when this type of CBPD is present:

1. Assess your degree of psychotic or quasi-psychotic symptoms.

2. Raise your awareness about medication and how to maximize its benefit to help you manage your psychotic symptoms.

3. Use grounding and mindfulness techniques to decrease the intensity of your psychotic or quasi-psychotic symptoms.

4. Apply reality-testing techniques to accurately assess your surroundings and determine the most advantageous response.

Building your knowledge, skills, and abilities in these four areas will help you manage and control your symptoms that make up this type of CBPD.

Severity of Your Psychotic or Quasi-Psychotic Symptoms

All symptoms aren't the same in how they're experienced and how they're expressed. This is true for all disorders, including your psychotic and quasi-psychotic symptoms that are associated with your CBPD. You know the different symptoms from reading the prior chapter. Now let's assess the degree to which they affect you so you can build insight into these symptoms and use the techniques outlined below to better control them.

Consider This: Psychotic, Quasi-Psychotic, and Cognitive Disturbance Symptom Severity

You'll use your journal to complete the exercise below to help you identify the severity of your psychotic, quasi-psychotic, and cognitive disturbance symptoms and to what degree they affect how you see yourself, others, and your world. At the top of a new page, write "My Symptom Severity." Then write each of the following psychotic, quasi-psychotic, and cognitive disturbance symptoms, leaving three to five lines between each—you'll find out why in a moment (you don't have to write out the definition of each symptom; it is included here to help you distinguish and best identify symptom severity):

- **dissociation** (a disrupted, nonpsychotic thought disturbance that includes impaired attention, recurrent illusions, a daydreaming-like state, and disturbance in memory). Two types are listed below:

  - **depersonalization** (a state in which your thoughts and feelings seem unreal or not belonging to you)

  - **derealization** (feeling detached from your environment and the objects and other people in it)

- **psychosis** (impaired reality testing, which includes the inability to differentiate yourself from others and internal from external stimuli and circumstances, and compromises your ability to maintain emotional control within different environments)

- **quasi-psychotic symptoms** (sensations that aren't actually present, misperceptions of your own body, or beliefs that irrelevant occurrences are directly related to you that last minutes to hours and are in response to actual or imagined abandonment while under extreme stress)

- **paranoid ideation** (perceived hostile intent in the speech, body language, casual glances, or behavior of others that appear nonthreatening to most others)

Next, to the right of the symptom, identify and write out the severity level of your symptoms using the scale below:

None	No symptoms at all.
Mild	Some symptoms, but they don't last long, cause you very little distress, and aren't noticeable to others.
Moderate	Symptoms cause discomfort, but you can still do the things you need to do to get through the day. These are noticeable to others, but especially to those closest to you.
Severe	Symptoms interfere with your ability to get through the day and are very noticeable to all others.
Extreme	Symptoms cause significant disruption in all areas of your life, you're unable to get through the day and need outside assistance to function, and symptoms and dysfunction are evident to all others.

Lastly, and this is why you left the spaces, identify the circumstances in which these symptoms manifest. Be as descriptive as you can and include people, places, or things that you feel are related to your symptoms being activated. Here's an example from Annalise's journal:

Derealization: Severe. I experience blanking-out when Carmon and I fight, and I get overcome with fear and rage that she's going to leave me forever.

The insight gained from this exercise further refines your understanding of your psychotic or quasi-psychotic symptoms. You can use this information to help you better manage your symptoms and empower you with choices on how to either avoid or minimize circumstances in which they occur.

Psychotic and quasi-psychotic symptoms are difficult to identify and manage, but if you did the above exercise, you were likely able to identify them. Sometimes you need help to manage your symptoms, and medication can be an ally when it's paired with the knowledge, skills, and abilities you're gaining throughout this book and this chapter. Let's move on to raising your awareness about medication by reviewing some strategies to maximize its potential to help you manage your psychotic or quasi-psychotic symptoms.

Managing Your Medications

Medication for CBPD that's made up of BPD plus psychotic, quasi-psychotic, and cognitive disturbance symptoms is challenging due to finding the right medication that works for you as well as the right dosage. However, it can be quite effective in helping you lessen symptoms so you can use the skills you're learning in this book to manage them. Research shows that medication can be mildly to moderately effective in reducing the symptoms and improving mental health functioning in people with BPD (Gunderson 2009). Medication is used to treat between 90 and 99 percent of individuals with BPD, and in 67 to 84 percent of the time, at least two or more types are prescribed (Bridler et al. 2015; Paton et al. 2015). The following guidelines, which are based upon research and my clinical experience, are designed to enhance the efficacy of medication(s) for BPD (Fox 2020; Gunderson 2009; Hopwood 2018). These strategies were designed to increase your awareness of your medication's use and its limitations and are vital aspects for you and your provider to consider.

1. Medication has been found to help lessen overt symptoms (surface content) related to anxiety, depression, impulsivity, and other symptoms; it should be supplementary and not the only part of treatment, as medication is not a cure.

2. Medication isn't effective to treat core content issues, which may include feelings of emptiness, abandonment, and low self-worth.

3. Collaboration between you and your provider is critical to identify a clear goal for the desired response to medications. Your provider won't know exactly what will work on which symptoms and to what degree they'll be impacted without your help.

4. You and your provider should develop a time line in which effects are likely to occur. For example, in two to four weeks, a reduction in the symptoms of anxiety that precede dissociation should be noticeable.

5. Your provider should clearly discuss side effects and possible alternatives to the medication. You're encouraged to be an active participant in the medication-decision process, as opposed to a passive recipient.

6. You're strongly encouraged to learn about the specific medications that are prescribed to you, the side effects, and the likelihood of you experiencing those side effects. (Remember Annalise's reluctance?)

7. Create a safety plan along with procedures to implement it in case psychotic or quasi-psychotic symptoms resurface or exacerbate. See the text box on the following page for instructions. Use the symptom descriptions outlined above as a guide as to when a safety plan needs to be activated.

8. Remain compliant on medication and take as prescribed. Remember that individuals with pure BPD and CBPD are more likely to be noncompliant or take the medication at various times and dosages for various reasons. This significantly decreases medication efficacy and the ability of the practitioner to accurately determine medication usefulness.

Create a Safety Plan

1.   At the top of a new page in your journal, write "Safety Plan."

2.   Identify your warning signs (thoughts, feelings, behaviors, and images) that indicate symptoms are worsening to a severe or extreme level.

3.   List your effective coping strategies (things you can do to lessen your symptoms; this chapter and book are full of strategies you can use).

4.   List people, services, and agencies you can contact who can help you (people you can count on to render assistance).

5.   Identify things you can do to keep your environment safe (for example, throw out old medication, don't keep old razors around, or use electric razors only).

6.   Write down the thing(s) that keeps you going and striving to manage your symptoms and grow beyond your CBPD.*

Please turn to the introduction and refer to the section titled "Suicidal Ideation or Intent" for resources that can help.

As you can see from this list, it's the collaborative effort between you and your provider that reaps the most benefit. Your outcome and likelihood of success are significantly strengthened when you're aware of your symptoms and the degree to which they impact you and your life. Medication is designed to treat surface content, while therapy is aimed at treating both surface and core content. This doesn't mean that medications aren't useful; they certainly are, as just discussed. It's important to be aware that there is no medication for pure BPD or CBPD. Although medication can help lessen symptoms, including psychotic and quasi-psychotic symptoms, it's not enough to completely manage the disorder. This means that you're going to have use strategies to lessen the symptoms you experience. This can be done using strategies called grounding techniques.

Grounding Your Symptoms

Grounding techniques are strategies that help you refocus your thoughts and feelings in the present when you feel detached or as if you're losing your grip on your thoughts, feelings, and behaviors. For example, the techniques could help after you just had a fight with your partner and they stomp out of the house in anger. Your core content of abandonment is activated, and you feel your symptoms worsening. Grounding often works to enhance self-control by strengthening focus on and awareness of the present.

Below are seven grounding techniques you can use to keep yourself in the present. Staying present empowers you with awareness and choice. Combining these two critical aspects gives you greater control over your thoughts, feelings, behaviors, and patterns. While you're doing these activities, thoughts are going to pop into your head. That's fine, but imagine the thoughts in balloons floating in your mind. Then pop them and let them fall so you can ground yourself.

1. **Cold water splash.** Splash cold water on your face or put your hands in a bowl of cold water. This is a great strategy to bring you to the present because it causes your body chemistry to change. Your heart rate immediately drops, and your parasympathetic nervous system is activated, which prompts a present-centered relaxation response. *Be very careful if you have sensitive skin or medical issues. Ask your doctor before trying this strategy.*

2. **Savory sips or bites.** Slowly drink coffee or eat something sweet, such as chocolate. It doesn't have to be coffee or chocolate; it can be whatever you wish. As you consume it, focus your attention on the temperature of the liquid or the sweetness of the food. Is it hot, cold, room temperature? Is it bitter, sour, sweet, or salty? Do you feel it on your tongue, sliding to the back of your mouth, and then down your throat? Do this with each sip or bite. Center your attention on the specifics of what you're doing and notice that your attention is present focused on the here and now.

3. **Slow pace wins the race.** Breathe using a slow, steady, and focused breath. When you breathe in, allow your stomach to expand, and when you breath out, allow your stomach to contract. Your chest should hardly rise or fall. When your chest rises and falls, you're using the upper third of your lungs, which sends a signal to your brain to prep for defense. Instead, you want to prep for awareness of the present, and focusing on your breath helps you control your body's response to stress, fear, and anxiety.

4. **Listen and hear.** Focus your attention and listen to what's going on around you. Do you hear music, traffic, wind, birds, or the stillness of your room? If you listen hard and there is no sound, you can hear your inner ear. This is when you hear a soft pitch that sounds like it's floating right outside your ear. It's the sound of listening to what you hear in your ear. This requires focus on the present and what's going on in the world around you.

5. **Pick a part.** Pick a body part, any part, and focus intently on it. Does it feel hot, cold, tingly, or still? Can you feel the blood flow in and out of it? Can you move it so slowly that only you know it's moving? Your attention is fixed on that body part and that body part alone. You're centered, calm, and with your picked part of you.

6. **The 5-4-3-2-1 method.** Identify five things you see around you, identify four things you can touch around you, identify three things you can hear right now, identify two things you can smell, and identify one thing you can taste.

7. **Touchy-feely.** Find an object that you can touch and maybe take with you, such as a keychain. Is the object soft, rough, smooth, cold, or fuzzy? As you feel the object, focus your attention on how it feels, then on your hand and fingers holding it; move it from hand to hand, but keep your focus on the item and how it feels. You're present, focused, calm, and in control.

Any of these seven grounding techniques can help you when your core content has been activated. Grounding techniques are like any other strategy: the more you do them, the better you get at them. Hone your skills regularly by practicing when you're not activated so when you are activated, you have the refined skill to fall back on. It's challenging or impossible to learn a skill in the midst of core content activation and symptom exacerbation.

Psychotic and quasi-psychotic symptoms hamper your capacity to understand and take in reality. Another very useful set of strategies you can use to do this is called reality testing. Let's learn some of these strategies now.

Bring Reality into It

Reality testing entails training yourself to differentiate between your internal thoughts, feelings, and ideas from the external triggering event. When you're in a situation where you feel trapped, controlled, hopeless, or overwhelmed, your CBPD is likely to distort your perception and prompt you to narrowly focus in on the worst possible outcome, such as your low sense of self-worth and that you'll be alone forever. This exercise will help you see the reality of the situation and resist the distortion often created by your CBPD.

Reality is often not as frightening and beyond your control as your distortion leads you to believe. For example, you just had an argument with your significant other. The fear aroused by your core content activation distorts your perception, causing you to catastrophize the situation and say to yourself, "She's going to leave me. I'll never see her again. I'll be alone forever. I'm worthless and unlovable." The reality is that couples argue, it doesn't mean she'll leave forever, and it doesn't mean you're unlovable. Challenge that distortion by using your personal power to push back and say to yourself, "She loved me, others have loved me, and this shows I'm lovable." This technique is what I call the "distortion pushback," and it's described below along with two other reality-testing strategies you can use. Use your journal to help you refine these strategies for you and specific issues in your life that your CBPD distorts.

The Distortion Pushback

1. Identify that your core content has been activated, such as feelings of abandonment, low self-worth, or emptiness.

2. Call out the distortion: "My distortion is that she hates, me, I'm worthless, and I have no value."

3. Be specific in your distortion pushback: "She got upset when I got home late and didn't call, and she was worried about me because she loves me. I felt guilty, so I acted defensively and tried to turn it on her, and we argued. I know this is something I shouldn't do. My behavior affects her, and I'm important to her and to me, so I'm going to apologize and tell her how I'll do it differently next time, showing her I value her and myself."

The Advantage of Vantage Points

1. Identify the situation, person, or event that caused the distortion.

2. Identify that your core content has been activated, such as feelings of abandonment, low self-worth, or emptiness.

3. Try to see the situation, person, or event from other points of view and ask yourself, "How can I see this differently?"

4. Resist the urge to fall into an old maladaptive pattern of distortion when your core content takes over. Identify evidence that supports this alternate viewpoint. Remember, when we get lost in a single perspective that's tied to our core content that we know distorts our perception, we're more likely to feel trapped, causing an increase in stress, which increases the probability of psychotic or quasi-psychotic symptoms to arise.

Think First, React Second

1. When you encounter intense stress or you're triggered, glue yourself in place and glue your lips together.

2. Don't engage in that immediate maladaptive response your CBPD is telling you to engage in.

3. Instead, take in a slow, steady, and focused breath.

4. Think and write out details about the situation, person, or event and the activated thoughts, feelings, and images.

5. Be solution focused and ask yourself, "What do I want out of this?" and "What's going to help me most?"

6. Lastly, plan to implement your next steps of engagement to manage the situation in a more effective way.

In this chapter, you learned to apply the knowledge you gained from chapter 7 to help you stay grounded and lessen distortions from your psychotic and quasi-psychotic symptoms. This chapter hopefully provided you with a clear understanding of the following:

•   how to build your overall skills to manage and control psychotic or quasi-psychotic symptoms associated with your CBPD

•   how to identify the degree of severity of your psychotic or quasi-psychotic symptoms

•   medication, its use, limitations, and vital aspects as well as how to get the most out of it to help you manage your symptoms

•   grounding and mindfulness techniques to decrease the adverse impact of your psychotic or quasi-psychotic symptoms

- how to use reality-testing techniques to clearly assess your surroundings and determine the most helpful response

It can feel as if your brain is against you when you're contending with this type of CBPD. The skills and strategies you learned in this chapter will help you build your sense of self-efficacy in controlling your symptoms. Your brain is just that, *your brain,* and you can control it instead of feeling like it's controlling you. Use the techniques in this chapter, and elsewhere in the book, to build mastery and recognize the power you have to influence your life and its course. Grasp your personal power to go forward with choice and a greater sense of control.

CHAPTER 9

Running the Endless Race with ADHD

"My motor's drowning me."

—Shelly, 29

Shelly arrived at the community clinic for their first appointment thirty minutes late. On the intake form, Shelly identified the preferred pronoun as "they/them." While they sat in the waiting room, they were in constant motion, fidgeting endlessly. When the psychologist came out to inform them of the abbreviated session, they said, "I get it. Sorry, Doc, I'm only on time by accident, and my motor's drowning me."

At the start of the session, Shelly said, "I'm at the end of my rope." They reported feeling desperate after they lost their last job at a data-entry company. They said, "Data entry! Can you believe that, Doc? This was my last hope at a job to pay the rent. Needless to say, I showed up late, turned in my data sheets late and incorrectly, and they let me go after three days." They went on to explain their long history of losing jobs: "I just don't focus. I don't see the finer details; it's like I'm in this dense fog and always out of touch. My attention is about as long as a gnat's leg, and I don't get what's being said to me unless it's the second, third, or even the fourth time. I don't sit still, and my mouth is on a motor that never runs out of gas." They hung their head in their hands and sobbed while their leg continually bouncing up and down and they incessantly shifted in their seat.

The psychologist didn't get much opportunity to speak, but interrupted them, leaned slightly forward, and asked them, "When did all of this begin?" They replied, "In elementary school, they put me in special education. I had a teacher's aide and everything. I was allotted extra time on tests and a special room to take tests, I was not given homework because I would always forget to do it, and my work was often read to me. I got through a lot of books that way. I read *Huckleberry Finn*, *Count of Monte Cristo*, *Little Women*, all those books you get to read in school, but I didn't read them; they were read to me. That counts, right?" The psychologist reoriented them to the question asked, and they continued, "I got breaks in my day to stretch my legs and move. I would disrupt the classes because I couldn't keep my mouth shut. My mouth, we'll talk about how my mouth has gotten me into trouble more times than I can count. I was able to graduate high school, but only because they were being nice, or wanted me out. I'm not sure which, but I wasn't going to ask either." Shelly went on to explain that they tried college for a year but were unable to keep up, showed up late to class, couldn't sit still in class, bothered the other students, blurted out answers, failed to finish assignments, and couldn't focus. All the things they went through in elementary school followed them into adulthood.

They recalled the medications they tried: "Everything my doctor could imagine." Some slowed them down but made them groggy. Others caused them to lose weight, to not be able to sleep, and to have stomachaches and headaches. They hadn't taken medication in ten years and were reluctant to try again. They explained that they never tried therapy to learn skills to help slow them down and manage the inattention and hyperactivity. They said, "I would've tried anything. I'm open to doing it, learning stuff. I'm here in an attempt to try and figure all this out. I need a track I can follow, walk, or run along. I like walking, and I walk often. I used to run regularly, but I got tired of doing it. I get bored with stuff easily. We live in a beautiful part of the country, and if things don't get figured out, I might be living in it, like, homeless." They began crying.

Shelly asked if they could pace in the office because sitting still was difficult for them while they explained how symptoms affected their romantic relationships. "My last relationship was with Taylor. When we met, we clicked. He could keep up, for a while. We had a whirlwind romance of sorts. Puppy love in the honeymoon phase, but he grew tired of me, but not until we had two kids together. He, like everyone else, got annoyed with me. I was in charge of the grocery shopping, but I would forget to make a list or not write stuff down, and when we needed stuff during the week for Taylor or the kids, we wouldn't have it. I was in charge of the finances for a little while, but that was a nightmare. We got hit with a ton of late fees, and our power got turned off because I didn't pay it for two months. Like all others in my life, I burn them out. I'm too much, can't follow through, don't pay attention, all the things that disrupted my schooling and employment wreck my relationships too. He's a good guy all in all; he just got tired. He pays for the kids and helps when he can. I'm still at the end of my rope and need some kind of help to get me from here to there, from work to rent money."

The abbreviated session ended, and Shelly agreed to return the following week, promising to be on time. While in the parking lot, they realized they had lost their keys. They retraced their steps from the parking lot to the waiting room and to the office and couldn't find them anywhere. After a ten-minute search, they checked the bathroom and found them in the sink, "I think they fell out when I washed my hands." Embarrassed, they walked out of the office.

Shelly never responded to the appointment confirmations and missed their next appointment. They showed up one day and one hour after their scheduled appointment, saying they had the wrong date and time written down. They said they had it in their phone, but explained, "I lost my phone again, and it took me a day to find it. I couldn't find which app it was in. It was supposed to be in the appointment app, but I have three, so I don't forget appointments, but I can't find where I wrote it." Another appointment was scheduled, multiple reminders were sent, and they arrived only five minutes late. During this session, a plan was created to help them learn attention and behavioral management skills, and Shelly agreed to see the clinic's psychiatrist. In the past, they had seen their primary care physician and never a specialist.

During the next few sessions, the psychologist often asked them to repeat back what was said, but they were unable to explain what was said or the steps involved. They would say, "Doc, if it's over three words, I'm outta town in my head. I drift and can't seem to keep my brain focused on one thing or in one place." Hearing this, the psychologist gave them a "session journal," where they would write down keywords related to what he was saying. Initially, they had difficulty doing this, as the tendency and habit to drift mixed with hyperactivity made it difficult to focus. The psychologist kept encouraging them and kept his own journal to show them how to do this, and over time, Shelly was able to do it. They got better at it, and it became almost automatic in session. The session journal was left with the psychologist, as they both agreed that was best due to the sensitive content but also to prevent it being lost. Shelly was given psychological tests to iden-tify areas of strengths and weaknesses. It was found that they had a learning disorder in reading and sentence comprehension as well as met criteria for attention deficit/hyperactivity disorder (ADHD), combined presentation.

Over the next year, the psychologist and Shelly worked together to build skills and manage their symptoms. A medication was found that could help lessen the symptoms to a level where they could use the strategies they were taught in therapy. They attended a reading class for adults at a local community college and finished it successfully. Employment continued intermittently for most of the year, with the average amount of time at each job slowly getting longer. Shelly eventually got a job they enjoyed and did well. Shelly's new employer worked with them regarding their tendency for distraction and agreed to accommodations regarding ADHD and their learning disabilities.

The Symptoms Identify the Diagnosis

The story of Shelly paints a vibrant picture of the challenges often experi-enced by those with ADHD. As you went through their story, you may have found many parallel circumstances or themes to your own. The difficulty marshaling your attention and controlling your "motor" is challenging. Shelly was actively seeking help and was driven to participate and do well, but their ADHD symptoms got in the way, preventing them from getting help and reaching their goals. They expressed despair when they said, "My motor is drowning me," showing insight into their issues and what's causing them.

They showed up late to their initial appointment, and this happens not out of disrespect or devaluing the psychologist's time, but due to the issue of hyperactivity and inattention. This is part of the problem that they couldn't control, which adversely impacts the initial session and could rupture rapport. However, the psychologist was understanding, didn't make broad generalizations about them being disrespectful, but recognized this as part of the pathology that Shelly was there to get help with. You may have numerous instances when your inattention and hyperactivity adversely impacted relationships, whether in your personal or professional life, just like Shelly.

Shelly was a good historian. They relayed their problems and issues to the psychologist that illustrated their problems with inattention. They turned in their data sheets late and incorrectly, and they had multiple scheduling apps but couldn't recall which one the appointment is in or even whether it was entered. These instances provide evidence of being unfocused and inattentive to tasks that lead to multiple mistakes and poor organizational skills. While talking about their past relationship problems and other occurrences, they were tangential and easily drifted to other topics. This shows an impaired ability to maintain focus on tasks or topics. They seemed to not be listening when someone was talking to them, whether the other person was making a statement, providing directions, or having a conversation with them, and this illustrates how their attention was easily diverted to unrelated topics or other things going on in the environment.

They have a long history of difficulties completing multistep tasks and following directions, such as homework in school, the finances of the household, and grocery shopping. The session journal was a positive management tool and kept at the psychologist's office so it wouldn't get lost, as they have a history of losing important items, such as schoolwork, phone, and keys. The psychologist devised this strategy to address their problem of listening when being spoken to, so they could comprehend needed information using the session journal. This wasn't an easy learning curve for Shelly, as it might not be for you, but proved to be effective, as it built their skills to extrapolate the needed information, as opposed to trying to take it all in at once because that typically caused them, as it may cause you, to feel overwhelmed.

The information outlined above clearly illustrates the adverse impact of their ADHD inattentive symptoms. These symptoms caused socioeconomic dysfunction, which is a critical diagnostic factor (see chapter 1 for more on socioeconomic dysfunction). They expressed frustration, fear, and embarrassment about not being able to hold on to their data-entry job and the problems in their personal and professional life ADHD has caused. The degree of socioeconomic dysfunction was so great that they were in constant disbelief, fear, and embarrassment and seeking help from a psychologist for the first time. You may have encountered that the same personal and professional barriers were put in place by your ADHD symptoms, and as much as you try, they continually manifest, draining your energy to maintain your focus, take in information, and stop your motor so you can work and take care of yourself and your family.

Shelly exhibited more than just inattentive symptoms; they had hyperactive/impulsive ones as well. They fidgeted; felt restless; had difficulty sitting still in session, at school, and at work; felt propelled by a motor; talked a lot during the session; reported a history of blurting out answers; and would disturb others who were trying to work. When we examine Shelly's full spectrum of symptoms, we see they meet criteria for ADHD, combined presentation, which means that both inattentive and hyperactive/impulsive symptoms are present and problematic.

There are three types of ADHD in the DSM-5 (APA 2013): predominately inattentive presentation, predominately hyperactive/impulsive presentation, and combined presentation. The first types of diagnoses are given when inattentive symptoms *or* hyperactive/impulsive symptoms predominate the clinical picture. It's possible to have one without the other or both, and this adds to the confusion that's often related to inaccurate diagnosis of

ADHD. Shelly had symptoms of both, so combined presentation was suitable in this case.

If you have inattentive symptoms that don't interfere with how you live your life, that have only been present as an adult, and that only occur in a single setting, say at work, it's unlikely that you qualify for ADHD inattentive presentation. The explanation for these symptoms could be that you hate your job or are bored with the work you do, so you daydream a lot and tend to not get your work done. If when you're home, you're focused on a hobby or sports, for example, and you get stuff done on time, it isn't inattentive ADHD. It's critical to discern this, as a disorder should never be diagnosed that doesn't meet the required criteria. For Shelly, their hyperactive/impulsive symptoms in conjunction with their inattentive symptoms intensified their problems in relationships and at work and had been present since they were in elementary school. This is very important, as it directly relates to the ADHD diagnosis, because symptoms need to be present before age twelve and occur in two or more settings, such as work, school, and with friends (APA 2013). They certainly do in Shelly's case. Do they occur that way for you?

Shelly first tried to manage their symptoms with medication, and they went to their primary care physician (PCP) for this, which is very common. They had a negative experience with medication and decided it was best to try to manage the symptoms without it. The symptoms persisted along with the related adverse consequences. Eventually, they decided that things had gotten so bad that something different needed to be tried, such as seeing a psychologist. You may have experienced this as well: you tried the same things for years, got very little out of them, decided to abandon seeking help, and then when things got so severe, you reached a point where you considered alternatives you would've discarded previously. The psychologist recognized the symptoms in Shelly and didn't hold it against them. Instead, the psychologist worked with them against the symptoms. He provided strategies to help them and recognized that a specialist, a psychiatrist, could also be helpful to manage their symptoms.

Most PCPs can manage ADHD symptoms because they see them often. However, in some cases, a specialist is needed to provide additional vantage points and services that your PCP can't. This isn't derision to PCPs but the recognition that certain cases require certain specialties that will open opportunities to treatment not considered previously. Shelly's story shows the benefit of collaboration toward their unified goal: symptom attenuation and management.

As the story of Shelly illustrates, their perseverance and strength to go forward and do things differently paid off. These aren't rare and unique traits in Shelly, as they may exist in you as well. Reading this book is an attempt to manage your symptoms, find clarity or a new vantage point, and learn skills to do it differently. As you can see through Shelly's story and the symptom and treatment explanation, ADHD is challenging, but when borderline personality disorder (BPD) is added to the mix, it gets even more confusing.

The ADHD-BPD Complexity

The overlap between BPD and ADHD is a complicated combination that poses many challenges for you and your treatment providers. ADHD is a neurodevelopment disorder characterized by hallmark symptoms of inattention and hyperactivity/impulsivity, and as you know, BPD is characterized by erratic and dramatic responses to internal and external stimuli that occur across situations for extended periods of time.

Approximately 4 percent of the general population meets criteria for ADHD, but it doesn't exist in isolation, as it's often comorbid with anxiety, depression, substance use, and personality disorders (Kessler et al. 2006). It's estimated that 38 percent of individuals with BPD have comorbid ADHD (Ferrer et al. 2010; Fossati et al. 2002), what we're calling complex BPD (CBPD), and 14 percent of those diagnosed with ADHD in childhood are later diagnosed with BPD (Matthies et al. 2011). As this data shows, ADHD and BPD occur together quite often, which adds to the difficulty in the identification and treatment for both yourself and the mental health providers you look to for help.

Shelly's story illustrates ADHD symptoms very well and clearly. In most therapeutic sessions, the information is erratic and disorganized, causing their PCP, psychiatrist, or mental health provider to be overwhelmed. Perhaps you've felt that way on more than one occasion. If everyone who's trying to provide treatment and understand the impetus for presentation of symptoms is overwhelmed, it's very difficult to make heads or tails of the connection and root to what's causing them. This significantly affects the ability to create a trajectory for successful treatment.

If you've been diagnosed with ADHD, BPD, or possibly both, but you can't seem to identify which is present, how often, and under what conditions, you're not alone. There's a lot of confusion about the intersection and co-occurrence of BPD and ADHD that make up this type of CBPD. In adolescents and adults, it's difficult to distinguish because both disorders share similar surface content and features (Fossati et al. 2002; Koerting et al. 2016; O'Malley et al. 2016; see chapter 2 for more on surface content).

The hallmarks of ADHD are inattentiveness and hyperactivity/ impulsivity. These symptoms manifest to such a degree that they impair your ability to concentrate, take in new information, follow directions, and complete needed tasks. These issues are also seen in those with BPD. You're reading this book likely because you experience some of them as well. You likely find it difficult to slow down enough to focus your attention, control your behavior, or just stop moving due to an intense need to get things done or avoid perceived adverse events. Things in your life change so quickly, causing your mind to race and jump so that you end up not getting anything done, which leaves you emotionally dysregulated (described below) by your thoughts, feelings, and mental images. This causes you to engage in maladaptive patterns to try to lessen those thoughts, feelings, and images, but in the end, the patterns actually make things worse.

Emotional dysregulation is associated with ADHD, but it's not a well-known byproduct of it like it is with BPD. Emotional dysregulation is an impaired ability to manage negative emotions, such as fear, anger, and sadness. In ADHD, emotional dysregulation builds quickly but doesn't go over that line where it's destructive to the same degree as it does in BPD.

For example, you're driven by your ADHD motor and your mind is wandering, someone tells you that you forgot to do something very important, and you feel sadness and regret because of it, but you're able to muster the energy to address and resolve the issue. This is somewhat similar in those with BPD, except the emotional dysregulation gets so intense and sometimes happens so quickly that they feel as though they're enveloped by it with nothing else to do but suffer through it until it passes, if it passes, or explode, harming themselves or others, or causing destruction in their life through other maladaptive means. In the example where you forgot something, the ensuing guilt and regret is so intense that you're unable to muster the energy to address it and fix it, and instead you act out or are frozen by it. The degree of difference in symptoms is what makes this a very complex aspect of this type of CBPD.

Low frustration tolerance and irritability are also overlapping symptoms of ADHD and BPD. These symptoms often work hand in hand to add to your difficulty in managing a wide variety of situations, whether they're related to work, school, or relationships. If you had ADHD alone, you'd experience your underlying low frustration tolerance and irritability as secondary to inattentiveness and hyperactivity/impulsivity, whereas if you had BPD alone, your irritability would intensely feed your low frustration tolerance, disrupting your ability to focus and concentrate on the issues you're contending with at any given time. When they occur jointly as CBPD, they're much more prominent and difficult to control and often interfere with daily functioning, as well as in how you relate to others across a wide variety of relationship types (including intimate, platonic, employment) and settings (such as home, work, in public and private). For example, when you get bad news and you're triggered, your irritability and low frustration tolerance get mixed with your ADHD symptoms of inattentiveness and hyperactivity/impulsivity. This increases the probability of you engaging in maladaptive patterns due to your impaired ability to take in all information, good and bad, related to the triggering event. Subsequently, you try to manage your emotional, cognitive, and behavioral response by engaging in those default maladaptive patterns (for example, an anger outburst or self-harm) that increase the probability of greater negative consequences (such as the loss of a relationship, job, or friendship).

Social intrusiveness and disorganization are also related to this type of CBPD. Social intrusiveness routinely manifests as interrupting others, but it can also be seen as a component of social awkwardness that's related to a tendency to misinterpret the environment or how to appropriately socially engage with others. For example, the social intrusiveness and awkwardness increase the likelihood that you'll experience rejection by others, which activates your issues of abandonment, which trigger the BPD part of your CBPD. This then becomes cyclical: social intrusiveness leads to your awkward social engagements, which increase the probability of rejection, which triggers your abandonment, causing you to engage in your maladaptive patterns. This cycle continues for years until you or a qualified professional helps you see the pattern and you learn to stop it.

Disorganization is highly disruptive to your mental health functioning. Disorganization adds to your sense of low self-efficacy (how well you feel you can engage in a required action to manage a situation), as your life often feels in disarray and outside of your control. Disorganization drives your feelings of being continually uprooted that leads to your sensation of being bombarded by stressors in all directions. When you feel like this, your BPD symptoms distort how you see yourself and your life, causing you to feel less able to gain control of yourself and your situations. This can leave you spiraling in an attempt to grasp your life, but control seems to continually slip away until you learn the skills of organization and self-efficacy, which we'll address in chapter 10. Both ADHD and BPD should be considered possible and likely comorbid conditions due to the high prevalence rate and degree of impairment that's often present when they co-occur. When treatment is considered, you and your provider must consider several derailing factors:

- the severity of impairment related to maladaptive patterns

- your access to helpful and supportive resources

- the degree of risk you're willing to take, whether physical, social, legal, or financial, to meet an urge or desire for excitement

- the strategies you've employed in the past that have been helpful and hindering

- stressors that impair your functioning

- your motivation to change

Even one of these issues can lead to poor acquisition of the knowledge and skills that would otherwise promote your progress in treatment, but when more than one is present, the likelihood of treatment success is significantly lessened. You can combat these issues and put yourself in a position to manage your CBPD by raising your awareness and insight into knowing the difference between ADHD with and without BPD. Shelly's first story illustrated ADHD only. Let's take a look at how Shelly's story changes when BPD co-occurs with ADHD.

Shelly's Complex Journey

Shelly arrived thirty minutes late to the community clinic for their first appointment. They were in constant motion, fidgeting endlessly while they waited. They asked the receptionist multiple times when the session would begin and how long they'd have to wait. The psychologist came out to inform them that due to arriving late, they would only meet for the remaining time allotted. Shelly said, "That's crazy! How is that fair to me? You probably don't want to meet with me anyway. I'm just another one of your broken clients. One thing you need to know about me is, I'm only on time by accident, and you're my last hope because my motor's drowning me."

They reluctantly agreed to participate in the shorter session, and once the office door was closed, Shelly sat on the couch and began sobbing while they explained why they were seeking treatment, "I can't do this! I can't keep it up. I just lost this stupid job doing data entry. Data entry! Can you believe that, Doc? Now I have no job to pay my rent. Guess why I got fired, wait don't answer that, I'll answer it for you. I showed up late, turned in my data sheets late and incorrectly, got in an argument with my boss, and they sat some girl next to me who smelled liked old pickles and sauerkraut. Can you even imagine what that smells like? You don't want to know, I'll tell you that. They're trying to force me to quit, I know it. I worked there for a total of three days, and then I gave them what they wanted. I quit." They went on to explain their long history of losing jobs and problems getting along with coworkers: "Most people I work for are stupid. They piss me off, and I'll let you know if you do me wrong. Like with you about this shortened session you're punishing me with. I can't, and don't, focus or see the finer details, and I live in this swamp shrouded by this dense fog. It hasn't drowned me yet, but water's rising, Doc. People say stuff to me, but I don't get it. It slides in and then right back out. They need to tell me stuff two, three, or sometimes four times. Then they look at me like I'm stupid, and that sets me off. I won't be judged by you, them, or anyone else. I don't sit still, and my mouth is on a motor that never runs out of gas." They hung their head in their hands and continued sobbing while their leg continually bounced up and down and they incessantly shifted in their seat.

As they sat there sobbing, they began hitting themselves in the head. The psychologist leaned forward, and in a calm voice said, "You feel like you're at the end of your rope. You feel trapped. Physically punishing yourself isn't the answer. You're here to do things differently, learn the skills to not hurt yourself and those around you. You can do this. I can already tell you're a determined person." Shelly stopped hitting herself and looked up, "I hope you're right. Not much more slack on this rope, Doc."

They wiped their tears away and continued telling the psychologist about their history and symptoms. "I've been messed up from day one. In elementary school, I was in special education. I had a teacher's aide, and she was cool, but she couldn't keep up. I was all over the place, up, down, and all around. I had scheduled time-outs and a 'cool-down room,' for when I got really pissed. I had other accommodations in school, like extra time on tests, a special room to take tests, no homework because I would always forget to do it, and my work was often read to me. They read to me because they knew I was dim-witted. You can't imagine being called dim-witted by teachers, family, and friends your whole life. Book stuff comes easy to you! Well, it doesn't for me, not a bit. School was a nightmare of validation of my sense of stupidity. Kids were horrid, my family is horrid, friends are fickle, and the only things of value were the boys I hooked up with. It's the only thing that made me feel connected. The more hookups I had, the more whole I felt." Shelly continued, "Oh yeah, school stuff. I got breaks in my day to stretch my legs and move. I would disrupt the classes and couldn't keep my mouth shut. I knew the principal by her first name. She called my mom all the time, who would never show up though she said she was 'on her way.' I was able to graduate high school, but only because they wanted me out and considered me a good riddance." Shelly went on to explain that they tried college for a year but were unable to keep up, showed up late to class, couldn't sit still in class, bothered the other students all the time, blurted out answers, failed to finish assignments, and couldn't focus. All the things they went through in school followed them into adulthood.

They recalled the medications they tried: "I've been on everything you can imagine, and it doesn't work on me. Never has. Some stuff slowed me down, but I would fall asleep or have headaches and stomachaches. I've been broken from day one. I haven't taken medication in ten years, and I don't plan on trying any." They explained that they never tried therapy to learn skills to help them slow down and manage the symptoms. They said, "The only reason I'm here is to try one last thing. I'm here in an attempt to try and figure all this out. I need a track I can follow, walk, or run along. I get bored with stuff easily. I'm not saying you have to entertain me. I'm saying if all we're going to do is dig up old dirt and you're going to throw it in my face, I'm not interested, but something's gotta help me. I can't be the only one you've seen with this, am I? Don't answer that. I don't want to know. I'm afraid if I don't sort this out, me and my kids are going to end up homeless."

Shelly asked if they could pace in the office because sitting still was difficult for them while they explained how symptoms affected their romantic relationships. "My last relationship was with Taylor. When we met, we clicked. He kept up with me for a while. We had a wild and passionate romance. We would get along one minute, he'd say or do something stupid, I'd check him on it, and we'd fight. We got into some pretty intense brawls.

Running the Endless Race with ADHD 155

He grew tired of me, like everyone does, but we had two kids together. I think the last straw was when we were arguing and I started hitting myself. He would yell and scream for me to stop, so I would step it up and show him how hurt I really was. Well, I hit myself really hard and gave myself a black eye. He freaked and took off. It could've been a good relationship, but he left like I knew he would. They all do; you'll leave me too."

The abbreviated session ended, which annoyed Shelly because they felt it was punishment for coming late. On the way out, they noticed someone waiting for their next appointment. *The psychologist wasn't lying*, they thought. Shelly agreed to return the following week. While in the parking lot, they realized they'd lost their keys. Annoyed and angry, they retraced their steps from the parking lot to the waiting room to the office, and couldn't find them anywhere. They began crying, berating themself, and after a ten-minute search, found them in the bathroom sink. Embarrassed, they walked out of the office and slammed the door behind them.

Over the next several sessions, Shelly continued to arrive between five and fifteen minutes late. During these sessions, a plan was created to help them learn attention and behavioral management skills. Though they sounded willing in session, they wouldn't follow through. They explained that there was just too much going on in their life to add another responsibility. The psychologist and Shelly processed the issue, and it was uncovered that underlying the anger was an intense fear of:

- failure

- abandonment related to others in their life as well as losing the psychologist if they succeeded in treatment

- emptiness that seemed to be intensifying

- moments when they felt detached from reality when under stress

- not knowing who they were or what they wanted out of life

The psychologist explained the increased challenge in learning new skills because of any possible learning disorders that might be present, based upon their reported history, as well as the presence of CBPD. They agreed to testing, and a reading and comprehension learning disorder was identified. Also, due to the added complexity of this type of CBPD, they were encouraged to see the clinic's psychiatrist and, though initially reluctant, they eventually agreed.

The psychiatrist was able to find medications that helped lessen the ADHD symptoms and some of the agitation with minimal side effects. The session journal was used extensively with a greater focus on emotional words and connecting those emotions to people and situations in their life. Encouragement and patience became a central component. The issue of self-harm, a surface content maladaptive issue, and its connection to core content was explored, and over time, it lessened significantly (see chapter 2 for an explanation of core and surface content).

Over the next three years, the psychologist and Shelly worked together to build skills and manage symptoms and behaviors. They attended a reading class and improved their skills, which improved their self-esteem. Employment remained a challenge due to CBPD symptoms and was an area of continual focus. Relationships improved as well as their ability to tolerate intimacy and accept their own and their partner's faults. Shelly was a success story as they learned to manage and control their symptoms, trust their providers, and eventually build their skills to feel empowered to change their life.

Not all of the symptoms and issues Shelly experienced and manifested may directly relate to you, but their story illustrates the added challenge of this type of CBPD. The psychologist recognized the changes to the course of treatment that needed to be made when he recognized that BPD was comorbid with ADHD. The approach continued to be one of compassion that focused on Shelly's drive to do well and get better. A particular focal point was the self-harm act while in session while simultaneously addressing their inattentive and hyperactive/impulsive symptoms. The presence of BPD, or any other personality disorder, adds to the amount of time treatment is going to take until symptom reduction can occur and stabilize. In Shelly's story, as well as in the other stories in this book, the time line is approximately three times longer when a personality disorder, such as BPD, is present.

The psychologist was also aware that ADHD is associated with impairment in social, academic, and occupational functioning (Barkley 2002). This is why the psychologist tested Shelly, identifying their reading and comprehension learning disorder. This is good and thorough practice because treatment progression would have been significantly impaired if it went ignored or unnoticed. When the psychologist gave Shelly something to read and they didn't do it, it could've been misconstrued as resistance, when in actuality it was the result of their learning impairment that's comorbid with their ADHD. You may be all too familiar with the assumption of your skills, whether it's what you can or can't do, will or won't do, and what you're able or unable to do.

We need to briefly discuss medication as it relates to this type of CBPD. Remember from chapter 2, when we discussed medication, personality, and personality disorders, and that it doesn't treat core content, such as feelings of abandonment or emptiness, but addresses surface content. ADHD is considered a surface content issue, which is why medication is often effective in lessening its symptoms. However, if it's believed you only have ADHD, but it's undiagnosed CBPD made up of ADHD and BPD, medication is only going to do so much, leaving you feeling frustrated, angry, or disappointed. Medication is often prescribed for those with ADHD, and research shows it to be effective in most cases, but when we consider the impact CBPD has on the individual and their symptoms and behavior, the importance of making the distinction between ADHD, BPD, and CBPD becomes even more apparent to planning a pathway for treatment success.

Making the ADHD and BPD Distinction

CBPD that's made up of ADHD and BPD is certainly confusing due to the overlap of symptoms, but there are symptoms that help distinguish between these two disorders. These distinguishing symptoms aren't exhibited in a nice orderly fashion, as you know. They're often presented when you encounter stress, fear, rejection, or any other triggering event or occurrence that activates your core content. Shelly's two stories show the added complexity when this type of CBPD is present, but they also illustrate the critical aspects needed to discriminate between the two.

History of aggressive behavior, paranoid ideation, episodes of dissociation, and being highly defensive to feedback are symptoms not often seen in those with ADHD but are common in those with BPD. Additional symptoms of distinction include past and present instances of self-harm, a tendency to exhibit a guarded presentation, wanting to be close but pushing others away, fear of disappointment from others, abandonment fears, feelings of emptiness, promiscuity to feel whole, and emotionally and physically intense relationships. You're at a higher likelihood to engage in these behaviors and exhibit these symptoms due to the internal turmoil you feel as a result of your BPD core content issues of abandonment and emptiness. All these symptoms and behaviors are often present and seen in those with BPD but not in those with ADHD.

Those with ADHD alone are unlikely to have these behaviors and symptoms due to the basic nature of the disorder, which is that it's difficult to focus on stressors when your attention continually wanes, you're constantly moving, and you're impulsively engaging in task after task but making little headway. This doesn't mean that those with ADHD don't feel stress; they certainly do, but the impact of the stressor is comparatively less due to the cognitively transient nature of ADHD. These behaviors and symptoms, as they relate to your BPD, are often a part of your maladaptive patterns that result from your core content being activated when you're under intense stress. The combination of core content activation and intense stress sends you into a BPD spiral, causing you to believe you don't have the time to think of an adaptive response, while you simultaneously feel propelled to engage in your default maladaptive patterns in an attempt to remedy the stress to calm your core content activation.

The final symptom related to your BPD but not ADHD is an unstable self-image. This symptom is unique to BPD and includes a sense of not knowing who you are or what you believe. Like all disorders, this is on a continuum, from mild to extreme. Mild cases may be situationally based, for example, when you're with someone you really want to like you, you change your beliefs and views to what you think that other person wants you to believe so they'll like you. At the extreme end, this is a continuous and deep-seated sense of not knowing the direction of your life, not being able to form an opinion out of fear it may alienate others, and a continual change in beliefs, values, and goals. As you try to find out who you are, you're continually blocked by your ever-changing self-image, so you feel constantly in flux. ADHD doesn't have this component because it's separate from the ability to recognize who you are, what you believe, and what you want to achieve. The ADHD symptoms may cause you to not achieve your goals, but you can identify them, and you have a firm sense of who you are.

Consider This: Identifying Your Inattention, Hyperactive/Impulsive, and BPD Symptoms

Symptoms identify the diagnosis, but many times these overlap, leading to misdiagnosis and time spent treating the wrong disorder. Knowledge and awareness of symptoms can help you better identify which symptoms are present, absent, or if they're occurring together, creating CBPD.

On a new page in your journal, draw a line down the middle of the page. Write "Inattentive Symptoms" at the top of the column on the left, and write "Hyperactive/Impulsive Symptoms" at the top of the column on the right. Number from 1 to 14 down the left side of the left column, and number from 1 to 10 down the left side of the column on the right. As you read each symptom listed below, put a T to indicate the symptom is true and something you experience often or an F if the symptom is false and something you don't experience often. Be sure to read the directions and take note of the time components, as these are critical to determining whether symptoms are situationally bound or occur across multiple contexts. Symptoms that occur across multiple contexts are likely related to mental health disorders, whereas those that are situationally dependent are likely due to the circumstance or location.

Only consider the presence of these symptoms and issues when you're not using drugs or alcohol or taking medication and when they are unrelated to a medical condition. This list isn't meant to be used for clinical diagnosis but to help you build insight into your symptoms and issues so you can better manage them and seek out appropriate mental health assistance.

Inattentive Symptoms

You've experienced the following for more days than not for six months or more.

1. I'm routinely unsuccessful in organizing things I need to get tasks done.

2. My work area, desk, or home is in disarray due to a failure to put things in their proper place.

3. I'm late to scheduled appointments or places I'm supposed to be.

4. It's difficult for me to follow a multistep task without losing track.

5. I avoid multistep tasks.

6. I hate having to do multistep tasks.

7. I have a tendency to lose things I need later.

8. My focus tends to diminish or drift to irrelevant topics or issues when I should be concentrating.

9. I tend to forget to do things that need to be done.

10. I tend to make mistakes at work or school.

11. It's hard for me to focus my attention, even when I really need to.

12. People tell me I seem distracted or spaced out.

13. I tend not to see things through to completion.

14. These symptoms cause socioeconomic dysfunction.

Hyperactive/Impulsive Symptoms

You've experienced the following for more days than not for six months or more.

1. I feel like I must keep moving.

2. I'm constantly in motion, going from person to person or activity to activity.

3. I'm fidgety and restless.

4. People say I talk a lot.

5. I can't wait until the question is asked completely before I answer.

6. It's very difficult for me to wait my turn.

7. I interrupt others while they're talking.

8. I interfere in what others are doing, whether invited or not.

9. I do things without asking for permission because I forget to ask.

10. These symptoms cause socioeconomic dysfunction.

Take a moment to go over your BPD symptoms from chapter 1 to help you clarify the separation of ADHD symptoms from BPD. Look over your ADHD symptom ratings and mark or circle the ones you indicated as true for you. These ratings are the significant symptoms that increase the likelihood of ADHD being an accurate diagnosis. Remember, this is an insight-building exercise, not a diagnostic one, and only a qualified mental health or medical provider can give you a diagnosis.

The last criterion is the universal symptom, and if you identified it as true for you, you're indicating that the other symptoms also identified as true significantly disrupt how you live your life. This increases the likelihood of meeting criteria for the full disorder. However, if you marked the universal symptom as false, you may have symptoms related to ADHD but they're not to the level of causing continuous disruption in your life. This still merits exploration, and you may benefit from reading the next chapter to learn management skills.

Listing your symptoms can be a very powerful experience because BPD and comorbid conditions can be overwhelming when seen as a whole. When understood as a combination of particular symptoms and issues, your CBPD is more manageable, and your efforts more impactful and focused as they target particular symptoms. This leads to greater symptom reduction and overall control of your CBPD.

Identifying your symptoms helps you create a management plan to lessen the adverse impact they have on you, your life, and those around you.

Your CBPD symptoms severely impair your ability to manage necessary tasks and focus your attention and energy, and they lower your sense of self-worth, which adds to the difficulty in learning new ways to manage your symptoms. In the next chapter, you'll learn skills that will give you the ability to manage your symptoms. CBPD that's made up of ADHD and BPD brings unique challenges and blockades to treatment, but these aren't insurmountable, and as you go through the next chapter, remind yourself that you can control these symptoms and you can do life differently. You've built your knowledge of empowerment; now let's put it into action.

In this chapter, we explored the following issues as they relate to CBPD when it's made up of inattentive and hyperactive/impulsive symptoms and BPD:

- inattentive and hyperactive/impulsive symptoms as they relate to your CBPD

- the complex combination of ADHD and BPD

- what distinguishes your ADHD from your BPD

- your inattentive, hyperactive/impulsive, and BPD symptoms

Your inattentive and hyperactive/impulsive symptoms that co-occur with BPD have made many aspects of your life hard to manage. Many times, you may have felt so overwhelmed that your focus, attention, behavior, and BPD symptoms all seemed to ignite, adding to your difficulty to control yourself and the situations you're in. It doesn't have to be this way. It's possible to learn about your CBPD and use adaptive strategies to strengthen your ability to influence your life in a positive way. The knowledge and insight you gained through this chapter are the first stepping stones to managing and controlling your CBPD made up of ADHD and BPD. Armed with this, you're ready to learn and utilize strategies to help you manage and control your symptoms.

CHAPTER 10

Activities to Win the Race

ADHD isn't only a childhood disorder. It may first be noticed in childhood, but in many cases, it continues into adulthood. It's estimated that 4.4 percent of adults between the ages of eighteen and forty-four meet criteria for ADHD (Kessler et al. 2006). This shows that you're not alone in contending with your ADHD as an adult. As we illustrated in the last chapter, CBPD that's made up of ADHD and BPD isn't a rare or unusual occurrence. You may have felt like the odd duck, but you're not. There are many, many ducks just like you out in the world. Let's take this knowledge and what you've learned about yourself from reading the last chapter and apply it to manage your CBPD symptoms.

The Impact of Your Symptoms

The last chapter helped you identify your inattentive, hyperactive/impulsive, and BPD symptoms and how often they occur. The next step is to consider in which environments they're exhibited. Most disorders that lead to socioeconomic dysfunction cause impairment across contexts, such as work, school, home, and public settings (restaurants or stores, for example), and may be more severe in some as opposed to others. In addition, certain people in your life may be impacted by your CBPD symptoms, such as friends, coworkers, family members, or significant others. Take a moment and think about how many different situations and people are impacted by the symptoms you identified in the previous chapter.

Consider This: Symptoms, Who, When, and Where

On a new page in your journal, make a four-column chart with the following headings: Symptom, Who, When, Where. In your chart, write each symptom you identified in the last chapter, and then write who it impacted, when it occurred, and where, such as home, work, or school. You can also download the "Symptoms, Who, When, and Where" worksheet at http://www.newharbinger .com/48558.

Here's an example from Shelly's story:

Symptom: I engage in recurrent behaviors of self-harm, such as cutting myself, banging my head, or burning myself.

Who: Taylor, David (son), Martin (son)

When: All year long

Where: Home and in public

As you examine your chart, ask yourself some key questions:

- Do your symptoms affect the same people at multiple times and in different settings?

- Do some symptoms affect more people than others?

- Are there particular times of the year that more symptoms are evident?

- Are there particular places where certain symptoms are expressed and others aren't?

Use this valuable information to determine the degree of impact your symptoms have on those in your life or if certain people elicit certain symptoms. The information from this exercise can also help you identify particular times and places that may be associated with your triggers.

As you look over your results from this exercise, consider that the more often your symptoms occur and the more people and places your symptoms impact, the more you may want to consider medication until you've learned coping and adaptive strategies to manage them.

Medication: Yes or No?

The typical first step for treatment of ADHD is medication. It's also very common to use medication to attempt to manage BPD symptoms as well. We're going to approach medication from the CBPD viewpoint, which means we have to recognize that medication impacts some, not all, symptoms. ADHD is different from BPD because it's not derived from an internal and longstanding wound, pain, loss, or trauma, but from a neurodevelopmental condition. ADHD is a surface content disorder that may have direct benefit from medication, but medication is a choice only you can make. The more severe your symptoms, the more weight you may want to put on your decision to try medication for your CBPD.

Consider This: Medication-Related Questions

If you decide to talk with your doctor about medication, there are some important questions to ask. At the top of a new page in your journal, write "Medication Questions" and copy the questions listed below. Don't worry about your doctor being upset or feeling awkward because you come in with a list. Most doctors actually like it when patients come in with questions that are clear and direct to the issue at hand. It shows you're invested in your wellness. Also, with ADHD, your attention is likely to drift away from the important questions you need answered.

1. What's the name of the medication I'm being prescribed?

2. What's it supposed to treat?

3. When should I expect my symptoms to start to decrease?

4. What are the primary short-term side effects I may experience?

5. What are the primary long-term side effects I should be aware of, such as sleep problems, decreased appetite, headaches and stomachaches, moodiness and irritability, and so on?

6. What can I do to minimize the side effects?

7. How and when should I take it?

8. Are there any foods, drinks, or other medications I need to avoid while taking it?

9. Should I take it with a full or an empty stomach?

10. Is it safe to drink alcohol while on this medication?

11. I'm currently using _____ (other medication you are taking). Is it safe to take this medication while using _____ (medication you are being prescribed)?

12. How do we monitor efficacy of the medication?

13. Under what conditions should I stop taking it?

14. Is there a generic version that's just as effective?

15. What should I do if I miss a dose?

When you are armed with the answerers to these questions, you gain immense knowledge to make a significant change in your symptoms. Fight that little voice inside that tells you your doctor is going to be mad or see you as foolish or whatever else it may be saying to convince you to not ask these questions. That is your BPD talking, wanting you to keep engaging in destructive thoughts and behaviors. You can make the choice to stop the patterns of destruction, just as you made the choice to empower yourself with the knowledge about your symptoms to do it differently.

Medication doesn't make CBPD symptoms and issues disappear. It lessens the symptoms to allow you to use strategies to better manage your focus, thoughts, feelings, and behaviors. This is where your adaptive strategies come into play. Research has shown that those with ADHD who were stabilized on medication reaped more benefits while participating in therapy compared to those who didn't (Safren et al. 2005).

Unblocking Your Blockades

CBPD that's composed of ADHD and BPD comes with unique growth-interfering thoughts, feelings, and behaviors that block your use of adaptive strategies that promote your psychological growth. Many of those thoughts, feelings, and behaviors are byproducts of your CBPD, and not the result of a conscious intent to disrupt or complicate your life and the life of others. Growth-interfering thoughts, feelings, and behaviors are just what they sound like: the things you think, feel, and engage in that create blocks in managing your CBPD core and surface content.

There may have been instances in your past where your medical or mental health providers, teachers, friends, significant others, coworkers, and even family members ascribed volition to these behaviors by saying things like, "You always do…," "You did…on purpose," or "Just stop doing…" Hearing these verbal blockades over the years may have worn away the belief that you can't master and control your CBPD symptoms, but you can. Don't let go of your desire to change your life. These growth-interfering thoughts, feelings, and behaviors may seem to be out of range for you to grab hold of and change, which adds to your frustration and doubt about being able to change them, but they're not. Resist those old thoughts, push back on that voice in your head that tells you, "You can't," and let's build the awareness and skills you need to unblock your blockades to managing your growth-interfering thoughts, feelings, and behaviors and get the most out of building your insight and core and surface content management skills.

Consider This: Hindrances and Helpers

You may feel that many of the issues related to your CBPD are just yours and yours alone, but they're not, and many people experience the same challenges you do. Problems are going to arise and hinder your progress. As you try to do things differently, difficulties are still going to happen. Doing things in an adaptive way doesn't mean there are no more hindrances, but if you focus on the ones that help you, you'll significantly increase the probability of your success.

Below is a list of common hindrances and helpers to address CBPD that's made up of ADHD and BPD. On the left is a list of common hindrances, and on the right is a list of what we'll call "helpers." These are thoughts, perspectives, and behaviors that will help you lessen the adverse impact of the hindrances.

These hindrances are likely a part of your default maladaptive patterns that you do without thinking twice. Because you've done them for so long, they've become default thoughts, perspectives, and behaviors. As you read the helpers below, add them to your daily routine. If you engage in the helpers often, they'll become a part of your default adaptive patterns, increasing the probability of positive outcome and greater self-control. You can also download this handout at http://www.newharbinger.com/48558.

Hindrances		Helpers
Arriving late to scheduled appointments	→	Keep a day planner or schedule with you, on paper or on your phone. Keep it up-to-date and turn on phone notifications. Add new information as you get it. *Don't wait.*
Not following through on tasks	→	Write out steps from start to finish for all tasks, even those that seem simple and quick. Once written out, do them.
Being hesitant or resistant to new ways of thinking and acting	→	Challenge old thoughts and behaviors by asking yourself, "How can I accept these ways and do it differently and adaptively?"
Waiting for others to solve problems and issues	→	Ask yourself, "What can *I* do in this situation to resolve it, control myself, and engage adaptively?" You need to focus on the problem and not wait for others. Link the problem to the solution and then engage.
Following through on impulsive and maladaptive urges	→	In every situation, even when not activated, stop, think, analyze, and then act to make sure you're using adaptive strategies.

Hindrances		Helpers
Reinforcing connections with unhealthy others	→	Recognize that unhealthy others strengthen dependency on maladaptive patterns. Distance yourself from them. Actively seek out those who build you up without strings attached.
Being hostile, argumentative, and resistant to helpful others	→	Fear is part of the process of change. Helpful others don't always want something in return, other than for you to be well. Resist old scripts and voices. Identify and trust those who want the best for you.
Failing to honor debts and promises	→	Learn to live by this affirmation: "I do what I say and say what I do."
Accepting excuses for procrastination	→	If something needs to get done, do it now. Keep a daily to-do list in your daily planner or scheduler. Prioritize the top three each day. It's rare that everything needs to get done right now. Live by this affirmation: "There's no better time than the present," and fulfill your goals in stages, not all at once.

As you went through the hindrances and helpers, you likely noticed many of your default thoughts, perspectives, and behaviors that keep you locked into your CBPD. Change is never easy, but it's certainly worthwhile when it's in a positive direction. When you employ the helpers on a daily basis and commit to adaptive and healthy change, you'll notice a difference not only in how you see yourself and live your life, but also in those around you.

Moving Mindfully

Mindfulness is a powerful technique that helps you bring your focus to the here and now. Your CBPD wants you to live in the past, stuck in the muck and mire of pain, misery, and fear. This negative way of thinking reinforces your CBPD core and surface content, but mindfulness can empower you to move beyond and take charge of you now.

Mindfulness *isn't* meditation. It's often confused with it, but it's not the same. It's not a passive process, but an active one that gives you tools to recognize where you are and what you're doing so you can engage with a clear mind. Your CBPD makes it hard to focus your attention and sit still. Many mindfulness techniques include focusing and being still, but that's probably contrary to what works for you when you have this type of CBPD. Below is a list of moving mindfulness activities to help you recognize the present and take charge of it.

When you're stressed, feeling overwhelmed, and spinning, try moving mindfully instead of losing touch and falling into those default maladaptive beliefs, behaviors, and patterns. As you do the activities below, breathe in and out slowly with your stomach, not your chest. Breathing correctly is very important. For more on breathing correctly, see the "Slow pace wins the race" technique in chapter 8 under "Grounding Your Symptoms." After you try one or all the activities listed, check in with yourself to see how much you've relaxed and are able to focus. The more you do these activities, the more you'll be able to control your inattention, hyperactivity/impulsiveness, and erratic and intensive thoughts, feelings, and behaviors. Now that you're pumped, let's get into it.

Mindful eating or drinking. Find something that tastes good to you; it could be a piece of chocolate or your favorite coffee shop drink.

1. First, feel the wrapper or container. Is it cold, warm, smooth, rough?

2. Next, unwrap it and touch it to your lips, but don't put it in your mouth yet. Breathe in, smell it. Is it sweet, fruity, robust?

3. Next, put it in your mouth but don't chew or swallow it. Feel the texture and temperature with your tongue and notice the flavor.

4. Lastly, let it slide over your tongue and down your throat. If your mind drifts, that's fine; just bring it back to your mindful eating or drinking.

Mindful moving. With or without shoes (your choice), take one step and feel the bottoms of your feet against the floor. Is the floor cold or warm, hard or soft, smooth or rough? Then take step two, then three, and so on. Focus on the rise and fall of each step and notice the movement in your legs and the rest of your body. If your mind drifts, that's fine; just bring it back to your mindful walking.

If you're in a wheelchair or use an apparatus to help you move, you can still do this. Instead of your feet rising and falling, notice your hands that help you move forward or the feeling of your wheelchair rolling over the surface while you focus on the movement going forward. If your mind drifts, that's fine; just bring it back to your mindful moving.

As you move, listen to the sounds, smell the scents, and notice the colors all around you. You are present focused and calm, and your mind is clear.

Glitter shake. Find an empty clear container, such as a Mason jar, plastic water bottle, or anything clear with a lid. Take off the lid and fill it with water almost to the top. Get a big spoonful of glitter and drop it in. Put the lid back on and tighten it. Shake the glitter. As it spins and flies from one side to the other, focus your attention on the glitter. Breathe in and out and move your attention back and forth from the glitter container to your breath. Allow thoughts to slide in and out of your mind. Your thoughts are like the glitter: they may rise, but they'll also fall. You control the rise and fall of your glitter. Shake it, watch it, and breathe, as much as you want. The more you do it, the more control you'll have over your focus and behavior.

In this chapter, you learned information, exercises, and activities that will help you gain control over your CBPD:

- the who, when, and where of your symptoms

- medication-related questions to help you and your medical provider decide whether medication is a suitable treatment course for you

- how to weaken and unblock growth-interfering thoughts, feelings, and behaviors while you avoid the hindrances and engage the helpers

- how to move mindfully to control your inattention, hyperactive/ impulsive, and erratic and intensive thoughts, feelings, and behaviors

Using this information and doing these exercises and activities one time will not be enough to create long-term sustainable change. Build them into your daily routine. This will be hard at first, but over time, you'll become used to using these adaptive and healthy strategies to control your CBPD that's made up of ADHD and BPD so do things differently.

CHAPTER 11

Living with More Than Broken Bones Through PTSD and C-PTSD

"It's love that broke me the most."

—Malcolm, 31

Previous chapters shared one person's story and their BPD symptoms to illustrate the added complexity that makes up CBPD. In this chapter, we focus on three separate individuals and their mental health conditions: Colby and post-traumatic stress disorder (PTSD), Karen and complex post-traumatic stress disorder (C-PTSD), and Malcolm and CBPD. These stories illustrate the differences in these disorders and hopefully lessen any confusion associated with the overlap. Please be aware that reading these stories may make you uncomfortable and bring up thoughts and issues related to your own trauma. If you're sensitive to reading about these issues and topics, you may want to skip the stories and focus on the symptom-identification and treatment parts of this chapter and the next.

A small trauma-focused therapy group was held at the local community treatment center run by Dr. Mathews, a licensed psychologist. Colby, a twenty-nine-year-old married unemployed veteran male; Karen, a thirty-three-year-old single unemployed female; and Malcolm, a thirty-one-year-old employed male signed up and were selected for the group. To be included in the group, they had to have a history of one or more traumatic experiences that impact their current functioning. The members arrived for the initial session at the same time, chose their chairs, which were set up in a circle, and waited for Dr. Mathews. He arrived, chose the chair that remained open, and introduced himself, "Hello, I'm Dr. Mathews, as all of you know from meeting individually, and this group is designed to help you identify your symptoms and issues associated with trauma and how it impacts you today." After explaining the group rules, each member was encouraged to describe their history and current symptoms. Colby volunteered to go first.

Colby looked at the other two group members and then at Dr. Mathews and said, "I'm Colby Jackson, and I was in the military for ten years. I've been out for almost a year. I did two tours overseas and participated in multiple combat missions. I'm proud of my service, and I know I did what I had to do when I had to do it, but that doesn't mean it was easy." Colby cleared his throat and continued. "I lost several of my friends while serving, and I did everything I could to save them, but I couldn't." Colby paused and sat up straight in his seat. "While in combat, I felt like it was going to be the end of me, but I witnessed the end of my friends instead. I see them losing their lives when I close my eyes and dream of it over and over. I wake up each night in a sweat and shaking, and it scares my wife. I won't go to the movies or watch anything that has explosions or gunfire. If I hear anything like that, I jump and start to sweat and get all shaky. Outside of that, I feel this weight on me all the time, and I don't know if it's shame, guilt, self-hate, fear, or what. I don't go fishing anymore or paint, and I forgot what it feels like to be happy. I can't work, and my marriage is on the rocks. All of this feels like it's too much for me, but I'm working to be okay with it, right, Doc?" Colby looked at Dr. Mathews, who nodded and smiled slightly.

Colby continued to describe how he tends to isolate himself and feel detached from his wife and children and other family members. "I prefer solitude and quiet, but I know I have to engage with the rest of you. You know, society, and I'm working on it." Colby looked uneasy that he had told them about his symptoms and experiences, but the group was supportive, and they admired his strength and his openness. Dr. Mathews said, "PTSD is a difficult disorder for many reasons, as its symptoms cause you, Colby, significant distress and impair your ability to get the things you need to get done, done. Remember, PTSD is a treatable disorder and learning about it and the strategies to manage it is an important part of this process." The first group session then concluded.

Karen started the next group meeting, saying, "I guess it's my turn. I have many of the same issues you do, Colby, but I wasn't in the military. I grew up in an abusive home. My mom was the one I was at war with, and now I'm at war with myself. It's like she's inside me, a part of me that lessens who I am. She makes me feel defunct, dirty, and broken; there's no other way to describe it or me." Karen looked at the floor, then raised her head and straightened her shoulders, and said, "In my house, I saw my mom get hit and beat, and after she got hurt, she would hurt me. Sometimes I wouldn't be able to go to school for the rest of the week because it was so bad. I see it all over again when I close my eyes. Just like Colby described. I have moments when I feel like I detach from myself, like she's just around the corner, any corner. I avoid loud noises; they make me really jumpy and sweaty too. I avoid arguments at all costs, even to the point that I let others get me into trouble. I've lost a lot of jobs listening to others who didn't have my best interests at heart. I haven't had a boyfriend in two years. They're all creeps and users and prey on my brokenness. I'm no good for anybody anyhow, so relationships don't really matter. I know they won't fill up my broken heart; no one can." Karen grew quiet and rubbed her hands on her jeans, wiping away the sweat.

She took a deep breath and continued, "My mom used to wear this perfume, Japanese Blossoms or something. I can't smell anything like it or I'm right back being a kid in that house and my anxiety goes to one hundred in the throes of her chaos. There's a soap that smells just like it, and I can't take it. I won't go anywhere near that bath and soap shop. I just can't, I won't. If I feel pushed, like by you, Doc, and you know this, you've lived it with me, I will retaliate and lose my cool. I call it going into 'rage mode.' All this stuff has left me alone and isolated, by choice mostly. It'd be nice to speak with my brother, but he has the same issues and problems I do. So I'm a loner in a group to try to get over my trauma and learn to 'unmode' my rage mode." Karen smiled at Dr. Mathews, who nodded in acknowledgment and said, "Complex PTSD is a disorder that you've struggled with for some time. You've been strong and open to learning to manage it. You've opened your mind and heart to new parts of you and to learning new and adaptive strategies to do it differently. That's what this group is all about." Dr. Mathews looked at Malcolm, who was watching the clock on the far wall. "Guess I start next session, Doc?" They each got up and left the session.

Malcolm arrived fifteen minutes late for the next session, saying, "I'm probably too late to start my stuff, and I don't need to waste everyone's time here. Let's get to the other stuff." Dr. Mathews looked at Malcolm with compassion and patience and said, "It's scary to tell others about our pain and trauma and what we've experienced. You're in a safe setting, and you've come a long way. Your story has value, and your words communicate this value. I speak for the group when I say each of us wants to hear your story, if you're ready." Malcolm looked quickly at Colby and Karen, skipped over Dr. Mathews, and stared at the clock on the wall. "It doesn't go any faster if you stare at it," Dr. Mathews said in a kind tone, smiling at Malcolm.

Malcolm stared at the floor and said, "I'm a cutter. I've been cutting myself since I was eight years old. It's love that broke me the most, and sometimes you live with more than broken bones. I've been abused and assaulted by everyone who was supposed to care for me. I've been their receptacle of hate and malcontent, hence my name Malcolm. I can't sleep for more than four hours at a time because I dream of them, my abusers. I relive my trauma with and without triggers, as I'm my own trigger. I feel unsafe in the outside world, so I avoid it and hardly go out, but I'm unsafe within the world inside myself, so I actively avoid any feelings if I can. I'm on the constant lookout for hate and pain. I jump at the smallest thing or feel a tidal wave of anxiety if something goes any way except the way I expect." Malcolm stopped and took a deep breath.

"Every relationship I'm in ends because I know it will, and I'll do anything for them not to leave me. I mean, the full text message onslaught, email bombardment, and phone call barrage. My significant others are heroes or zeros, right, Doc? But it doesn't matter because I can't win. I want them close, but then I push them away. The higher I place them on the pedestal, the further they fall, and the more it hurts." Malcolm started tearing up. "I have a hole inside of me that won't fill. I'm always empty. I got kicked out of Duke because of it. I got involved with a professor, it didn't work out, and I lost myself, flunked out of Duke, and my life. I was fixated on her, and I believed if I tried hard enough, showed her how much I'd put myself through for her, she'd come back. She didn't. She filed charges, and I was dismissed from Duke. I was eventually able to get into another school and get my degree in software engineering. This is perfect for me because I work from home and master my domain, until I don't and I'm not. I'm a social chameleon, and I change colors, so to speak, to fit in, to keep people close, regardless of how horrid they are." Malcolm looked up at the clock and sighed in frustration. Dr. Mathews motioned for him to continue.

"I have a lot of the same symptoms as both of you. When I'm stressed, I lose touch and time. I see my abusers when I close my eyes. I know they're inside me, and I'm working with Doc to get them out. I'm reminded of them all the time because they call me, my abusers, and I think I hear them. I will not refer to them by any other name, just by what they are: abusers. I never return their calls, texts, or emails, and yes, they try to contact me all the time. They broke me, and I'm broken. I'm the Humpty Dumpty, and no one can put me back together. My memory is like Swiss cheese. I remember the feeling of the trauma, but the incidents have holes. Maybe that's good; maybe it's bad. I don't know. My mind is all over the place; I can't focus." Malcolm stopped and looked at the clock, then to Dr. Mathews.

Dr. Mathews looked over the three members of the group and then looked directly at Malcolm and said, "BPD is a challenging disorder on its own, but one that can be successfully treated. When we add PTSD, which is also included as part of C-PTSD, and BPD, we get what's called complex BPD. Recognizing this helps us both understand the condition and be more impactful in ascribing steps for management of your conditions. You're doing the work by learning about your condition and your responses when things go awry, but also when they go your way and you don't trust them. Our goal in this group is to support one another in replacing our maladaptive patterns with adaptive ones. To do that, we have to know what causes our maladaptive patterns, and to do that, we need to explore our core content—the underlying components that drive us to think, feel, and behave in particular ways. First, we need to understand our conditions by building insight and recognizing how and when they impact our life and those we share it with, and how to overcome and replace the maladaptive patterns. I'm not going to tell you it's easy, but by putting your time, attention, and energy toward doing it differently, you can do it. Let's get started."

The Symptoms Identify the Diagnoses

The stories of Colby, Karen, and Malcolm illustrate the similarities and differences in PTSD, C-PTSD, and BPD. As you read each of the stories, you may have related to one more than the others or to all three. Learning about the stories of others can help put your own issues in perspective and shows how each disorder is similar in many ways. They all have experienced multiple instances of trauma but are varied in how it affected their life and those within it.

These three diagnoses are unique. PTSD and BPD are both in the *DSM-5* (APA 2013), but C-PTSD isn't, as it's only in the *International Classification of Disorders (ICD-10)* manual, which is now in its tenth edition (World Health Organization 1992). C-PTSD was first proposed by Judith Herman (1992a) to describe a group of occurring symptoms seen in survivors of sustained and repeated trauma. To qualify for C-PTSD, the individual must meet criteria for PTSD plus have experienced prolonged events without the possibility of escape along with an intense and continuous difficulty managing emotions; have a tendency to see themselves as weak and worthless in conjunction with feelings of shame, guilt, or failure; and have problems in relationships and feeling close to others. The *ICD-10* has the diagnosis of PTSD but not BPD. It has a similar disorder called emotionally unstable personality disorder (EUPD) with two subtypes: impulsive type and borderline type. The impulsive type focuses on characteristics of emotional instability and poor impulse control, whereas the borderline type pertains to an individual with uncertain and variable self-image, issues of abandonment and emptiness, unstable relationships, and self-harm or suicidal threats. In this chapter, we're using information from both manuals to provide a complete picture and understanding of all these diagnoses. CBPD isn't in either manual and is being introduced in this book (see chapter 1 for more details).

There is certainly confusion about these three disorders, as they have considerable overlap, but they have distinguishing factors as well, which are discussed in this chapter. These three disorders fit together in this way: PTSD can stand alone. To qualify for C-PTSD, you must meet criteria for PTSD and meet additional specific criteria, which we will discuss below. CBPD can be made up of a variety of different disorders, as you've learned by going through this book. As it relates to trauma and post-traumatic stress, it's possible for someone to have CBPD that's made up of PTSD, C-PTSD (PTSD plus additional criteria), and BPD. If it's still unclear, don't worry; the stories of the three group participants will help tease it all out.

Colby meets criteria for PTSD but not C-PTSD or BPD. Colby is a combat veteran and recalls experiencing, and the subsequent impact of seeing, his fellow soldiers and friends killed on the battlefield. He talks about waking up at night shaking, sweating, and being hypervigilant. These experiences of reliving the trauma are linked to recurring, uncontrolled, and invasive dreams. These are also linked to distress that's the result of internal or external cues associated with the trauma related to his diagnosis of PTSD. Avoidance is another component often seen in those with PTSD, and Colby illustrates this by not going to the movies or watching anything with explosions or gunfire. He also has changes in his thoughts and moods that are connected to the trauma because he feels stress associated with guilt, shame, self-hatred, lack of happiness, and other unidentified emotions, and he no longer does things he once enjoyed, such as fishing or painting. These symptoms are the direct result of the trauma, and all fit into the diagnosis of PTSD. He also meets criteria for the most universal criterion for any disorder, socioeconomic dysfunction, as he's unemployed, and his marriage is "on the rocks" as a result of his PTSD symptoms.

Karen meets criteria for C-PTSD. She reported growing up in an abusive home, with abuse perpetrated by her mother, and she witnessed her mother being abused for an extended period. She meets criteria for PTSD: experiencing and witnessing traumatic events, repetitive uncontrolled anxiety-provoking dreams or images, and dissociative reactions and flashbacks, as she feels detached from herself and that her mother is just around the corner. She avoids loud noises as much as she can because if she encounters any, she becomes jumpy and breaks out into a sweat. She avoids the smell of Japanese Blossoms because the scent reminds her of her mother's perfume, as this is an intense trigger for her. She becomes aggressive, what she calls "rage mode," and is hypervigilant when activated or when she encounters something that seems associated with her trauma. She has socioeconomic dysfunction because she's unemployed, has had relationship problems in the past, and classified herself as a loner due to her trauma. She has low self-worth; sees herself as defunct, dirty, and broken; and has problems with intimacy and maintaining relationships due to the abuse.

To make the distinction between Colby and Karen, the specific components of C-PTSD aren't reported or illustrated in his story, so he doesn't meet criteria for C-PTSD but he does for PTSD. Also, a C-PTSD-specific issue is Karen's avoidance of close relationships and difficulty with intimacy due to the trauma.

Malcolm's CBPD is made up of C-PTSD and BPD. Malcolm experienced direct traumatic events by growing up in an abusive home. This trauma caused significant sleep difficulties and hypervigilance. He can't sleep for more than four hours at a time due to dreams of the abuse and his abusers. He feels threatened and unsafe in the outside world, and this causes him to avoid it by rarely going outside. He also struggles with feeling safe within his own skin and with his emotions, thoughts, and control over his behavior, and he says he's afraid of his inside world as well. Malcolm's always on the lookout for hurt and pain and jumps "at the smallest thing." He has "Swiss cheese" memory problems—holes in his memories related to the trauma—and he has low self-worth and shame about his past abuse.

Malcolm meets criteria for C-PTSD, as he feels his name brands him with low self-worth and value, and he sees himself as a "receptacle" for his abusers' hate and malcontent. Because of the abuse, he harbors misbeliefs about himself that manifest as being unworthy of love or happiness. He also struggles with feeling damaged, broken, and deserving of the pain he suffered at the hands of his abusers, which are also criteria specifically related to C-PTSD. He has intimacy-related issues connected to his past trauma, also a criterion specific to C-PTSD, as evidenced by the intense relationship with the professor at Duke that got so out of hand that he was removed from the university.

To add even greater complexity to his mental health challenges, Malcolm meets criteria for BPD. His symptoms occur outside PTSD and C-PTSD and are linked to his concept of self, his core content, and his surface content beliefs, behaviors, and patterns. He engages in cutting behaviors and has intense fear of abandonment. He believes that all relationships will end, and he became fixated on the relationship with the professor at Duke. When it ended, he bombarded her with texts, emails, and calls to attempt to restore it. You may have felt a similar push and pull. You want to be close, so you try to pull them to you, but your fear of abandonment drives you to push them away. You engage in this enough times that they leave, which you feel validates your fear of abandonment. When that fear of abandonment becomes so great, you may self-harm, which gives you a false sense of self-control and distraction from the internal hurt of feeling rejected once again. Malcolm had the same experience. Malcolm didn't connect his cutting to his fear of abandonment in his story to the other group members, but it's something he and Dr. Mathews discussed during his individual therapy sessions.

Malcolm tells the group that he feels he has a hole he can't fill even though he tried in his relationship with the Duke professor. He feels empty inside, and he struggles with how he sees his significant others: as heroes or zeros. He idealizes them when they meet his unspoken needs and then devalues them when they don't or when they trigger his core content of fear, loneliness, abandonment, and emptiness. Malcolm calls himself a "social chameleon" to fit in with others. This illustrates an unstable self-image. When under stress, he loses "touch and time," and when he closes his eyes, he sees his abusers and feels they're inside of him. These are components specific to BPD and may be ones you've experienced as well.

Through the identification and exploration of symptoms, we're able to identify the diagnoses that are present in the three group members. Accurate diagnosis helps guide impactful treatment and management strategies. These three stories illustrate the challenges and each individual's determination to take on their diagnoses and surmount them. You can do the same. It's possible to manage your conditions, get control of your life, and do it differently. Just as Colby, Karen, and Malcolm went through their process, you can go through yours. A first step is to recognize the overlap and distinction often seen in CBPD that's made up of C-PTSD and BPD (remember, when we say C-PTSD, we're including PTSD because C-PTSD includes all the conditions of PTSD plus additional criteria).

C-PTSD and BPD Complexity and Distinction

There is great confusion about trauma and BPD. It's not a required criterion that you experience trauma to meet criteria for BPD, and not all individuals who experience trauma, with or without BPD, meet criteria for PTSD or C-PTSD. However, those with BPD are at a higher likelihood to have experienced childhood adversity, which certainly qualifies as traumatic. A recent study found that approximately 71 percent of those diagnosed with BPD experienced at least one instance of childhood adversity, which includes emotional, physical, or sexual abuse, or neglect. Within this group, approximately 49 percent reported physical neglect, 42 percent reported emotional abuse, 36 percent reported physical abuse, 32 percent reported sexual abuse, and 25 percent reported emotional neglect (Porter, Palmier-Claus, et al. 2020). These results show the frequency in which those with BPD have experienced abuse, which adds to the complexity of symptom presentation and diagnosis.

Living with CBPD that's made up of C-PTSD and BPD is a challenge for many reasons. It may be difficult for you to find a knowledgeable mental health provider with whom you feel comfortable working. You may feel that you're only partially understood by those in your life and those to whom you reach out for help. You may feel the constant push and pull of the CBPD symptoms that cause you to feel overwhelmed by your symptoms when your core content is triggered. All these issues are genuine concerns and experienced by many people trying to manage their issues just like you. You're not alone. It's estimated that PTSD co-occurs in 24 to 58 percent of those with BPD (Grant et al. 2008; Pagura et al. 2010; Zanarini et al. 1998; Zanarini et al. 2004; Zlotnick, Franklin, and Zimmerman 2002). Trauma is common in, but not a prerequisite for, BPD.

A study that focused on distinguishing PTSD, C-PTSD, and BPD found that almost 55 percent of those who had BPD also met criteria for PTSD and 45 percent of those with BPD met criteria for C-PTSD (Cloitre et al. 2013). Symptom confusion often follows the high prevalence of comorbidity. The good news is that there is information in this book on C-PTSD and BPD comorbidity that can help you understand the condition and lay the foundation to identify management strategies to help you control it.

C-PTSD and BPD Complexity

Trauma is impactful, and it has certainly affected your life and how you live it in many ways. Your C-PTSD and the associated adverse changes in how you think and feel about many aspects of your life that started or were exacerbated by your trauma may make you feel alone, but you're not. The confusion you're experiencing in discerning whether your thoughts, feelings, images, and behaviors are due to C-PTSD, BPD, or CBPD is common.

Due to the high degree of comorbidity of trauma and C-PTSD in those with BPD, we need to examine the symptoms that cause the complexity and subsequent confusion that accompanies this type of CBPD. Dissociative symptoms are likely to be experienced by those with both C-PTSD and BPD. For those with C-PTSD, dissociations are often in the form of flashbacks or reoccurrences of the traumatic event. Those with BPD dissociative symptoms tend to have more of a global sense of disconnection with the self and the world around them when under stress as opposed to being related to a trauma flashback. The confusion here is that if you have CBPD made up of C-PTSD and BPD, you may experience both types of dissociative experiences.

Disrupted sleep is another common overlapping complex symptom. Although it's not part of the "official" *DSM-5* criteria, sleep disturbances are often associated with BPD symptoms (Bromundt et al. 2013; Selby 2013). The BPD symptoms that disrupt your sleep are likely to be due to impaired ability to manage emotions and ruminating about "what if's" and "could be's," and this may be associated with your past trauma. This is very similar to those with C-PTSD who experience nightmares linked to their past traumatic experiences. Additionally, internal and external cues that drive psychological distress overlap both disorders as well. Those with C-PTSD may hear loud noises, screams, or something on TV that's similar to their traumatic event, which ignites psychological symptoms that impair their functioning. This is similar to what occurs with BPD symptoms as well. When you encounter something that prompts your core content, whether specific or nonspecific to your past event, hurt, or trauma, it drives your surface content psychological symptoms. For example, you see a happy couple on TV that reminds you of a recent breakup, and you suddenly feel overwhelmed with negative thoughts of self-contempt, sadness, loneliness, and abandonment.

Intensive perpetual negative thoughts and emotions can cause poor memory; global pessimistic beliefs and outlook; emotional detachment; self-recrimination; sustained anger, hate, and shame; and impaired ability to enjoy things you once did. They can blunt or dissolve feelings of joy. These symptoms and consequences are often seen in those with C-PTSD and BPD, creating a complex picture of identification that can lead to poorly planned and executed treatment.

When your core content gets activated, driving your surface content to manage it, the result can be extreme irritability, explosive or impulsive behavior, impaired ability to focus, and feeling as if you're on high alert, which could be related to C-PTSD, BPD, or CBPD that's made up of both. The overlapping symptoms we just explored create a complex conundrum to understanding the root of your CBPD, but learning about these symptoms and their overlap helps build insight and knowledge so you can enhance your skills to manage them. Before you go to the next chapter and get into management strategies, we need to deconstruct the overlap and focus on discerning between C-PTSD and BPD so you have a greater understanding of not only your symptoms but also the issues that are problematic for you.

Discerning Between Your C-PTSD and BPD Symptoms

When you consider the extensive overlap between C-PTSD and BPD and how often they co-occur, it's no wonder there is so much confusion about these two disorders. However, you never want to assume that if one is present so is the other, and this requires separating out your symptoms and the severity of their impact. Discerning when and what symptoms first became evident is key to connecting them to either C-PTSD or BPD. Relationship problems, self-control issues, sleep difficulties, paranoia, and memory and dissociative issues that were present before the trauma should be attributed to personality and not as derived from the trauma.

Many individuals with BPD experienced prolonged childhood trauma, and because their personality wasn't solidified until they were much older, uncertainty remains about whether the initial presentation of symptoms is due to C-PTSD or BPD. In these cases, we have to look at the symptoms themselves. This is where we examine the BPD-specific symptoms that aren't part of C-PTSD to know whether BPD is present or not. These BPD-specific symptoms include:

- intense fear of abandonment

- continuous feelings of emptiness

- seeing significant others as heroes or zeros

- not knowing who you are, your values, or what you believe in

There are C-PTSD symptoms that aren't present in those with BPD as well. We can use these to tell the difference between C-PTSD and BPD. The following C-PTSD symptoms must occur for more than one month and cause disruption in how the individual interacts with others or is able to sustain employment or academic success:

- flashbacks of the trauma

- avoidance of trauma reminders, including people, places, sounds, or smells

- a continuous sense of threat or fear that manifests a feeling of being on high alert

- poor recall of the traumatic event

- avoidance of intimacy or relationships

- seeing themselves as damaged, worthless, or deserving of pain as a result of having experienced the trauma

These key symptoms that differentiate between C-PTSD and BPD can be used to help you lessen the confusion associated with the complexity that makes up your CBPD.

Consider This: Identifying Your C-PTSD Symptoms

Symptoms identify the diagnosis, but many times these overlap, leading to misdiagnosis and time spent treating the wrong disorder. Knowledge and awareness of symptoms can help you better identify which diagnoses are present, which are absent, or if they're occurring together, creating CBPD.

On a new page in your journal, write "PTSD/C-PTSD Symptoms" at the top and number from 1 to 28 down the left side of the page. As you read each symptom listed below, put a *T* to indicate the symptom is true and something you experience often or an *F* if the symptom is false and something you don't experience often. Be sure to read the directions and take note of the time components, as these are critical to determining whether symptoms are situationally bound or occur across multiple contexts. Symptoms that occur across multiple contexts are likely related to mental health disorders, whereas those that are situationally dependent are likely due to the circumstance or location.

Only consider the presence of these symptoms and issues when you're not using drugs or alcohol or taking medication and when they are unrelated to a medical condition. This list isn't meant to be used for clinical diagnosis but to help you build insight into your symptoms and issues so you can better manage them and seek out appropriate mental health assistance.

PTSD/C-PTSD Symptoms

At least one of the statements in numbers 1 through 4 must be marked as true to qualify for PTSD/C-PTSD.

1. I've directly experienced at least one life-threatening situation that included but wasn't limited to violence, injury, or sexual assault.

2. I've seen others go through at least one life-threatening situation that included but wasn't limited to violence, injury, or sexual assault.

3. People in my family, or that I'm close to, have experienced a traumatic event that significantly altered their life.

4. I've experienced prolonged trauma that included but wasn't limited to childhood abuse, domestic violence, or being a prisoner of war that has significantly disrupted how I live my life.*

The symptoms listed below must be present for at least one month.

1. I experience nightmares or intense memories that are a direct result of having experienced trauma.

2. I feel like I'm reliving the trauma.

3. While I'm reliving the traumatic experience, I lose touch with myself and the world around me; I space out.

4. I feel extreme anxiety, sorrow, or pain when something is said or done that reminds me of the trauma.

5. I feel extreme anxiety, sorrow, or pain when something inside of me, such as a memory or sensation, reminds me of the trauma.

6. My heart rate increases, I begin to sweat, and my stomach may hurt when something is said or done that reminds me of the trauma.

7. My heart rate increases, I begin to sweat, and my stomach may hurt when something inside of me, such as a memory or sensation, reminds me of the trauma.

8. My memories of the trauma are incomplete, fuzzy, or confused.

9. I blame myself for the trauma.

10. I believe I should've known better or prevented the trauma.

11. Since the trauma, it's hard for me to feel joy or happiness.

12. I feel sad, depressed, shame, or guilt because of the trauma.

13. Since the trauma, I'm angry, irritable, and likely to lose my temper.

14. Since the trauma, I engage in behaviors that are likely to have severe negative consequences for me.

15. Since the trauma, I feel like I'm on high alert, always on the lookout for harm and danger.

16. Since the trauma, I'm jumpy.

17. Since the trauma, it's hard for me to concentrate.

18. I try to avoid or prevent thoughts, feelings, or memories related to the trauma.

19. I try to avoid people, places, and things that might bring up thoughts, feelings, or memories related to the trauma.

20. The trauma was made up of a series of incidents that I couldn't escape from and thought I'd never live through.

21. Due to the trauma, I'm having trouble controlling my emotions.

22. Due to the trauma, I feel worthless, weak, broken, ashamed, guilt-ridden, and like a failure.

23. Due to the trauma, I can't keep a relationship going because I feel distant and detached.*

24. These symptoms cause socioeconomic dysfunction.

* These symptoms are specific to C-PTSD.

Take a moment to go over your BPD symptoms from chapter 1 to help you clarify the separation of PTSD/C-PTSD symptoms from BPD. Look over your PTSD/C-PTSD symptoms ratings and mark or circle the ones you indicated as true for you. These ratings are the significant symptoms that increase the likelihood of PTSD/C-PTSD being an accurate diagnosis. Remember, this is an insight-building exercise, not a diagnostic one, and only a qualified mental health or medical provider can give you a diagnosis.

The last criterion is the universal symptom, and if you identified it as true for you, you're indicating that the other symptoms also identified as true significantly disrupt how you live your life. This increases the likelihood of meeting criteria for the full disorder. However, if you marked the universal symptom as false, you may have symptoms related to PTSD/C-PTSD, but they're not to the level of causing continuous disruption in your life. This still merits exploration, and you may benefit from reading the next chapter to learn management skills.

Listing your symptoms can be a very powerful experience because BPD and comorbid conditions can be overwhelming when seen as a whole. When understood as a combination of particular symptoms and issues, your CBPD is more manageable and your efforts more impactful and focused because they target particular symptoms. This leads to greater symptom reduction and overall control of your CBPD.

Trauma and managing all the things that come with it and after it are certainly overwhelming. They can cause you to question the value and worth of others, people you once trusted, and your belief in yourself. The exercise you just completed is designed to empower you with knowledge. Teasing out your most impactful symptoms helps you focus your energy to gain control over them so you can choose how to best use your strength and energy to go forward on your terms, empowered.

In this chapter, we explored the following issues as they related to CBPD when it's made up of PTSD or C-PTSD symptoms and BPD:

- the difference between PTSD, C-PTSD, and CBPD

- the interplay between trauma and BPD

- the similarities and differences between C-PTSD and BPD that creates your CBPD

- the symptoms related to your PTSD or C-PTSD

The next chapter is going to help you address and regain a sense of safety, tap into your inner strength, manage your distorted perceptions, expand your range of behavioral responses, and embrace your worth.

CHAPTER 12

Activities to Triumph over Your Trauma

This chapter is going to provide you with the tools to help you manage and control the CBPD symptoms derived from your PTSD or C-PTSD and BPD. CBPD tends to produce simultaneous symptom expression. In some other forms of CBPD, one disorder's symptoms can severely derail treatment if not dealt with first. For example, with CBPD that's made up of bipolar disorder and BPD, the bipolar symptoms need to be addressed and stabilized first or else the process of increasing insight and maximizing treatment is significantly lessened. Recognizing concurrent symptom presentation in CBPD that's made up of PTSD or C-PTSD and BPD is critical to developing a management plan that not only focuses on symptom presentation, whether from one disorder or the other, but also addresses the central aspects associated with your trauma and BPD. This chapter outlines an five-step sequence to help you lessen the impact of your CBPD while restoring your sense of security, building your mastery of symptoms, and enhancing your personal empowerment so you rule your conditions instead of them seeming to dominate you.

This five-step sequence is hierarchical, meaning that one level is built on the previous one to move forward. For example, it's hard to confront your sense of helplessness if you don't feel safe. However, this doesn't mean that issues of safety will not arise while learning and mastering cognitive and behavioral flexibility, for example. If a reemergence of an earlier step occurs, it absolutely doesn't mean failure, and you should resist your BPD filling you with negative self-talk that tells you so. Issues of trauma aren't all the same; they're just like your symptoms—they're on a spectrum—and some may push harder to the surface when you're learning a new skill or engaging in a new behavior. As you go through this process, be patient and kind to yourself. Embrace your bravery to explore these issues and remember that managing CBPD takes time and repetition. One and done isn't enough. Continually revisiting these issues is critical. It's like going to the gym to build your biceps. You have to keep going and focusing on them to help them grow.

Restoring Your Sense of Safety

Trauma often produces a longstanding byproduct of fear due to the loss of safety. This fractured sense of safety can be in how you believe you can control yourself, see others, or manage your world. Safety is the sensation, belief, or view that you're in control of yourself and your world and that you can protect yourself from harm. Even though it was ruptured by trauma, you can start to restore it by identifying the "what" and the "who" of safety.

Consider This: The What and Who of Safety

Building your sense of safety is a central part of managing and overcoming your trauma. To do this, you need to break down the "what" and "who" that make up your components of safety. At the top of a new page in your journal, write "My What and Who of Safety." Write the answer to each question below in your journal to the best of your ability. Examples from the group members from the last chapter are provided to help you.

As you go through this exercise, you may feel pushback from your BPD. This is normal and expected. You may feel discouraged as your negative self-talk surfaces to discredit the positives, or you may feel torn by a split (see things as all good or all bad) and not write anything. If this happens, try some of the exercises in chapter 8 under "Grounding Your Symptoms." When you feel ready, let's get started.

1. What does safety feel like for you? *Colby described safety as knowing who's in the room, being in situations that are low volume, slow-paced, and have little or no drama.*

2. What place(s) help you feel safe? *Malcolm feels safe when he's in his backyard.*

3. What objects help you feel safe? *Karen has an old teddy bear from when she was little that's soft and cuddly.*

4. What can you do to feel safe? *Karen has a nightly routine she follows to make sure her doors are locked and her alarm is on.*

5. What can you do to make a situation safer? *Colby likes to know the exits of any room and sit with his back to the wall.*

6. What can you do to help yourself feel safe? *Karen takes tae kwon do and kickboxing classes.*

7. Who in your life helps you feel safe? *Colby feels safe when he's with his wife.*

8. Whom do you trust to keep you safe? *Malcolm has a childhood friend whom he trusts to keep his secrets.*

9. What can you change in your life that will increase your sense of safety? *Karen defined her boundaries with others, particularly with significant others and family, about what's healthy and unhealthy for her.*

10. On a scale from 1 to 10, with 1 being very unsafe to 10 being completely safe, rate those in your life (pets included) on how safe you feel with them around you. *Colby rated his wife a 10, his boss a 5, and Dr. Mathews an 8.*

You may have never thought to ask yourself these questions or explored the what and who in your life gives you a sense of safety, but it's of great value because it lessens the sensations of loneliness, fear, emptiness, and other emotions and core content related to your CBPD.

Identifying the what and who of your safety helps you build insight and knowledge for an increased sense of security and protection. We also have to consider the specific components of your CBPD that disrupt building a sense of safety: feelings of abandonment and emptiness. Below is a tool to help you lessen these feelings and give you a sense of comfort whenever you need it.

Consider This: Pillow of Comfort and Safety

CBPD adds a level of distortion that causes you to see abandonment as imminent and emptiness as omnipotent. The reality is that people may leave you in your life and that may make you sad and even afraid, as they may have been a source of safety that helped push back on your trauma symptoms. However, there are many things you can do to get a sense of safety and comfort. Pets are certainly one of them. Another one is the comfort and safety of a pillow that's just for you to hold, squeeze, cry into, or do whatever else you need to feel comforted and safe. Below are the steps to create your pillow of comfort and safety.

1. Buy a pillow specifically for this reason. Don't use an old one, as it may have memories or a scent. You want to a brand-new one. Body pillows are particularly good for this.

2. Buy a cologne or perfume that no one else you know wears but that you like. You don't want it to remind you of someone or something, as you want a unique pillow with a unique scent.

3. Spray your pillow with your "pillow-specific" cologne or perfume and hug it, squeeze it, and let yourself be absorbed by it.

This is an effective way to feel a sense of safety and comfort and create something that's uniquely yours.

Your Power in Revelation

This next stage of managing your trauma entails telling your story without judgment, shame, guilt, fear, or any of the other negative thoughts, feelings, and images you have experienced since it occurred. Having a good foundation of safety is an important first step before engaging in this exercise. If you're not sure whether you're ready to reveal your story, then you don't have to. You can skip this step and come back to it later, if you wish. You're empowered with choice to not reveal it if you choose not to. You have the right to decide how, when, and to what degree you tell your story.

This step is more than just revealing your trauma; it's a step toward empowerment to not only tell your story as it needs to be told, but also to give it the honor, respect, and attention it deserves. It's common to avoid talking or thinking about your trauma. However, when CBPD is present, your BPD tends to use your trauma against you by distorting it and using it to misrepresent how you see yourself and your world. Revealing it helps you recognize and embrace your courage to see it with open eyes and to see that it's no longer a source of self-contempt but a sign of your strength of perseverance because you survived it. All those negative thoughts and feelings fester in the dark. Shining a light on them helps you see them and manage them.

As you proceed, you may want to do this with the assistance of a trained mental health professional or have access to one or another supportive resource. The process of revealing isn't easy, and it's not something that should be done without having systems of support in place. On a new page in your journal, write "My Systems of Support" and the answers to the following questions. Some examples are listed to help you.

- What adaptive strategies can I use to manage any increase in my trauma-related thoughts, feelings, urges, or images? *These can include mindfulness, exercise, and watching a funny movie.*

- Who can I call when distressed? *Friend, therapist, or suicide lifeline.*

- Where can I go if I feel a strong increase in my trauma-related thoughts, feelings, urges, or images? *Emergency room, make an appointment with my therapist, go for a walk to a relaxing place, or go to a gym.*

Now that you've identified your systems of support and have defined your sense of safety, you're ready for the next "Consider This" exercise.

Consider This: The Fortitude of Revelation

Revealing your trauma isn't just a retelling from start to finish. It's recognizing what occurred, the symptoms derived from it, and the strength and courage you used to survived it. You may have had more than one traumatic experience, as many people do. It is helpful to do this activity for each trauma separately. Don't mix traumas in your retelling; do one at a time. As you go through this exercise, you'll rate your thoughts and feelings. This is to keep you vigilant about your reactions to what you're writing and to help you stay present and focused. Use the scale below:

1	2	3	4	5	6	7	8	9	10
Mild			Moderate			Severe			Extreme

On a new page in your journal, write "My Revelation" at the top. Write the event that occurred and include your age. Write only as much as you feel comfortable. Don't worry about editing it for spelling or grammar. Just write what feels right. When you're done, write "Thoughts:" and "Feelings:" beneath what you wrote. Take a self-assessment of the intensity of your thoughts and feelings associated with writing down this event and how it feels at that very moment. For example, you may give a rating of an 8 for thoughts and a 9 for feelings because your thoughts and feelings about this traumatic event and what occurred are particularly vivid. Whereas perhaps your writing about another traumatic event, such as surviving a natural disaster, is a 3 for thoughts and a 2 for feelings because they're not as intense.

Beneath your ratings, write "How I Survived" and describe what you did to make it through the experience and identify your resilient traits. Some examples include:

- refusing to give up

- fighting for myself

- reaching out for help when I need it

- practicing patience and self-compassion

- embracing acceptance of the pain and that it wasn't my fault

Beneath this description, do another self-assessment and rate your thoughts and feelings just like you did previously. In most cases, the number is lower because when we focus on our fortitude in relation to traumas or other life adversities, we see that we're powerful, able, and a force for change in our life—even with traumas in our rearview mirror.

Unearthing your traumas and recognizing your strength to get through them is something to embrace and hold up high because you're a survivor. You're a person of strength and courage who decides their own course. Part of that decision is using control mechanisms to help manage your CBPD thoughts, feelings, and behaviors, and that's what we're going to do next.

Controlling Your Split

Trauma is an external event that has an internal impact. CBPD leaves you feeling as though you have no control over your life. Whether your trauma is a single instance or composed of multiple occurrences, it adds a layer of derailment to your view on life, others, and your world. When BPD is added, that internal impact adds a layer of distortion that's hard to see through, and this distortion directly impacts your perspective of control.

Your distorted view of control is usually housed in a tendency to split. Splitting is seeing something or someone as all good, all bad, never gonna make it, always being horrible, and so on. Splitting feeds your view of no control, that you'll never have any, you can't get any, or you'll always be broken and alone. You know you're splitting because your view has extreme terms: "always," "never," "can't," "every," "forever," and so on. Seeing with balance expands your horizons and options.

CBPD core and surface content are challenging to work through and control. You know you're strong. You've made it this far in this book. You've enhanced your safety, revealed your trauma, and now it's time to embrace your control. Your tendency to split is a maladaptive method that empowers your CBPD and adds to your confusion. Control is taking hold of the view of your life and challenging it for what it is: not all despair, but not all roses and sunshine either. It's a balance. Control is balance in how you see yourself, others, and your world beyond your CBPD core and surface content. A balanced view has terms like "could be," "might be," "may be," and so on.

Controlling the split can be scary because it's something you're not used to. Your CBPD isn't going to like you doing this, and it's going to raise your fears, doubts, shame, guilt, and all those other feelings that keep you locked into your maladaptive patterns. Seeing things as only one-sided may seem like it simplifies things, leading to less anxiety, depression, and other symptoms, but in reality, it cuts your world in half. If you see only half your world, you can't live in the other. Your whole world is balance, and that includes acceptance of yourself for who you are, including your fears, flaws, fortitude, and strength.

Consider This: De-Splitting the Split

Adding balance to your view is creating a new adaptive, healthy, and powerful habit. Splitting is something that was very protective when you were younger or shortly after your trauma. It's a coping strategy that served a purpose, but over time it became a maladaptive one. Splitting someone as good or bad helped you weed out the people who might have hurt you. This is problematic because it becomes habitual and, when used indiscriminately, lessens your experiences and gives you a false sense of your world as all bad. It's time to take back your life and build a balanced view by de-splitting your split.

On a new page in your journal, write "My Balanced View." Describe a situation or person in as much detail as you feel comfortable with, then use the percentage scale to determine your outlook, or how positively you perceive it. Then, using the control scale on the next page, write a percentage of the degree of control you feel you have, or had, over the situation or person.

0%	50%	100%
Nothing Positive		All Positive

0%	50%	100%
No Control		Total Control

Look at what you wrote and ask yourself, "Did I use extreme terms, such as 'always,' 'never,' 'can't,' 'forever,' 'impossible,' 'terrible,' and so on?" Circle the extreme terms to help you identify the split. Here's Malcolm's example about his mother.

Split: She never listens to me and is always so defensive.

Outlook: 10%. Control: 2%.

Like Malcolm, it's likely that your perception is closer to you feeling as though you have no control due to the split. Splitting doesn't help you see things clearly or empower you; it does the opposite. Well, let's de-split it.

Replace those extreme splitting terms with balanced terms, such as "sometimes," "could be," "might be," "may be," and so on. Review what you wrote using balanced terms: Is your perspective more positive? Do you feel you have more control? Do you feel you have more room for choice? Do you see other options and possibilities? Here's Malcolm's balanced example:

Balanced: She listens when she's not upset, and she tends to be afraid of other people taking advantage of her because of her past abuse.

Outlook: 50%. Control: 40%.

Malcolm's outlook increased a lot in positivity, as did his sense of control. It's not realistic to think they would be 100 percent positive. That would be a split, and there are very few situations or people that are 100 percent negative or positive. The goal is to empower you with seeing situations in a more balanced way to improve your perspective and sense of control that splitting takes away. Malcolm recognized his mother's tendencies and issues, where they come from, and why they're there. This helped him see his mother in a balanced way and that she isn't evil or always dismissive. He took this information and adjusted his approach to her, being vigilant when dealing with her but having control of his anger and frustration when he feels unheard and attacked. By seeing the balance, he raises his sense of control, providing him with choices on how to interact effectively with his mother.

This is a powerful activity, and the more you do it, the more you'll begin to see you have choice regarding the situations you're in and the people you interact wiith. Split perspectives tend to have a high percentage of negativity and low perceived control. This exercise shows you that the more balanced your perspective, the more options, choices, and control you have.

Your CBPD wants you to believe that you're not safe, that you must keep your trauma a secret and in the dark, and that you have no control over your life. It's time to push back on that now that you know your balanced view removes the distortion created by your CBPD. You're ready to add flexibility to the mix.

From Fixed to Flexible

Now we're going to take all that you've learned and apply it to your fixed behavioral patterns to turn them into empowered flexible ones. Flexibility in how you see yourself, others, and your world can help you broaden your options, which, because of your CBPD, you have believed are narrow. It's likely that your CBPD causes you to see and respond in a very fixed manner, using maladaptive patterns that increase the probability of negative consequences. As mentioned previously, the more you do something, the greater the likelihood it'll become a habit and you'll engage in it automatically. This includes your maladaptive patterns. These maladaptive patterns directly, or indirectly, reinforce your view of yourself and your life.

Your behavioral patterns, and everyone else's, are designed to justify how you see yourself and your world. For example, if you believe all people are going to abandon you, you engage in behaviors to scare or push others away until they leave. These behaviors may include self-harm in overt and drastic ways, picking fights, or showing extreme displays of aggression or rude behavior when you know the other person doesn't like it or is afraid of it. Engaging in these patterns repeatedly drives the other person away, and once they leave, you say to yourself, "See, everyone abandons me. I'll always be alone." However, if you engaged in more flexible behavioral patterns that are situationally adaptive, you'd weaken the distorted view created by your CBPD. It's all connected in a tapestry of thoughts, feelings, images, behaviors, and patterns. The next step toward making choices to reconnect with yourself and others by embracing your empowerment is a big one to outgrowing your CBPD.

Conditioning yourself to go from fixed-behavioral responses to flexible ones is a challenging task, but not impossible. Your reactions to situations are more than just simplified stimulus and response, like a bug flying up your nose. If this happens, your body immediately responds with intense nasal exhales and rubbing your nose profusely to get it out. The events and situations you find yourself in are rarely that simple. Outside of the bug-in-the-nose situation, you initially encounter an event or a situation that triggers an activator, which may include what you see, hear, or smell, but it also activates thoughts, memories, images, and emotions. Once activated, your fixed pattern comes into play when unchecked. This is typically your CBPD maladaptive pattern of angry expression, acting out, self-blame, and contempt. Ask yourself, "Do my fixed response patterns increase the probability of a positive outcome?" It's likely the answer is no. This clearly illustrates the need to increase your flexibility in these situations going forward, but you need to know how.

Increasing your flexibility entails not just waiting until the event or situation happens but also planning for it and visualizing your response to it, as opposed to using a limited set of fixed-maladaptive responses across multiple situations. Adapting to your events and situations and preparing for them expands your response options while increasing the probability of a positive outcome.

Consider This: From Fixed to Flexed

On a new page in your journal, write "Flexing" at the top. Like working out, you're going to show and build your muscles, your adaptive strategy muscles. To do this, you must first identify an event or a situation, what's activated inside of you, the fixed response pattern you tend to use to try to resolve the event or situation, and the probability of a positive outcome using your fixed pattern. Next, describe two or three options for flexible response patterns and the assessed probability of a positive outcome after using them. Finally, take a moment and notice the difference in probability between steps 4 and 6. How do we know there was an increase in probability? Because using flexible response patterns causes an increase in the probability of positive outcomes.

There are seven parts to this exercise, which are described below, along with Malcolm's examples to help. Number from 1 to 7 down the left side of your "Flexing" page and write the title for each step, such as "Event or situation" for number 1, followed by your response. Include as much or as little detail as you feel comfortable.

1. Event or situation: Duke professor breaking up with me. People breaking up with me, abandoning me.

2. Activators (sight, sound, scent, memory, emotion, thought, taste, touch, urge): I saw her walk away. She broke up with me and then just walked away. I heard her say, "It's over." I smelled her perfume; it was a floral scent. In my head, I see my mom leaving the house for the last time; she's not coming back. I'm not important enough for her to stay or to care. I feel the same pain I felt from her leaving me with my dad. My urge is to fix it, and only she [Duke professor or girl I'm in love with who's leaving me] can fix it. I feel empty inside, broken, shamed, and alone.

3. Fixed pattern: See them as heroes or zeros. I reach out to them continuously until they respond. I send texts, call them, drive by their house, and show up at their office or place of business.

4. Probability of a positive outcome 0 to 10 (with 0 being absolutely nothing positive and 10 being completely positive): 0

5. Flexible pattern (alternate responses): Make one or two attempts to contact her via text or phone and then give her some space. Reach out to my friends who make me laugh. Play a video game online to get some social contact so I don't feel so alone. Divert my attention to work or working out. Journal the heck out of it: write out what I want to say to her, how I feel, and how this makes me feel; get it out of me so it doesn't fester.

6. Probability of a positive outcome 0 to 10 (with 0 being absolutely nothing positive and 10 being completely positive): 8

7. What caused the increase in probability from step 4 to 6? I feel a greater sense of control over myself. I use other outlets to manage my thoughts and feelings. If I did these things, I'd still be at Duke. I'd be proud of myself for the self-control, and I wouldn't have fanned the flames of my emptiness, brokenness, shame, and aloneness.

This exercise will help you break the pattern that reinforces your CBPD and expands your response options. The more you do this, the more you'll see that you have the power of choice to impact how you respond when activated. You're more than the maladaptive patterns that have kept you locked in place and that reinforced all those negative beliefs, behaviors, and patterns about your trauma and who you are because of it. You're doing it differently.

The flexibility you gained through doing this exercise, and the others in this chapter and book, can be life changing. Going through this chapter and doing these exercises helps push back on your CBPD that's made up of PTSD or C-PTSD and BPD. They help you create a foundation to make the choice to reconnect with the world and step outside again—a key piece to recognizing your internalized worth.

Your Reconnection to Worth

Trauma is a destructive element and one, particularly when coupled with BPD, that disrupts many aspects of your life. One aspect is your sense of worth that affects your trust in your ability to find and connect with others. As you've gone through this chapter and built the foundational factors to help you manage your CBPD, you're ready to go inward and explore your worth and use the tools to raise your sense of self-worth to take it outward into the world to the degree you want and are comfortable, not to the level dictated by your CBPD. You're a survivor and warrior for your empowerment and freedom. Judith Herman (1992b) said it best in her book *Trauma and Recovery*:

The survivor no longer feels possessed by her traumatic past; she's in possession of herself. She has some understanding of the person she used to be and of the damage done to that person by the traumatic event. Her task now is to become the person she wants to be. In the process, she draws upon those aspects of herself that she most values from the time before the trauma, from the experience of the trauma itself, and from the period of recovery. Integrating all of these elements, she creates a new self, both ideally and in actuality (202).

This is a powerful quote and one that you can take with you as you define and build your worth to embrace your empowerment going forward.

Consider This: Letter to Your Integrated Self

On a new page in your journal, write letters to the two sides of yourself: the side that experienced the trauma and the side of your recovered self. Write the first letter as though you're writing to another person who experienced the trauma, in the second person. Say the things that side of yourself needs to hear. This often includes words of encouragement, empathy, understanding, and compassion. For example, *I'm so sorry you went through that and had to endure such a traumatic pain. It's hard when it feels like no one hears you calling out for help.*

The next letter is to your recovered self. Again, write this letter as though you are writing to someone else, in the second person. This letter often includes words of praise, pride, excitement, and strength. For example, *I'm so proud of you for mastering your issues and overcoming your pain. You really showed your true colors and strength through your perseverance and by conquering your demons.*

These letters can be as long or as short as you'd like. You may find it challenging to write one or the other. This is to be expected, and it depends upon where you are in your process of healing. Know that wherever you are, it's okay because you're doing this in your way, on your own timetable.

Next, you are going to write a third letter. The final letter is your integration letter from you to you. Merge the two letters into one. This isn't done word for word, but it's a series of collected sentiments to tell yourself you recognize the trauma and pain along with the admiration and worth you now possess. For example, *I went through a lot of pain and endured trauma that derailed my life, and no one heard me calling for help. I mastered my issues, slayed my demons, and overcame the pain. My true self is strong and determined, and I'm worth being seen and treated with respect and valued by others and myself as well.*

The first two letters are important to provide you the foundation and outlook to your experience to create the final letter to yourself that builds you up, reminds you of all you are, and empowers you going forward, living beyond your CBPD.

Your worth will become more self-evident the more you do the exercises in this chapter, which are designed to give you the tools to enhance your abilities to do things differently, overcome your trauma, manage your BPD, and go forward knowing you've mastered your CBPD.

In this chapter, you learned the following tools to help you manage your CBPD:

- how to restore your sense of safety

- how to increase your insight into finding safety and comfort

- how to reveal your trauma and recognize your resilience

- how to manage the fallacy of safety in splitting

- how to respond to situations to maximize your flexibility and benefit

- how to reconnect with your worth

This goal of this chapter, and this book, is to help you not only find your voice, but also, in many ways, rediscover yourself. Trauma is disruptive to the knowledge and belief you have of yourself and in the things you can and can't do. After completing this chapter, you've hopefully discovered more of your true self, a self that's determined to grow beyond CBPD and feel liberated from the pain and violence that you were subjected to. It's my sincere hope that this chapter gave you, or helped you find, a protected space in which to explore yourself and grow to honor your experiences, to reach out when you need to, and to comfort yourself when necessary. Remember, you define you, and that's an empowering faith to hold on to.

CHAPTER 13

The Complicated Complication

As you went through the prior chapters and learned about your CBPD, it's likely occurred to you that you may have more than two co-occurring conditions—a further complication of an already complicated condition. Don't let this dishearten you, as it should fill you with relief, because you're not alone. Forty-two percent of those diagnosed with BPD have two or more comorbid conditions (Fyer et al. 1988).

The purpose and scope of this book is to introduce you to the various types of CBPD, the inherent challenges, and how to manage and overcome them. As you went through these chapters, you raised your awareness about how CBPD impacts your life and your specific symptom presentation. You also learned that the successful treatment of CBPD doesn't rest solely on BPD management but must consider and include the other conditions that are also present. This chapter adds an important piece to the puzzle by helping you pull together the information you gathered so far and then use it to successfully manage the symptoms associated with your CBPD. The first step is recognizing the conditions and symptoms that make up your specific CBPD when it includes more than one co-occurring condition.

Consider This: The Complete Complexity

At the top of a new page in your journal, write "My Co-Occurring Conditions." Below that, you're going to list each co-occurring condition and your total symptom score. Malcolm's scores are provided below as an example, and the total possible score for each condition is listed in parentheses for reference. Below that, write each co-occurring condition we examined throughout this book followed by the symptoms you rated with a T (for True) from that chapter's checklist. How to outline and the total number of symptoms for each checklist is listed in parentheses below to give you a perspective on the severity of the condition based on your scores. Break up the disorders that are made up of separate underlying conditions, such as bipolar disorder that's made up of mania and major depressive disorder, and list them below the more global one, as shown below.

BPD (27 total symptoms): 19

Bipolar disorder:

   Mania (11 total symptoms): 1

   Major depressive disorder (16 total symptoms): 14

Major depressive disorder (16 total symptoms): 14

Psychosis (15 total symptoms): 4

ADHD:

   Inattention (14 total symptoms): 3

   Hyperactive/Impulsive (10 total symptoms): 3

C-PTSD:

   PTSD (23 total symptoms): 19

   C-PTSD (5 total symptoms): 5

As you can see from Malcolm's co-occurring conditions list, he has a preponderance of symptoms associated with BPD, major depressive disorder, and C-PTSD. Doing this exercise gave Malcolm a wealth of knowledge about his conditions in one clear picture. It'll do the same for you. Try the activity now before going forward in the chapter.

Next, we're going to examine the groundwork of the knowledge you've gained.

Knowledge Is the Foundation

Throughout this book, you've gained knowledge about the conditions you're contending with that adversely impact your life. When you look at your conditions, you see all these symptoms, and it can seem like a swarm of killer bees buzzing around your head that you can't run away from fast enough. It's normal and expected to feel overwhelmed. To lessen this, we have to narrow all the symptoms that make up the conditions you've identified. This makes them more manageable and helps you streamline and target your approach to managing those symptoms and conditions.

Also, not all of your symptoms affect you the same way or to the same degree. Some may only be present in the morning or at work, and others may occur all day and severely negatively influence you getting through your day and how you relate to others. For example, if major depressive disorder was one of your related co-occurring conditions, the symptom "I lose weight due to not eating and having no appetite" may not be as impactful as "I feel sad, hopeless, and helpless most of the day, nearly every day," although both were true. Let's sort out the bees buzzing around your head because they're not all killer bees, although taken together they may seem that way. We'll do this by identifying your most impactful symptoms.

Consider This: Your Top Ten Symptoms

In this exercise, you're going to identify the symptoms that have the greatest influence on your conditions and your overall functioning. Identifying your top ten symptoms helps you narrow the field of confusion and gives you a manageable metric to gauge your movement forward in growing beyond your CBPD. To help you tease out your most impactful symptoms, use the following top ten identifying criteria:

- I spiral downward when this symptom is activated.

- I have extreme difficulty controlling my thoughts, feelings, and behaviors when this symptom is activated.

- I feel that this symptom strongly defines my mental health.

- This symptom worsens all my other symptoms.

- This symptom strongly impacts me and those around me.

- This symptom has been present and recurring in my life for a long time.

- My perception of the future is adversely affected by this symptom.

- I feel a sense of hopelessness and powerlessness when this symptom is activated.

- This symptom impairs my ability to work, go to school, or attain socio-economic stability.

- This symptom disrupts my relationships when activated.

Let's consider one of Malcolm's top ten symptoms related to his BPD: "I engage in behaviors out of desperation to prevent actual, possible, or perceived abandonment." This symptom was identified as true for him and it's one of his core content areas; it causes him to spiral downward and have difficulty controlling his thoughts, feelings, and behaviors when it is activated. He feels that this symptom strongly defines his mental health and exacerbates his other symptoms. Alternatively, he also rated the depressive symptom "I oversleep; hypersomnia" as true, but it doesn't impact him and his functioning to the same degree, and it doesn't meet any of the criteria above, so he didn't include it in his top ten.

Now it's your turn to explore your symptoms and create your top ten symptoms list. On a new page in your journal, write "My Top Ten Symptoms." To find your top ten symptoms, do the following:

1. Go through your journal and review those symptoms you identified as true for each co-occurring condition.

2. Assess whether each symptom identified as true meets all the top ten identifying criteria listed above. This isn't going to be a quick task. Take your time and really think about how each symptom is related to the top ten identifying criteria.

3.   If it meets seven or more of the top ten identifying criteria, write it down on your top ten list.

You may be asking yourself, "What if I have more than ten top symptoms?" This is certainly possible, and if you encounter this scenario, write down all the symptoms that meet the top ten identifying criteria, and then from that list, separate out those that are most impactful.

The goal is to identify your top ten most impactful symptoms at this time in your life. This isn't a task to only do once and then never do again. As you grow and develop more adaptive strategies, issues and concerns are still going to arise, just like they do for all of us. You may have some symptoms that arise later that are more impactful than they were, and some intense symptoms will weaken as well. This is part of the growth process. Growing beyond your CBPD takes time, and although it's not a smooth, linear growth process, going through these steps to increase insight and build skills and abilities has tremendous payoff for you and those in your life. Just like it took time for those maladaptive patterns to become habitual responses to stress and other activating situations, it will take time for your adaptive strategies to override the maladaptive ones and become strengthening responses and positive perceptions.

These two activities can be draining. Take a moment, look at your ten most impactful symptoms, and take a breath. If your CBPD is driving self-deprecating comments, use your strategies from the previous chapters to counter them. Hold on to the skills you've learned and use them often. Take a wellness time-out to do the quick relaxation exercise provided below to help you.

Sit, Breathe, and Feel

This short exercise, about one to two minutes, will help you relax and decrease the sense of being overwhelmed you may be experiencing after doing the previous exercises. If you're not feeling overwhelmed, this is still a helpful exercise to do now so you can use it in the future when you do find yourself overwhelmed.

1. Find a relaxing space and sit in whatever way is most comfortable for you. This could be on the grass, on a mattress, on a floor, or anywhere that's a comfortable place to be.

2. Rest your hands on your thighs.

3. Focus on your breath and breathe in through your nose. As you do this, move your hands up, away from your knees, toward your hips about three inches.

4. Hold for three seconds.

5. Exhale through your mouth and move your hands forward over your thighs, toward your knees.

6. As you continue breathing, focus your attention on your hands on your thighs. Do your pants (or skin, if wearing shorts) feel rough, dry, smooth, or cold? Describe the feeling to yourself. Focus on the details of the sensation of your touch on your legs. If your attention drifts, that's fine; bring it back and focus on your breath and your touch.

7. After one to two minutes, take an emotional inventory of yourself. When you feel ready, move on in the chapter.

Now that you've pulled back the curtain on your most impactful symptoms, it's time to lessen their impact and continue your journey of growing beyond your CBPD.

Weakening Your CBPD and Strengthening Yourself

It's common for your CBPD to use the symptoms associated with it against you. This is part of its trickery in keeping itself present and impactful in your life. This next section is designed to help you weaken your CBPD. As it weakens, you have an opportunity to empower yourself by using the adaptive strategies provided below to help you go forward today and in the future.

Too Many Choices. What Do I Do First?

Even with ten symptoms narrowed down from so many others, you may still feel confusion about which ones to address first or when and how to go about addressing them. When your most impactful symptoms are activated, they have a tendency not only to override your ability to make the choice to use adaptive strategies but also to cause you significant confusion and stress that leads you to engage in your maladaptive patterns almost automatically, as if by default. Due to the emotional turmoil that comes with your top ten symptoms, you're likely to miss the times you're actually able to control them or mitigate their impact. Remember, not all bees are the same, although they may seem that way.

Holding on to this belief is part of the deception of your CBPD. The truth is that you do have moments where you're able to manage the adverse impact of your top ten symptoms when activated; you just don't recognize it. To increase your ability to identify and mitigate the impact of your top ten symptoms, you need to stop and see them for what they are when you're not in the throes of them. It's easier to study the bees when they're not swarming and trying to sting you, but when they're docile and at bay.

Consider This: The Clarity of Success

This insight-enhancing exercise will help you recognize what it looks like when your symptoms aren't at their height of turmoil. This is because when you're not in the throes of emotion, you're better able to lessen the adverse influence of those maladaptive urges, gain control over them and your CBPD, and see your success clearly. On a new page in your journal, write "Symptom Reduction Identifiers" at the top. Then write down the following statement for each of your top ten symptoms:

I would know _____ (one of your top ten symptoms) has lessened when _____ (a clear and concrete identifier of when the symptom has lessened).

Here are two of Malcolm's top ten symptoms and his identifiers of when they're lessened and controllable.

- I would know I lose weight due to not eating and having no appetite has lessened when I'm eating three healthy meals a day and monitoring my weight, and it's stable.

- I would know I feel sad, hopeless, and helpless most of the day, nearly every day has lessened when I'm more patient with myself and others, I'm playing guitar more often, I have more energy to go outside, I'm able to concentrate better, and my sex drive returns.

Notice that Malcolm's not focused on "the how" in this exercise, but on "the what." His lessened identifiers are signals that he's moving in the right direction. They provide markers of success. Without clear definition of what it looks like when you succeed, how would you know when you get there or that you're heading in the right direction?

Be sure to keep your list near you and refer to it routinely so you can stay apprised of your success.

Growth beyond your CBPD isn't a singular process of success only. Staying the course, staying aware, and continuing to use adaptive and empowering strategies will get you there, even when your CBPD inner voice is pulling you down.

Destroying Negative Value Judgments

You may often feel lonely and isolated by your CBPD. This is a common feeling, but you're not alone and you have the ability to connect to others in healthy and adaptive ways. It's possible, and this book is proof of that. All the symptoms, conditions, and techniques in this book are designed to help lessen the impact of CBPD and do your life differently. Knowing that your CBPD is pulling your symptom strings and driving the maladaptive patterns that keep it in place empowers you to do it differently. You now know your CBPD tries to use your pathology against you, to judge you, and make you feel inadequate, powerless, and fearful. It's about to learn it's sorely mistaken.

Consider This: Destroying Destructive Judgment

This is a three-step exercise.

Step 1. Tear out a blank page from your journal. Look over your top ten symptoms and write down the associated destructive value judgments your CBPD tells you. Write them in different colors and sizes, any way you want. It can be neat or messy. This is a no-holds-barred activity. Get that judgment out and destroyed, using the steps below.

1. Cut out or tear out the destructive value judgments so each one is on a single piece of paper. For example, *No one loves you* is on its own piece of paper.

2. One at a time, cut them up and drop them into the toilet or throw them in the trash.

3. As you do this, say each destructive value judgment aloud and counter it with an adaptive empowering statement before you destroy it.

Step 2. On a new page in your journal, write "Adaptive Empowering Statements" at the top. Next, write out encouraging, empowering, validating statements that explain how you feel after destroying those destructive value judgments.

Step 3. Read your empowering statements to yourself in the mirror. This may feel weird at first because you're not used to saying adaptive empowering statements to yourself, but that was then and this is now. You're doing it differently. You're purging yourself of those old destructive value judgments and replacing them with honest, authentic, empowering statements that encourage adaptive functioning.

Here are some of Malcolm's destructive value judgments along with his adaptive empowering statements:

Destructive Value Judgment	Adaptive Empowering Statement
You're worthless and unlovable.	Many people in my life love and care about me.
You're helpless and inept.	I got into Duke. I'm successful at my job and people notice it.
Your mother was right. You're weak.	I'm strong, able, and committed to doing my life differently.

Malcolm loved this exercise! It was empowering for him, and he did it often. He was able to get a sense of his self-control and of feeling free of the destructive value judgments that he carried inside for so long.

Verbalizing affirmations of success and empowerment is an important thing. Using verbalizations is one effective method, and now let's do another: visualization. The most successful people in history use this technique on a daily and routine basis to keep them moving in the direction to achieve their goals. You're no different from the Oprah Winfrey, Steve Jobs, Elon Musk, Bill Gates, Muhammad Ali, or Michael Jordan's of the world. You just have barriers, but you're using strategies to surmount them.

The Sight of Success

I often use the analogy of planning a trip to Disneyworld to describe the importance of knowing the road ahead to reaching a destination. During one session, I asked a client who was struggling with defining his course through treatment to tell me how he'd know he reached Disneyworld, and his response was terrific. He said, "I'd see it." I asked him to describe what Disneyworld looks like, and he described it in clear detail; he'd been a few months ago. I then asked him to use this same strategy in his mind with his goals for controlling his top ten CBPD symptoms. He was able to see himself unchained by regret, fear, and doubt and saw himself on top of a mountain of symptoms. He stood with his arm bent and his fist against his hip, looking upward toward possibilities. He then drew a picture of what was in his mind. He'd be the first to tell you he's no artist, but artistry wasn't the point. A picture of his end goal was now in his mind. He'd made it to the Disneyworld beyond his CBPD.

The sight of success is a powerful motivator. Your CBPD thrives on the inaccurate and distorted picture of yourself and often uses this against you. Using visualization helps clarify your end goal and your plan to get there.

Consider This: Transcending Your CBPD

On a new page in your journal, write "Getting Over It." Draw yourself standing over a pile of your symptoms. Imagine what you'd look like having beaten your CBPD. To help you define your picture, use the questions below. This isn't an art exercise. Artistic ability is irrelevant here. Drawing a picture of you surmounting your symptoms and beating your CBPD is what matters most.

- What's your facial expression?

- What are you wearing: a T-shirt and jeans, suit, a superhero outfit with a cape?

- What about your shoes: boots, high heels, no shoes?

- What does your pile of beaten symptoms look like: a trash heap, broken glass, crooked letters?

- What's in the background? Is it a road, an ocean, a castle? Are you leaving it or going there?

- What's in the sky, or are you in space or on a new planet?

- Are other people in the picture with you? Are they helpful or hurtful others, are they large or small, and are their faces mean, happy, sad?

This activity is limitless. The more detail you add, the better. This is a good exercise to go back to from time to time to update or recreate as you grow beyond your CBPD. You may be surprised how it changes over time, as you build your inner strength.

Seeing yourself as a success and breaking the bonds of your CBPD is empowering. Using these techniques, activities, exercises, and skills on a routine basis will help you continue to progress beyond your CBPD and the symptoms that disrupt your life. When you're in charge of your life, you make decisions that increase the probability of your success.

The Work You've Done and Are Doing…

As you've gone through this book, you've learned a lot about yourself and your symptoms. Your knowledge has increased exponentially, as have your skills and abilities in managing maladaptive symptoms and patterns. There is one more step to uncomplicate your once-complicated complication. With so many skills and abilities, you can get lost, feel overwhelmed, and then not use any of them. That's the last thing we want you to do. So let's target the skills and abilities that are the most helpful now, and they may change as you grow beyond your CBPD.

Consider This: Targeted Skills and Abilities

On a new page in your journal, write "Top Three Skills and Abilities." Review the skills you learned from the various chapters in the book that you'll use to manage your top ten symptoms. Then, identify the top ten exercises and activities that fit your lifestyle, available time in your schedule, and so on. Practice these at least three to four times a day. About every three months, revisit the symptom checklists to see how many you would still identify as true.

When you build adaptive skills and abilities and pinpoint specific symptoms, you're likely to find that other symptoms have decreased as well. Symptoms and growth are interrelated. That's the thing about skill building: it gives you the ability to manage not only the symptoms you've targeted but also those you haven't.

Identifying your BPD and co-occurring conditions is a complex task that likely often overwhelmed you to the point that you tended to give up and "just deal" with the symptoms and issues. Perhaps, you defined yourself by your symptoms or submitted to their reign over your thoughts, feelings, images, behaviors, and patterns. You know that knowledge is step one, and from there, building skills and abilities are what allow you to manage and control your symptoms. Your approach to managing your CBPD is and will be unique to you, but you are not alone.

You Don't Have to Do This Alone

Although this book is directed at you, other people, including loved ones, would likely find great benefit in learning more about your CBPD and in turn learning about you. You can share this book with them, show them your journal, if you feel comfortable, or use this material in therapy to help you.

If you're working with a therapist, the next chapter addresses how to use the information you learned in this book in therapy so you can enhance your probability of success. However, if you can't find or don't have the option to access mental health providers for a variety of reasons, know that other forms of treatment are available. I've written a workbook specifically for those with BPD, aptly titled *The Borderline Personality Disorder Workbook* (Fox 2019), that you may find helpful as an additional resource to build your knowledge, skills, and abilities to manage and control your BPD.

In this chapter, you enhanced your insight, growth, skills, and ability to control and manage your CBPD symptoms, even when they're part of more than two co-occurring conditions.

- You identified your co-occurring conditions by pulling together your most salient symptoms to create a clear picture of your complete CBPD.

- You enhanced your knowledge by identifying your top ten symptoms.

- You learned strategies to weaken your CBPD and enhance your personal strength and awareness.

- You recognized when your top ten symptoms are weakened and when you control them, as opposed to only seeing them as intense, overwhelming, and uncontrollable.

- You learned how to push back against your negative value judgments and develop adaptive empowering strategies.

- You used visualization to see your end goal of overcoming your CBPD.

You've broadened your world as you've enhanced your awareness and learned the strategies to manage your symptoms of CBPD. This expansion includes your authentic and honest self that will help you see the true possibilities that lie ahead for you. The continual practice of your adaptive strategies will further empower you going forward and will change how you live your life in a productive way. Growing beyond your CBPD is an attainable goal and one that remains within reach, growing ever closer as you continue to grow beyond your CBPD.

CHAPTER 14

When It's Not Just a Singular Endeavor

BPD is considered a *treatment-seeking* condition. This means that those with it often reach out to a mental health provider to learn about themselves and their world. The challenge can sometimes be that associated maladaptive patterns have a deep hold on you, and this grip can feel so tight and strong that you stop pushing back and seeking help. As you've dealt with your CBPD over the years, you've learned more about it and yourself. By going through this book, you've discovered the associated conditions that define your unique type of CBPD. Knowing your co-occurring conditions, learning skills, and enhancing your ability to manage your symptoms are terrific and empowering endeavors. However, CBPD isn't a simple disorder, and you may need a qualified professional to help you. This chapter addresses common areas of concern so you can avoid the pitfalls and disruptions when seeking help that are often experienced by others with CBPD.

Am I Passive or Active?

In the past, as you've gone through therapy, you may have felt directionless and not gotten the input and focus you wanted from your therapist. You're not alone in this feeling, and there is something you can do about it. It comes down to perspective. Therapy isn't a passive process, but an active one. You must be more than just a consumer of insight; instead, think of yourself as a utilizer of insight who puts it into action to make life changes.

You're not a patient in the therapeutic process, but a client. A patient is defined as an individual who's a receiver of treatment; it is passive. A client is a present and active participant who engages the advice, suggestions, or services of a professional; it is active. For example, your medical doctor considers you her patient, and she performs medical tests on you and gives you treatment in the form of medication, which is what occurs in approximately 73 percent of all medical doctor visits (Rui, Kang, and Ashman 2016). You passively received the treatment she gave you. Your mental health provider should see you as a client, as an active participant who takes in the information explored and uses it to determine psychological and behavioral responses to core content activations. It's a very active process, much like finding a suitable therapist for yourself.

Since CBPD is a new concept, many mental health providers may not be familiar with it, so referring to BPD with co-occurring conditions is sufficient when wanting to discuss issues, concerns, and treatment related to it.

Consider This: Finding a Therapist

All around the world, there are varying views of BPD that range from completely false to research supported. Different therapists hold differing views of BPD and those who have it. Successful treatment is often highly related to working with a therapist who's aware of current research and recognizes the treatment-seeking aspect in you and others with CBPD. There are some things you can do, and should avoid doing, to help increase the probability that you'll find a therapist who fits for you and can help you manage your CBPD.

On a new page in your journal titled "Me, My Therapist, and Therapy," write your answers to the questions and prompts below.

- Ask your friends and colleagues for therapists they know and like.

- Call a university psychiatry or psychology department and ask for recommendations for people trained in the program who may specialize in personality disorders or BPD.

- If you're employed, see if your employer has an employee assistance program (EAP) and see if someone there specializes in personality disorders or BPD.

- Research some different local therapists. Avoid randomly picking a name from your insurance company; explore who they are and what they do. Consult the individual's or practice's website to see their specialties. Are personality disorders, or BPD, listed?

- Online therapy is another viable alternative and broadens your access to experts in personality disorders and BPD. Research has found that online therapy is as useful and successful in treating mental health and medical illnesses with psychiatric comorbidities as in-person treatment (Kumar et al. 2017).

- If you are helping a friend or family member find a therapist, consider going to the initial appointment with them.

Questions for the Therapist

Finding a therapist is a great first step, but knowing what information to consider and what questions to ask is also important. Below is a list of questions to ask the therapist to help you determine whether they are a good fit.

- Are you licensed?

- How long have you been in practice? (CBPD is a complex disorder and can be overwhelming for newly licensed therapists, unless they've had specified supervision in this area.)

- Have you received supervision or been exposed to treatment approaches for people with BPD or personality disorders?

- Do you specialize in BPD?

- What kinds of treatments do you use? Cognitive behavioral, interpersonal, transference-focused, dialectical behavior therapy (DBT), schema therapy (all efficacious treatments for BPD), or others?

- Do you take insurance?

- What are your fees? How do you accept payment? What is the fee for missed appointments?

Questions to Ask Yourself

In addition to asking your future therapist questions, you need to do some self-exploration as well. Below are some thought-provoking questions to consider after you've spoken to the therapist.

- Did I feel comfortable enough with this person to open up?

- Did I feel listened to?

- What do I want out of going to therapy? (Paint as clear a picture as you can.)

- What are my expectations of therapy?

- Were there any red or pink flags? (Pink flags are those little things that are not quite red yet and that made you hesitant with that person or that require more exploration.)

Do this for each therapist with whom you're thinking about working. Your responses for each therapist will quickly become a valuable resource when making the decision about which therapists to work with.

Consider This: Treatment Success and Impediments

Now that you've identified your therapist, there are several important questions to ask yourself as you engage in the active process of growing beyond your CBPD with a mental health provider. Your answers to these questions are important to share with your therapist so you don't repeat past frustrations and disappointments and so you reengage in what has worked or helped you in the past.

Title a new page in your journal "Treatment Successes and Impediments," and write your answers to the following questions.

- Did you like it when your therapist was more emotive, cognitive, or an equal mixture of both? An emotive therapist tends to focus more on feelings than thoughts, whereas a cognitive therapist focuses on thoughts.

- What techniques were helpful and frustrating for you in the past?

- What did you like and dislike about therapists in the past?

- Did you trust your past therapists? What made you trust them or not?

- What medications have you taken in the past that have been helpful, harmful, or no help at all? List all those you've taken and put them in one of these three categories.

- What self-help resources have you used that have been helpful, harmful, or no help at all?

You may have come to therapy not considering what has worked and what has impeded your growth and progress in the past. If so, you're not alone in this approach, and it's one most often missed because the expectation is that your mental health provider will know what works, what doesn't, and what is irrelevant. The reality is that they don't know and you can spend valuable therapy time and money going over the old roads that got you nowhere, as opposed to being on the roads that move you forward.

How Will I Know If Therapy Is Working?

As you begin therapy, you should establish clear goals with your therapist. Remember, certain goals require more time to reach than others. You and your mental health provider should decide at what point you may expect to begin to see progress. This is a tough question for anyone to answer, particularly for someone outside yourself. The benefit of this question is that it opens the dialogue to defining your progress and expectations. Too many times, these are things that are implicit and believed to be equally understood to the same degree, but rarely are.

Openly discuss what the process of therapy is like for you and how you feel going forward on a regular basis. Working through CBPD isn't an easy process, and you're likely to get frustrated with it, as is the person accompanying you on this journey, your mental health provider. This is expected, but exploring this together can bring you closer and provide a sense of safety for you. If (and when) you both get frustrated with the process, or the CBPD symptoms keep resurfacing, it doesn't mean the treatment is a "lost cause." That's your CBPD talking.

It's a good sign if you begin to feel a sense of relief and a sense of hope. It's also a good sign to feel fear and apprehension. Your maladaptive patterns have been with you a long time, and they once served a purpose, but they also created intensely adverse consequences for you. Negative feelings are part of the increased discomfort of moving away from being comfortable with maladaptive patterns and moving toward the adaptive strategies that'll take their place. This is likely going against what you heard growing up and what you believe about yourself and your CBPD. Your therapist is a resource to help you identify your therapeutic success and normalize all those thoughts and feelings associated with the therapeutic process of growing beyond your CBPD.

It's Not a Linear Process

Hold on to the hope that this process provides a mixture of feelings that are good, bad, overwhelming, fearful, and everything in between. Staying the course and using your adaptive strategies coupled with strong therapeutic support will get you there. The process of treatment isn't a linear process filled only with forward steps. You're going to slide backward, and it's at these times that your mental health provider can be most impactful to encourage you to go forward and fight through the tendency to embrace your old maladaptive patterns. Together, you'll both work to reengage the process of therapy so you can continue your growth without recrimination, self-contempt, and all those falsities about yourself and your world.

The Curse of "I Don't Know"

You may have developed an indirect support system for your maladaptive patterns without even knowing it. When you're overwhelmed, you may shut down and say, "I don't know," to yourself and others. When "I don't know" becomes a habit, it blocks you from exploring all options and gives you the implicit permission to shut down. This shutting down increases the probability of falling back and using your default maladaptive behaviors, which can create a cycle where you feel less in control of your thoughts, feelings, and behaviors. This leads to feeling as if you're cursed with bad luck, have no options, and are doomed to repeat a cycle that supports your CBPD.

The great thing about therapy is that you're likely to be caringly challenged to explore the moments you use your "I don't know" curse and find out that breaking free from that mind-set encourages the use of adaptive skills. The steps to do this are listed below, and you don't need frogs' legs or witches brew to do them.

1. Be mindful of when you think or say, "I don't know," to yourself or others.

2. When you think or say, "I don't know," ask yourself, "If I did know, what would I say?"

3. Be open-minded to challenges to explore options.

4. Try to stay energized to push back and not shut down. Notice the things that prompt you to say, "I don't know."

5. Ask your mental health provider to help you be aware of when you say, "I don't know," and to caringly challenge you.

You can do steps 1 through 4 on your own and step 5 in sessions with your mental health provider. Breaking the curse is within your grasp. This will help you engage in your world more fully, and by doing that, you're better able to recognize your ability to produce a desired and intended result.

The Broadest Barrier

One of the greatest impediments to overcoming your CBPD is substance abuse. It needs to be addressed here because it's most often overcome successfully with mental health and medical support. Research estimates that approximately 28 to 63 percent of individuals with BPD have a co-occurring alcohol abuse disorder, and approximately 28 to 72 percent have a co-occurring drug use disorder (a substance use disorder other than alcohol; Trull et al. 2018). Substances are often used as a means of coping, and as you know, over time, dependency is likely to develop. Due to the intensity of working on CBPD and addressing core content, your primary coping mechanisms are going to call out to you and beckon you to use them to lessen the dissonance associated with growing beyond your CBPD. If substance abuse is your primary, or even secondary, maladaptive coping strategy, it'll be significantly more difficult for you to remain in, and complete, the process and work required to grow beyond your CBPD because you'll be called to it each time core content is activated, which will be often. This is why the broadest barrier is substance abuse and why *it's recommended to be addressed first*, before any work on CBPD core content can be done.

Getting your substance abuse under control and you on the road to sustained sobriety is a critical first step. Failure to do this, or to tell your therapist you have a co-occurring substance use issue, will lead to continued ruptures and backslides because when your core content is activated, you're going to be drawn to this maladaptive coping mechanism. If your sobriety stabilization is part of your therapeutic process and goals, both you and your mental health provider can build adaptive strategies, skills, and support resources that are most helpful for achieving and maintaining your sobriety. As in all things, there is more than one way to address this issue.

Synchronous Approach

You may be asking yourself, "Can't I work on my sobriety and my CBPD at the same time?" In this situation, knowledgeable mental health and medical providers are critical. If you elect the synchronous approach, a balance will be needed between the degree of exploration and unearthing of the depth and origin of core content issues and the drive to resolve the surface content thoughts, feelings, images, and behaviors often resulting from, and habitually used to manage, these issues.

The greater the degree of substance dependence, the harder it'll be to successfully engage in the synchronous approach. To do this, newer, healthier, and adaptive strategies must be put in place first to build up viable response options so when your core content is activated, these new strategies become your go-to resources and you avoid the old maladaptive ones of substance abuse.

Consider attending therapy two to three times a week; you may only need two half-hour sessions and one full-hour session. The half-hour session is supportive of your growth, whereas the hour-long one is for exploration into core content activation and surface content response.

In session, or outside of it, title a new page in your journal "Breaking My Broad Barrier," and write the responses to the following prompts below.

- Identify the situations in which you're driven to use substances.

- List core content activations that drive you to want to use.

- Identify new adaptive strategies you can do instead of using.

- In what situations can you practice these adaptive strategies routinely, when triggered and when not?

- How can you rebuild your interpersonal circle with those who are sober?

Difficult never means impossible. The synchronous approach is possible with the right team of support combined with your drive to attain sobriety and contend with and surmount your CBPD.

There are many people just like you, who want to do it differently and struggle with addiction to substances, who have overcome their CBPD issues and concerns. The fact that you're reading this book shows you have a desire to prepare for action or to engage in it. This is commendable and shows your motivation to do things differently. Motivation is the critical factor that determines success in overcoming your CBPD. Embrace and encourage your motivation, as it'll get you through this and help you overcome your CBPD.

Two Types of Withdrawal

Cold turkey isn't recommended. Most substances have physically and psychologically addictive properties. Withdrawal from certain substances can cause death, alcohol included. As you think about and engage in sobriety to address your CBPD, it should be done with a physician who's knowledgeable about withdrawal or at an inpatient setting.

Physical withdrawal symptoms can follow the discontinuation of many substances. They can include nausea, diarrhea, body aches, chills or shakes, delirium tremens (DTs, these can include physical effects such as shaking, shivering, irregular heart rate, confusion, and sweating), and others. Psychological withdrawal symptoms are very different, and often more intense for those with CBPD.

Over time, you've become emotionally tied to the substance and your mind fixated on the produced effect of being free of the negative thoughts, feelings, images, and behaviors that are often the result of core content activation. This is the reason for psychological withdrawal. Psychological withdrawal symptoms manifest as intense emotional turmoil that drives you to engage in behaviors to lessen or reconcile your dissonance. These symptoms can include headaches, anxiety, irritability, restlessness, loss of appetite, denial, inability to imagine coping without the substance, fixation on the substance and perceived need for it, insomnia, poor concentration, social isolation, depression, and so on.

Knowing these two withdrawal types is important. Different substances have different withdrawal time lines. Some symptoms come soon after abstinence, and others can come hours to days later. Due to the variability and severity of response to withdrawal, don't do this alone. Consult a trained physician for help.

Symptom Vigilance and Treatment

The ideal therapeutic scenario is you and your mental health provider working together against your CBPD. Being vigilant of your core content activations and surface content responses will enhance the probability of your success and mitigate the destructiveness of your maladaptive beliefs, behaviors, and patterns.

Problem Identification

Your growth beyond CBPD is a fluid process. As we addressed earlier, there's going to be an ebb and flow of successes and challenges as new problems arise. You'll want to use your therapeutic sessions to explore these problems and attach them to your adaptive strategies. Walk through how you'll use them to help yourself grow in as much detail as you can. Your default maladaptive patterns are going to have a stronger draw initially, which is where your mental health provider comes into play. They can serve as a reality-coping filter to not only identify your problems but also teach you how to best implement adaptive strategies that you learned from this book, or elsewhere, so you come out even stronger than before. However, doing this will awaken your stray cat.

Your Stray Cat

Your CBPD is like that stray cat that doesn't want to go away after you stop feeding it. When you start to address your CBPD core and surface content, the intensity and number of symptoms you feel are likely to increase. This isn't a bad thing but an indicator that your stray cat doesn't want to let go and that it's starting to get scared you're moving on. These symptoms may cause you to feel as if you're being stalked by your stray cat of problems. Remind yourself of the truth: It'll move on as you persevere, and you're not doing this alone. You have the help of a trusted other, your mental health provider.

In session, you and your therapist should work to connect your problems to your core content activations using a structured process. Title a new page in your journal "From Problems to Core Content," and write the responses to the following prompts below.

- When problems first arise, explore and write down the immediate thoughts, feelings, images, and drive to respond.

- What core content is activated?

- Assess for any degree of distortion of the problems: Are you catastrophizing, splitting, overgeneralizing, personalizing, blaming, and so on?

- Rate the intensity of your perceived need to resolve the issue on a scale of 0 to 10, where 0 is none at all and 10 is intense immediate need.

- Which adaptive strategy from this book, or elsewhere, can you use to calm yourself, clear out any distortion, and open your mind to positive resolution?

- Is there anyone in your life who is helping or hurting your process of managing your core content activation?

- Are there any unhealthy and hurtful others in your life who encourage maladaptive strategies? How can you distance yourself from them?

- Write, in as much detail as you can, how you'll implement an adaptive strategy to resolve the problem. Include helpful and healthy others in this process if appropriate.

- Clearly describe what your life will look like when the problems have resolved and what you expect to happen next.

Going through these steps with your therapist in a structured fashion encourages your sense of control over your problems and yourself. That stray cat doesn't want order; it wants panic and disorganization, which is why you fed it. Feeding days are over!

A Gift to Therapy

There's a "Clinician's Guide" that accompanies this book. It's a free supplement that I wrote for mental health providers to help them approach CBPD using the information in this book. The purpose of the "Clinician's Guide" is to increase the probability of you and your therapist being on the same page going forward. It's designed to be a resource to help you and your therapist contend with and grow beyond your CBPD while your mental health provider gains understanding of your condition, to help you both outline a treatment approach that fits for you and to provide a framework for identification of core and surface content as therapy progresses.

You can access this material using this link: http://www.newharbinger .com/48558. Send it to your therapist, and both of you can work through this book and its contents together.

This chapter is pretty unique compared to many other self-help resources. It provided you with the steps to identify a mental health provider who fits with your interests, approach, and issues. In this chapter, you learned:

- how to find a therapist

- questions to ask the mental health provider and yourself to increase the probability of a good fit

- how to recognize and discuss your previous therapy successes and impediments to enhance your growth and prevent wasted therapy time

- metrics to help you determine whether therapy is working

- the deleterious effects of saying, "I don't know," and how to counter them

- the importance of sobriety in clearing the way so you can address core content issues

- suggested guidelines related to the synchronous approach using mental health and medical providers to contend with your CBPD issues, substance abuse, and maladaptive patterns

- how to engage with your therapist so it's both of you against those intractable maladaptive patterns

The therapeutic relationship is a special one. It's founded on the basis of objectivity, kindness, caring, and hope. These components are tried and true in identifying and working through CBPD issues. Your relationship with your therapist isn't a friendship, but a source of steadfast support to foster your growth beyond your CBPD. It's normal to be afraid to connect to someone in this way, as you've likely experienced abandonment that enhanced your sense of emptiness in the past. Confronting this fear is part of the process, but so is allowing the hope, kindness, and caring of someone in your life whose goal aligns with yours: overcoming your CBPD.

References

Allport, G. W. 1937. *Personality: A Psychological Interpretation*. New York: Holt, Rinehart, and Winston.

APA (American Psychiatric Association). 2001. *Practice Guideline for the Treatment of Patients with Borderline Personality Disorder*. Washington, DC: American Psychiatric Association.

APA (American Psychiatric Association). 2013. *Diagnostic and Statistical Manual of Mental Disorders*. 5th ed. Washington, DC: American Psychiatric Association.

Baer, L. H., J. L. Shah, and M. Lepage. 2019. "Anxiety in Youth at Clinical High Risk for Psychosis: A Case Study and Conceptual Model." *Schizophrenia Research* 208: 441–446.

Baer, R. A., J. R. Peters, T. A. Eisenlohr-Moul, P. J. Geiger, and S. E. Sauer. 2012. "Emotion-Related Cognitive Processes in Borderline Personality Disorder: A Review of the Empirical Literature." *Clinical Psychology Review* 32, no. 5: 359–369.

Baer, R. A., and S. E. Sauer. 2011. "Relationships Between Depressive Rumination, Anger Rumination, and Borderline Personality Features." *Personality Disorders: Theory, Research, and Treatment* 2, no. 2: 142.

Barkley, R. A. 2002. "Major Life Activity and Health Outcomes Associated with Attention-Deficit/Hyperactivity Disorder." *Journal of Clinical Psychiatry* 63, Supplement 12: 10–15.

Bateman, A., and P. Fonagy. 2016. *Mentalization-Based Treatment for Personality Disorders: A Practical Guide*. Oxford, UK: Oxford University Press.

Bieling, P. J., G. M. MacQueen, M. J. Marriot, J. C. Robb, H. Begin, R. T. Joffe, and L. T. Young. 2003. "Longitudinal Outcome in Patients with Bipolar Disorder Assessed by Life-Charting Is Influenced by DSM-IV Personality Disorder Symptoms." *Bipolar Disorders* 5, no. 1: 14–21.

Bonde, J. P. E. 2008. "Psychosocial Factors at Work and Risk of Depression: A Systematic Review of the Epidemiological Evidence." *Occupational and Environmental Medicine* 65, no. 7: 438–445.

Boon, S., and N. Draijer. 1993. "The Differentiation of Patients with MPD or DDNOS from Patients with a Cluster B Personality Disorder." *Dissociation* 6, no. 2/3: 126–135.

Brand, B., and R. J. Loewenstein. 2010. "Dissociative Disorders: An Overview of Assessment, Phenomenology, and Treatment." *Psychiatric Times* 27, no. 10: 62–69.

Bridler, R., H. Häberle, S. T. Müller, K. Cattapan, R. Grohmann, S. Toto, and W. Greil. 2015. "Psychopharmacological Treatment of 2195 In-Patients with Borderline Personality Disorder: A Comparison with Other Psychiatric Disorders." *European Neuropsychopharmacology* 25, no. 6: 763–772.

Bromundt, V., A. Wirz-Justice, S. Kyburz, K. Opwis, G. Dammann, and C. Cajochen. 2013. "Circadian Sleep-Wake Cycles, Well-Being, and Light Therapy in Borderline Personality Disorder." *Journal of Personality Disorders* 27, no. 5: 680–696.

Chanen, A. M., M. Berk, and K. Thompson. 2016. "Integrating Early Intervention for Borderline Personality Disorder and Mood Disorders." *Harvard Review of Psychiatry* 24, no. 5: 330–341.

Chanen, A. M., and L. McCutcheon. 2013. "Prevention and Early Intervention for Borderline Personality Disorder: Current Status and Recent Evidence." *The British Journal of Psychiatry* 202, no. s54: s24–s29.

Charles, S. T., J. R. Piazza, J. Mogle, M. J. Sliwinski, and D. M. Almeida. 2013. "The Wear and Tear of Daily Stressors on Mental Health." *Psychological Science* 24, no. 5: 733–741.

Cloitre, M., D. W. Garvert, C. R. Brewin, R. A. Bryant, and A. Maercker. 2013. "Evidence for Proposed ICD-11 PTSD and Complex PTSD: A Latent Profile Analysis." *European Journal of Psychotraumatology* 4, no. 1: 20706.

Coid, J., M. Yang, P. Tyrer, A. Roberts, and S. Ullrich. 2006. "Prevalence and Correlates of Personality Disorder in Great Britain." *British Journal of Psychiatry* 188: 423–431.

Costa, P. T., and T. A. Widiger, eds. 1994. *Personality Disorders and the Five-Factor Model of Personality.* Washington, DC: American Psychological Association.

Cuijpers, P., M. Sijbrandij, S. L. Koole, G. Andersson, A. T. Beekman, and C. F. Reynold. 2013. "The Efficacy of Psychotherapy and Pharmacotherapy in Treating Depressive and Anxiety Disorders: A Meta-Analysis of Direct Comparisons." *World Psychiatry* 12, no. 2: 137–148.

Dahl, A. A. 1985. "Diagnosis of the Borderline Disorders." *Psychopathology* 18, no. 1: 18–28.

De Maat, S., J. Dekker, R. Schoevers, and F. De Jonghe. 2006. "Relative Efficacy of Psychotherapy and Pharmacotherapy in the Treatment of Depression: A Meta-Analysis." *Psychotherapy Research* 16, no. 5: 566–578.

Doering, S., S. Hörz, M. Rentrop, M. Fischer-Kern, P. Schuster, C. Benecke, A. Buchheim, et al. 2010. "Transference-Focused Psychotherapy v. Treatment by Community Psychotherapists for Borderline Personality Disorder: Randomised Controlled Trial." *The British Journal of Psychiatry* 196, no. 5: 389–395.

Elzy, M. B. 2011. "Examining the Relationship Between Childhood Sexual Abuse and Borderline Personality Disorder: Does Social Support Matter?" *Journal of Child Sexual Abuse* 20, no. 3: 284–304.

Ferrer, M., Ó. Andión, J. Matalí, S. Valero, J. A. Navarro, J. A. Ramos-Quiroga, R. Torrubia, et al. 2010. "Comorbid Attention-Deficit/Hyperactivity Disorder in Borderline Patients Defines an Impulsive Subtype of Borderline Personality Disorder." *Journal of Personality Disorders* 24, no. 6: 812–822.

Few, L. R., J. D. Miller, J. D. Grant, J. Maples, T. J. Trull, E. C. Nelson, T. F. Oltmanns, N. G. Martin, M. T. Lynskey, and A. Agrawal. 2016. "Trait-Based Assessment of Borderline Personality Disorder Using the NEO Five-Factor Inventory: Phenotypic and Genetic Support." *Psychological assessment* 28, no. 1: 39

Fossati, A., L. Novella, D. Donati, M. Donini, and C. Maffei. 2002. "History of Childhood Attention Deficit/Hyperactivity Disorder Symptoms and Borderline Personality Disorder: A Controlled Study." *Comprehensive Psychiatry* 43, no. 5: 369–377.

Fox, D. J. 2019. *The Borderline Personality Disorder Workbook*. Oakland, CA: New Harbinger Publications.

Fox, D. J. 2020. *Antisocial, Narcissistic, and Borderline Personality Disorders: A New Conceptualization of Development, Reinforcement, Expression, and Treatment*. New York: Routledge.

Fruzzetti, A. E., C. Shenk, and P. D. Hoffman. 2005. "Family Interaction and the Development of Borderline Personality Disorder: A Transactional Model." *Development and Psychopathology* 17, no. 4: 1007–1030.

Fyer, M. R., A. J. Frances, T. Sullivan, S. W. Hurt, and J. Clarkin. 1988. "Comorbidity of Borderline Personality Disorder." *Archives of General Psychiatry* 45, no. 4: 348–352.

Giffin, J. 2008. "Family Experience of Borderline Personality Disorder." *Australian and New Zealand Journal of Family Therapy* 29, no. 3: 133–138.

Grant, B. F., S. P. Chou, R. B. Goldstein, B. Huang, F. S. Stinson, T. D. Saha, S. M. Smith, D. Dawson, A. J. Pulay, P. Pickering, and W. J. Ruan. 2008. "Prevalence, Correlates, Disability, and Comorbidity of DSM-IV Borderline Personality Disorder: Results from the Wave 2 National Epidemiologic Survey on Alcohol and Related Conditions." *Journal of Clinical Psychiatry* 69, no. 4: 533–545.

Greaney, J. L., R. E. Koffer, E. F. Saunders, D. M. Almeida, and L. M. Alexander. 2019. "Self-Reported Everyday Psychosocial Stressors Are Associated with Greater Impairments in Endothelial Function in Young Adults with Major Depressive Disorder." *Journal of the American Heart Association* 8, no. 4: e010825.

Gunderson, J. G. 1994. "Building Structure for the Borderline Construct." *Acta Psychiatrica Scandinavica Supplementum* 379: 12–18.

Gunderson, J. G. 2009. *Borderline Personality Disorder: A Clinical Guide.* Washington, DC: American Psychiatric Publishing.

Gunderson, J. G., and C. Berkowitz. 2011. *A BPD Brief: An Introduction to Borderline Personality Disorder—Diagnosis, Origins, Course, and Treatment.* https://www. borderlinepersonalitydisorder. com/wp-content/uploads/2011 /07/A_BPD_Brief_REV2011-1.pdf.

Gunderson, J. G., and P. D. Hoffman. 2016. *Beyond Borderline: True Stories of Recovery from Borderline Personality Disorder.* Oakland, CA: New Harbinger Publications.

Gunderson, J. G., I. Weinberg, M. T. Daversa, K. D. Kueppenbender, M. C. Zanarini, M. T. Shea, A. E. Skodol, et al. 2006. "Descriptive and Longitudinal Observations on the Relationship of Borderline Personality Disorder and Bipolar Disorder." *American Journal of Psychiatry* 163, no. 7: 1173–1178.

Hale, M. 2013. *The Single Woman: Life, Love, and a Dash of Sass.* Nashville, TN: Thomas Nelson.

Hartley, S., C. Barrowclough, and G. Haddock. 2013. "Anxiety and Depression in Psychosis: A Systematic Review of Associations with Positive Psychotic Symptoms." *Acta Psychiatrica Scandinavica* 128, no. 5: 327–346.

Herman, J. L. 1992a. "Complex PTSD: A Syndrome in Survivors of Prolonged and Repeated Trauma." *Journal of Traumatic Stress* 5: 377–391.

Herman, J. 1992b. *Trauma and Recovery.* New York: Basic Books.

Hopwood, C. J. 2018. "A Framework for Treating DSM-5 Alternative Model for Personality Disorder Features." *Personality and Mental Health* 12, no. 2: 107–125.

Ibrahim, J., N. Cosgrave, and M. Woolgar. 2018. "Childhood Maltreatment and Its Link to Borderline Personality Disorder Features in Children: A Systematic Review Approach." *Clinical Child Psychology and Psychiatry* 23, no. 1: 57–76.

Imel, Z. E., M. B. Malterer, K. M. McKay, and B. E. Wampold. 2008. "A Meta-Analysis of Psychotherapy and Medication in Unipolar Depression and Dysthymia." *Journal of Affective Disorders* 110, no. 3: 197–206.

Joyce, P. R., R. T. Mulder, S. E. Luty, J. M. McKenzie, P. F. Sullivan, and R. C. Cloninge. 2003. "Borderline Personality Disorder in Major Depression: Symptomatology, Temperament, Character, Differential Drug Response, and 6-Month Outcome." *Comprehensive Psychiatry* 44, no. 1: 35–43.

Kaess, M., R. Brunner, and A. Chanen. 2014. "Borderline Personality Disorder in Adolescence." *Pediatrics* 134, no. 4: 782–793.

Kernberg, O. F., and E. Caligor. 2005. "A Psychoanalytic Theory of Personality Disorders." In *Major Theories of Personality Disorder,* edited by J. F. Clarkin and M. F. Lenzenweger, 114–156. New York: Guilford Press.

Kessler, R. 1999. "Comorbidity of Unipolar and Bipolar Depression with Other Psychiatric Disorders in a General Population Survey." In *Comorbidity in Affective Disorders,* edited by M. Tohen, 1–25. New York: Marcel Dekker.

Kessler, R. C., L. Adler, R. Barkley, J. Biederman, C. K. Conners, O. Demler, S. V. Faraone, et al. 2006. "The Prevalence and Correlates of Adult ADHD in the United States: Results from the National Comorbidity Survey Replication." *American Journal of Psychiatry* 163, no. 4: 716–723.

Kessler, R. C., P. Berglund, O. Demler, R. Jin, D. Koretz, and K. R. Merikangas. 2003. "The Epidemiology of Major Depressive Disorder: Results from the National Comorbidity Survey Replication (NCS-R)." *Journal of the American Medical Association* 289, no. 23: 3095–3105.

Kingdon, D. G., K. Ashcroft, B. Bhandari, S. Gleeson, N. Warikoo, M. Symons, L. Taylor, et al. 2010. "Schizophrenia and Borderline Personality Disorder: Similarities and Differences in the Experience of Auditory Hallucinations, Paranoia, and Childhood Trauma." *The Journal of Nervous and Mental Disease* 198, no. 6: 399–403.

Koenigsberg, H. W., L. J. Siever, H. Lee, S. Pizzarello, A. S. New, M. Goodman, H. Cheng, J. Flory, and I. Prohovni. 2009. "Neural Correlates of Emotion Processing in Borderline Personality Disorder." *Psychiatry Research* 172, no. 3: 192–199. https://doi.org/10.1016/j.pscychresns.2008.07.010.

Koerting, J., R. Pukrop, P. Klein, K. Ritter, M. Knowles, A. Banzhaf,
    L. Gentschow, et al. 2016. "Comparing Dimensional Models Assessing
    Personality Traits and Personality Pathology Among Adult ADHD
    and Borderline Personality Disorder." *Journal of Attention Disorders*
    20, no. 8: 715–724.

Korzekwa, M. I., P. F. Dell, P. S. Links, L. Thabane, and P. Fougere. 2009.
    "Dissociation in Borderline Personality Disorder: A Detailed Look."
    Journal of Trauma and Dissociation 10: 346–367.

Kumar, V., Y. Sattar, A. Bseiso, S. Khan, and I. H. Rutkofsky. 2017. "The
    Effectiveness of Internet-Based Cognitive Behavioral Therapy in
    Treatment of Psychiatric Disorders." *Cureus* 9, no. 8: 1-14.

Kuo, J. R., J. E. Khoury, R. Metcalfe, S. Fitzpatrick, and A. Goodwill. 2015.
    "An Examination of the Relationship Between Childhood Emotional Abuse
    and Borderline Personality Disorder Features: The Role of Difficulties
    with Emotion Regulation." *Child Abuse and Neglect* 39: 147–155.

Lahera, G., A. Benito, A. González-Barroso, R. Guardiola, S. Herrera,
    B. Muchada, N. Cojedor, et al. 2012. "Social-Cognitive Bias and Depressive
    Symptoms in Outpatients with Bipolar Disorder." *Depression Research and
    Treatment* 2012: 1–6.

Lenzenweger, M. F., M. C. Lane, A. W. Loranger, and R. C. Kessler. 2007.
    "DSM-IV Personality Disorders in the National Comorbidity Survey
    Replication." *Biological Psychiatry* 62, no. 6: 553–564.

Levy, K. N., K. B. Meehan, K. M. Kelly, J. S. Reynoso, M. Weber, J. F. Clarkin,
    and O. F. Kernberg. 2006. "Change in Attachment Patterns and Reflective
    Function in a Randomized Control Trial of Transference-Focused
    Psychotherapy for Borderline Personality Disorder." *Journal of Consulting
    and Clinical Psychology* 74: 1027–1040.

Linehan, M. M. 1993. *Cognitive Behavioral Therapy of Borderline Personality
    Disorder.* New York: Guilford Press.

MacIntosh, H. B., N. Godbout, and N. Dubash. 2015. "Borderline Personality
    Disorder: Disorder of Trauma or Personality, a Review of the Empirical
    Literature." *Canadian Psychology/Psychologie Canadienne* 56, no. 2: 227.

Mantere, O., K. Suominen, S. Leppämäki, H. Valtonen, P. Arvilommi, and
    E. Isometsä. 2004. "The Clinical Characteristics of DSM-IV Bipolar I and II
    Disorders: Baseline Findings from the Jorvi Bipolar Study (JoBS)." *Bipolar
    Disorders* 6, no. 5: 395–405.

Matthies, S., L. T. van Elst, B. Feige, D. Fischer, C. Scheel, E. Krogmann,
    E. Perlov, et al. 2011. "Severity of Childhood Attention-Deficit Hyperactivity

Disorder—A Risk Factor for Personality Disorders in Adult Life?" *Journal of Personality Disorders* 25, no. 1: 101–114.

Menon, P., B. Chaudhari, D. Saldanha, S. Devabhaktuni, and L. Bhattacharya. 2016. "Childhood Sexual Abuse in Adult Patients with Borderline Personality Disorder." *Industrial Psychiatry Journal* 25, no. 1: 101.

Niemantsverdriet, M. B., C. W. Slotema, J. D. Blom, I. H. Franken, H. W. Hoek, I. E. Sommer, and M. Van Der Gaag. 2017. "Hallucinations in Borderline Personality Disorder: Prevalence, Characteristics and Associations with Comorbid Symptoms and Disorders." *Scientific Reports* 7, no. 1: 1–8.

O'Malley, G. K., L. McHugh, N. Mac Giollabhui, and J. Bramham. 2016. "Characterizing Adult Attention-Deficit/Hyperactivity-Disorder and Comorbid Borderline Personality Disorder: ADHD Symptoms, Psychopathology, Cognitive Functioning and Psychosocial Factors." *European Psychiatry* 31: 29–36.

Pagura, J., M. B. Stein, J. M. Bolton, B. J. Cox, B. Grant, and J. Sareen. 2010. "Comorbidity of Borderline Personality Disorder and Posttraumatic Stress Disorder in the U.S. Population." *Journal of Psychiatric Research* 44: 1190–1198.

Paton, C., M. J. Crawford, S. F. Bhatti, M. X. Patel, and T. R. Barnes. 2015. "The Use of Psychotropic Medication in Patients with Emotionally Unstable Personality Disorder under the Care of UK Mental Health Services." *The Journal of Clinical Psychiatry* 76, no. 4: 512–518.

Pearse, L. J., C. Dibben, H. Ziauddeen, C. Denman, and P. J. McKenna. 2014. "A Study of Psychotic Symptoms in Borderline Personality Disorder." *The Journal of Nervous and Mental Disease* 202, no. 5: 368–371.

Peckham, A. D., S. L. Johnson, and I. H. Gotlib. 2016. "Attentional Bias in Euthymic Bipolar I Disorder." *Cognition and Emotion* 30, no. 3: 472–487.

Pfohl, B., W. Coryell, M. Zimmerman, and D. Stangl. 1986. "DSM-III Personality Disorders: Diagnostic Overlap and Internal Consistency of Individual DSM-III Criteria." *Comprehensive Psychiatry* 27, no. 1: 21–34.

Porter, C., J. Palmier-Claus, A. Branitsky, W. Mansell, H. Warwick, and F. Varese. 2020. "Childhood Adversity and Borderline Personality Disorder: A Meta-Analysis." *Acta Psychiatrica Scandinavica* 141, no. 1: 6–20.

Porter, R. J., M. Inder, K. M. Douglas, S. Moor, J. D. Carter, C. M. Frampton, and M. Crowe. 2020. "Improvement in Cognitive Function in Young People with Bipolar Disorder: Results from Participants in an 18-Month

Randomised Controlled Trial of Adjunctive Psychotherapy." *Australian and New Zealand Journal of Psychiatry* 54, no. 3: 272–281.

Roberts, T., R. Shidhaye, V. Patel, and S. D. Rathod. 2020. "Health Care Use and Treatment-Seeking for Depression Symptoms in Rural India: An Exploratory Cross-Sectional Analysis." *BMC Health Services Research* 20, no. 1: 287. https://doi.org/10.1186/s12913-020-05162-0.

Robertson, C. D., N. A. Kimbrel, and R. O. Nelson-Gray. 2013. "The Invalidating Childhood Environment Scale (ICES): Psychometric Properties and Relationship to Borderline Personality Symptomatology." *Journal of Personality Disorders* 27, no. 3: 402–410.

Ross, C. A. 2007. "Borderline Personality Disorder and Dissociation." *Journal of Trauma and Dissociation* 8, no. 1: 71–80.

Ross, C. A., L. Ferrell, and E. Schroeder. 2014. "Co-Occurrence of Dissociative Identity Disorder and Borderline Personality Disorder." *Journal of Trauma and Dissociation* 15: 79–90.

Rui, P., K. Kang, and J. J. Ashman. 2016. *National Hospital Ambulatory Medical Care Survey: 2016 Emergency Department Summary Tables.* Atlanta: Centers for Disease Control and Prevention.

Safren, S. A., M. W. Otto, S. Sprich, C. L. Winett, T. E. Wilens, and J. Biederman. 2005. "Cognitive-Behavioral Therapy for ADHD in Medication-Treated Adults with Continued Symptoms." *Behaviour Research and Therapy* 43, no. 7: 831–842.

Samuels, J., W. W. Eaton, O. J. Bienvenu III, C. H. Brown, P. T. Costa Jr., and G. Nestadt. 2002. "Prevalence and Correlates of Personality Disorders in a Community Sample." *British Journal of Psychiatry* 180: 536–542.

Şar, V., G. Akyuz, N. Kugu, E. Ozturk, and H. Ertem-Vehid. 2006. "Axis I Dissociative Disorder Comorbidity in Borderline Personality Disorder and Reports of Childhood Trauma." *Journal of Clinical Psychiatry* 67, no. 10: 1583–1590.

Scalabrini, A., M. Cavicchioli, A. Fossati, and C. Maffei. 2017. "The Extent of Dissociation in Borderline Personality Disorder: A Meta-Analytic Review." *Journal of Trauma and Dissociation* 18, no. 4: 522–543.

Selby, E. A. 2013. "Chronic Sleep Disturbances and Borderline Personality Disorder Symptoms." *Journal of Consulting and Clinical Psychology* 81, no. 5: 941–947. https://doi.org/10.1037/a0033201.

Selby, E. A., M. D. Anestis, T. W. Bender, and T. E. Joiner Jr. 2009. "An Exploration of the Emotional Cascade Model in Borderline Personality Disorder." *Journal of Abnormal Psychology* 118, no. 2: 375.

Skodol, A. E., J. G. Gunderson, B. Pfohl, T. A. Widiger, W. J. Livesley, and L. J. Siever. 2002. "The Borderline Diagnosis I: Psychopathology, Comorbidity, and Personality Structure." *Biological Psychiatry* 51, no. 12: 936–950.

Skoglund, C., A. Tiger, C. Rück, P. Petrovic, P. Asherson, C. Hellner, D. Mataix-Cols, and R. Kuja-Halkola. 2019. "Familial Risk and Heritability of Diagnosed Borderline Personality Disorder: A Register Study of the Swedish Population." *Molecular Psychiatry* 1: 999-1008.

Slotema, C. W., M. B. A. Niemantsverdriet, J. D. Blom, M. Van Der Gaag, H. W. Hoek, and I. E. C. Sommer. 2017. "Suicidality and Hospitalisation in Patients with Borderline Personality Disorder Who Experience Auditory Verbal Hallucinations." *European Psychiatry* 41: 47–52.

Soloff, P. H., K. G. Lynch, T. M. Kelly, K. M. Malone, and J. J. Mann. 2000. "Characteristics of Suicide Attempts of Patients with Major Depressive Episode and Borderline Personality Disorder: A Comparative Study." *American Journal of Psychiatry* 157: 601–608.

Starcevic, V., and A. Janca. 2018. "Pharmacotherapy of Borderline Personality Disorder: Replacing Confusion with Prudent Pragmatism." *Current Opinion in Psychiatry* 31, no. 1: 69–73.

Stern, A. 1938. "Psychoanalytic Investigation of and Therapy in the Borderline Group of Neuroses." *The Psychoanalytic Quarterly* 7, no. 4: 467–489.

Tackett, J. L., S. Balsis, T. F. Oltmanns, and R. F. Krueger. 2009. "A Unifying Perspective on Personality Pathology Across the Life Span: Developmental Considerations for the Fifth Edition of the Diagnostic and Statistical Manual of Mental Disorders." *Development and Psychopathology* 21, no. 3: 687.

Tamam, L., N. Ozpoyraz, and G. Karatas. 2004. "Personality Disorder Comorbidity Among Patients with Bipolar I Disorder in Remission." *Acta Neuropsychiatrica* 16, no. 3: 175–180.

Terr, L. C. 1991. "Childhood Traumas: An Outline and Overview." *American Journal of Psychiatry* 148: 10–20.

Trull, T. J., L. K. Freeman, T. J. Vebares, A. M. Choate, A. C. Helle, and A. M. Wycoff. 2018. "Borderline Personality Disorder and Substance Use Disorders: An Updated Review." *Borderline Personality Disorder and Emotion Dysregulation* 5, no. 1: 15.

Trull, T. J, S. Jahng, R. L. Tomko, P. K. Wood, and K. J. Sher. 2010. "Revised NESARC Personality Disorder Diagnoses: Gender, Prevalence, and Comorbidity with Substance Dependence Disorders." *Journal of Personality Disorders* 24, no. 4: 412–426.

WHO (World Health Organization). 1992. *The ICD-10 Classification of Mental and Behavioural Disorders: Clinical Descriptions and Diagnostic Guidelines.* Geneva: World Health Organization.

WHO (World Health Organization). 2008. *The Global Burden of Disease: 2004 Update.* Geneva: World Health Organization.

Witt, S. H., F. Streit, M. Jungkunz, J. Frank, S. Awasthi, C. S. Reinbold, J. Treutlien, et al. 2017. "Genome-Wide Association Study of Borderline Personality Disorder Reveals Genetic Overlap with Bipolar Disorder, Major Depression and Schizophrenia." *Translational Psychiatry* 7, no. 6: e1155–e1155.

Zanarini, M. C., F. R. Frankenburg, E. D. Dubo, A. E. Sickel, A. Trikha, A. Levin, and V. Reynolds. 1998. "Axis I Comorbidity of Borderline Personality Disorder." *American Journal of Psychiatry* 155, no. 12: 1733–1739.

Zanarini, M. C., F. R. Frankenburg, D. B. Reich, M. F. Marino, R. E. Lewis, A. A. Williams, and G. S. Khera. 2000. "Biparental Failure in the Childhood Experiences of Borderline Patients." *Journal of Personality Disorders* 14, no. 3: 264–273.

Zanarini, M. C., F. R. Frankenburg, L. Yong, G. Raviola, D. Bradford Reich, J. Hennen, J. I. Hudson, and J. G. Gunderson. 2004. "Borderline Psychopathology in the First-Degree Relatives of Borderline and Axis II Comparison Probands." *Journal of Personality Disorders* 18, no. 5: 439–447.

Zanarini, M. C., T. F. Ruser, F. R. Frankenburg, and J. Hennen. 2000. "The Dissociative Experiences of Borderline Patients." *Comprehensive Psychiatry* 41, no. 3: 223–227.

Zimmerman, M., and J. I. Mattia. 1999. "Psychiatric Diagnosis in Clinical Practice: Is Comorbidity Being Missed?" *Comprehensive Psychiatry* 40: 182–191.

Zlotnick, C., C. L. Franklin, and M. Zimmerman. 2002. "Is Comorbidity of Posttraumatic Stress Disorder and Borderline Personality Disorder Related to Greater Pathology and Impairment?" *American Journal of Psychiatry* 159: 1940–1943.

Daniel J. Fox, PhD, is a licensed psychologist in Texas, international speaker, and award-winning author. He has been specializing in the treatment and assessment of individuals with personality disorders for more than twenty years in the state and federal prison system, universities, and in private practice. His specialty areas include personality disorders, ethics, burnout prevention, and emotional intelligence. He has published several articles in these areas, and is author of *The Borderline Personality Disorder Workbook* and *The Clinician's Guide to Diagnosis and Treatment of Personality Disorders*; along with the award-winning *The Narcissistic Personality Disorder Toolbox*; and the award-winning *Antisocial, Borderline, Narcissistic and Histrionic Workbook*.

Fox has been teaching and supervising students for more than twenty years at various universities across the United States, some of which include West Virginia University, Texas A&M University, University of Houston, Sam Houston State University, and Florida State University. He is currently an adjunct assistant professor at the University of Houston, and maintains a private practice that specializes in the assessment and treatment of individuals with complex psychopathology and personality disorders. Fox has given numerous workshops and seminars on ethics and personality disorders; personality disorders and crime; treatment solutions for treating clients along the antisocial, borderline, narcissistic, and histrionic personality spectrum; emotional intelligence; narcissistic personality disorder (NPD) and its impact on children and partners; managing mental health within the prison system; and others. Fox maintains a website and is on social media to present various treatment interventions focused on working with and attenuating the symptomatology related to individuals along the antisocial, borderline, narcissistic, and histrionic personality spectrum. Learn more at www.drdfox.com.

FROM OUR PUBLISHER—

As the publisher at New Harbinger and a clinical psychologist since 1978, I know that emotional problems are best helped with evidence-based therapies. These are the treatments derived from scientific research (randomized controlled trials) that show what works. Whether these treatments are delivered by trained clinicians or found in a self-help book, they are designed to provide you with proven strategies to overcome your problem.

Therapies that aren't evidence-based—whether offered by clinicians or in books—are much less likely to help. In fact, therapies that aren't guided by science may not help you at all. That's why this New Harbinger book is based on scientific evidence that the treatment can relieve emotional pain.

This is important: if this book isn't enough, and you need the help of a skilled therapist, use the following resources to find a clinician trained in the evidence-based protocols appropriate for your problem. And if you need more support—a community that understands what you're going through and can show you ways to cope—resources for that are provided below, as well.

Real help is available for the problems you have been struggling with. The skills you can learn from evidence-based therapies will change your life.

Matthew McKay, PhD
Publisher, New Harbinger Publications

**If you need a therapist, the following organization can help you
find a therapist trained in acceptance and commitment therapy (ACT).**

Behavioral Tech, LLC
please visit www.behavioraltech.org and click on *Find a DBT Therapist*.

**For additional support for patients, family, and friends,
please contact the following:**

BPD Central
Visit www.bpdcentral.org

Treatment and Research Advancements Association for Personality Disorder (TARA)
Visit www.tara4bpd.org

National Suicide Prevention Lifeline
**Call 24 hours a day 1-800-273-TALK (8255) or
visit www.suicidepreventionlifeline.org**

MORE BOOKS from
NEW HARBINGER PUBLICATIONS

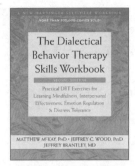
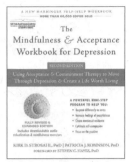
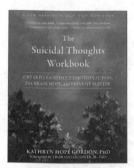

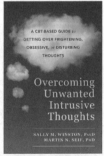

Did you know there are **free tools** you can download for this book?

Free tools are things like **worksheets**, **guided meditation exercises**, and **more** that will help you get the most out of your book.

You can download free tools for this book— whether you bought or borrowed it, in any format, from any source—from the New Harbinger website. All you need is a NewHarbinger.com account. Just use the URL provided in this book to view the free tools that are available for it. Then, click on the "download" button for the free tool you want, and follow the prompts that appear to log in to your NewHarbinger.com account and download the material.

You can also save the free tools for this book to your **Free Tools Library** so you can access them again anytime, just by logging in to your account! Just look for this button on the book's free tools page.

+ Save this to my free tools library